The
Barry Diller
Story

The Life and Times of America's Greatest Entertainment Mogul

GEORGE MAIR

JOHN WILEY & SONS, INC.
New York • Chichester • Weinheim • Brisbane • Singapore • Toronto

The author acknowledges permission to reprint the following:

Excerpt from "Barry Diller: TV's Smart Agent," by Don West and Mark Berniker. Reprinted with permission from BROADCASTING AND CABLE, copyright 1996 Cahners Publishing Company, a division of Reed Elsevier Inc. BROADCASTING AND CABLE is a trademark of Cahners Publishing Company, a division of Reed Elsevier Inc. All rights reserved.

Excerpt from "Delaware Law: From a Muddle, Owners Win," by Floyd Norris, *New York Times* (November 28, 1993).

Excerpt from "Disconnected: After Seeing Barry Diller's Plan for the QVC Home Shopping Network, It's Hard to Believe This Is the Same Man Who Created the Fox Network." © 1993 ASM Communications, Inc. Used with permission from ADWEEK.

Excerpt from "Playboy Interview: Barry Diller," by Kevin Sessums, *Playboy* (July 1989), p. 51 ff.

This text is printed on acid-free paper.

Library of Congress Cataloging-in-Publication Data:

Mair, George, 1929–
    The Barry Diller story : the life and times of America's greatest entertainment mogul / by George Mair.
      p. cm.
    Includes bibliographical references.
    ISBN 0-471-13082-6 (cloth : alk. paper)
    1. Diller, Barry. 2. Chief executive officers—United States—
Biography. I. Title.
PN1992.4.D46M35   1997
384.55'4'092—dc21
   [B]   96-49770

Printed in the United States of America

10 9 8 7 6 5 4 3 2 1

Contents

Introduction   1

1   An Issue of Privacy   9

2   The Mailroom and Beyond   19

3   Reinventing the Wheel   35

4   At the Movies   51

5   The "Killer Dillers"   71

6   Aboard the Twentieth-Century Express   89

7   Setting the House in Order   107

8   Creating the Fourth Network   119

9   Truth or Consequences   139

CONTENTS

10 The Plots Thicken 151

11 "Don't Have a Cow, Man" 167

12 In Development Hell 179

13 Saying Goodbye 201

14 The Odyssey 211

15 "What's the Idea?" 229

16 Of Paramount Importance 245

17 Breakfast at Tiffany's: The Bid for Black Rock 285

18 Silver King 311

Notes 331

Index 343

Introduction

In the spring of 1975, writer-director Elia Kazan had just completed shooting *The Last Tycoon,* F. Scott Fitzgerald's final, unfinished novel about the dark side of Hollywood. Harold Pinter had written the screenplay for legendary producer Sam Spiegel, and Kazan, who had previously directed *Streetcar Named Desire* and *On the Waterfront,* had insisted that the lead role of Monroe Stahr go to Robert De Niro. Despite the combined talents of such an illustrious team, the filming had been difficult for all concerned.

The producer, director, and writer were at odds about the key cast members: Spiegel characterized De Niro as "willful and arrogant," and criticized Theresa Russell, his own choice for one of the major women's roles, for being "hopeless, even embarrassing." Although Kazan had originally opposed Spiegel's choice of Ingrid

Boulting for the other female lead, he changed his mind after seeing her work, much to the distress of Pinter, who strongly felt that she was wrong for the part. To add to the tension, Kazan had serious reservations about the strength of the love story at the heart of the movie. He had written to Pinter about his concerns and twice traveled to England with Spiegel to discuss the script. But Pinter ignored his comments and made none of the changes Kazan sought.

For all of his doubts and fears, after viewing the rough cut in early March, Kazan wrote in his diary, "The picture hangs together. . . . the film has . . . subtlety, and even emotional power."

But the true seal of approval was to come three months later, on June 1, when Sam Spiegel screened the movie for Barry Diller, who was then in his second year as chairman and chief executive officer of Paramount Pictures. Diller telephoned Kazan the very next day. "It's a wonderful picture," he declared.

Kazan's relief was short-lived. Subsequent audiences composed of close friends and colleagues within the film industry, as well as the European distributors, were unanimous in their disappointment. The movie was a failure. It opened to decidedly mixed reviews and bombed at the box office.

What did Barry Diller see in *The Last Tycoon* that others did not? Why the enthusiastic endorsement from the *wunderkind* of the movie industry, who was just one month shy of his thirty-second birthday when he was plucked out of television to head up Paramount? Perhaps Diller was particularly drawn to the character of Monroe Stahr, the genius, work-obsessed studio head whom Fitzgerald had so patently modeled after Irving Thalberg. Thalberg, considered "the most influential man in Hollywood" for almost a decade beginning in 1924, could well have been a role model for Barry Diller.

Promoted to MGM's chief of production at the age of 25, Thalberg was meticulous almost to a fault. He involved himself in every aspect of film-making, from originating concepts to casting and editing classics such as *Grand Hotel, The Barretts of Wimpole Street, The Good Earth,* and *Camille.* Thalberg had many foes and came in for his share of criticism. Some said his movies were all glitz and glamour—empty, bland vehicles that borrowed too much from Broadway theater. But writers and directors appreciated his canny, diplomatic approach to improving scripts and rushes. He also propounded the radical idea that a successful studio like MGM—the only one of the major studios to turn a profit during the Depression—could occasionally afford the luxury of producing a movie that would run far above budget, so long as it added to MGM's prestige and glory.

Like Irving Thalberg and the fictitious Monroe Stahr, Barry Diller was only in his mid-20s when, as vice president of prime-time programming at ABC Television, he was charged with making financial and creative decisions that involved millions of dollars and shaped the viewing habits of vast numbers of Americans. While at ABC, Diller virtually invented the concept of the *Movie of the Week,* as well as that of the miniseries.

He moved from the William Morris Agency to ABC as personal assistant to Leonard Goldberg, who had just been named head of programming for the network. Diller quickly became known at ABC as a man who got results. Even then, his style was to demand, cajole, pressure, and intimidate in order to achieve his goals, making it clear to those with whom he dealt that he would not accept excuses or refusals. Goldberg would later say that Diller was every executive's dream assistant.

In the mid-1970s, Diller returned to Hollywood, where he saved Paramount Pictures from fiscal disaster and revolutionized the process by which the studio acquired scripts. A decade later, despite a string of hits, Diller ran into trouble at Paramount; after the sudden death of his boss Charles Bluhdorn, a bitter conflict—the first of several that dogged his career—erupted between him and Martin Davis, the new head of Gulf & Western, Paramount's parent company.

Eager to escape from an increasingly untenable situation, he was enticed by oil magnate Marvin Davis to become chief executive officer of Fox, Inc., where he was immediately and unexpectedly faced with a corporate debt of six hundred million dollars. An ugly power struggle between Diller and Davis culminated in the purchase of Fox by Australian newspaper titan Rupert Murdoch. In 1987, he and Murdoch made television history when they launched the fourth television network. Fox-TV soon became known for its edgy humor and offbeat programs, including *Married . . . with Children* and *The Simpsons,* the animated cartoon created by Matt Groening. At the same time, Diller, as head of Fox's movie studio, was also green-lighting hits such as *Home Alone* and *Big.*

Then, in February 1992, he stunned both Hollywood and Wall Street when he left Fox to spend the next several months driving across the United States, accompanied only by his newest toy, his Apple Powerbook®. Amazement turned to shock when, in December of that same year, he acquired a 3 percent stake in QVC, a home shopping network, and became its chief executive officer. *Multichannel News,* an industry publication, voiced the question being asked by so many others who had followed Barry Diller's career: "What interest could the former chairman of Fox, Inc. possibly have in running a cable network that peddles ceramics and fake diamonds?"

In the months that followed, Diller tried to provide an answer as he articulated his vision for the future of television, which he believed would be "dominated by the interests of cable." He spoke of expansion and interactivity, of information services and the evolution of programming. And yet the skeptics wondered why Barry Diller, one of Hollywood's most powerful, respected, and feared individuals, a man whose closest friends were a select group of the industry's power elite, would exile himself to a shopping network in the backwaters of West Chester, Pennsylvania.

The picture seemed to come more sharply into focus later that year when Diller, backed by his QVC partners, played the spoiler in the proposed Viacom-buyout of Paramount Communications. Although Diller denied that his bid to buy Paramount was fueled by personal motives, his friends spoke off the record about his well-known animosity toward his former employer, Martin Davis. The battle between Diller and Sumner Redstone, Viacom's chairman, raged in the Delaware courts and on Wall Street until February 1994, when Redstone's bid of roughly 10 billion dollars finally forced Diller to drop out.

"They won. We lost. Next," Diller proclaimed, serving notice that he would continue the search for a suitable corporate partner for QVC. Although Diller publicly betrayed no signs of doubt, questions resurfaced among veteran Diller-watchers: How could he have so badly miscalculated his position in a deal of this magnitude? And was he truly as sanguine about his future as he professed to be?

His next move, a proposed marriage with CBS, seemed like a match made in heaven. "It's a real merger," said CBS chief executive Laurence Tisch, in an obvious attempt to warn off other bidders. He would stay on at CBS as chairman but publicly committed himself to leaving the company within the next two years. "Barry is going to be the boss here," he said. "It's time to move on."

By the close of trading on the day of Tisch's announcement, Wall Street registered its excitement with prices that jumped 19 percent for both CBS's and QVC's stock. The two companies scheduled board meetings to vote on the proposal. But in an eleventh-hour surprise move, one of Diller's own partners made a rival bid. Stockholders hardly had time to consider the offer before the *Wall Street Journal* was predicting the outcome by calling Diller "a mogul in search of an empire."

Why had the CBS deal fallen through? And why would Brian Roberts, the man who'd wooed him to join QVC, suddenly turn against him? Was Diller losing his touch? Would he ever attain his stated goal of being his own boss?

Six months later, when the QVC-Comcast deal finally became a reality, Diller was richer by a hundred million dollars, and the press was still speculating about his next move. Though some had him renewing his pursuit of CBS, his war chest was still far short of the two billion dollars needed to gain control of the company.

Diller bided his time, scheming and spinning his dreams until the summer and fall of 1995, when he became the owner of Silver King Communications and Savoy Pictures, and gained a controlling interest in the Home Shopping Network. The ever-watchful press was quick to weigh in with their questions and comments about Diller's media empire *manqué*. "How much room is there for Barry?" asked *BusinessWeek,* while the *Economist* dubbed him "the would-be network king." Diller, guarded as always about his strategy, would only say that he intended to create his new network "from the bottom up with local programming."

However his plans for the future play out, the man who's known in Hollywood as "Killer Diller" has already left an indelible mark on the entertainment industry. Dawn Steel, another of Diller's Paramount protégés and currently president of Columbia Studios, said of her former mentor's contribution to the movie industry, "He created the 'advocacy system' within motion picture studios. He taught movie executives how to put some passion into their jobs. The business is a better place because of Barry."

Many would disagree with her. Diller has always had his enemies, although few will go public with their complaints.

There are no end of stories about Diller's perfectionist nature, fiery temper, and abrasive tongue. Like Irving Thalberg, once Hollywood's ultimate micromanager, Diller insists on exerting such total control that during his tenure at Fox, he personally chose the graphics for the shows, as well as the color schemes for the sets. He is often described as a bully and emotionally abusive. Once, also while at Fox, he became so enraged at a key associate that he flung a videocassette at his errant aide with such ferocity that it made a dent in the wall.

Diller is aware of his reputation for being a son of a bitch, an expression that comes up time and again in conversations about him. He professes surprise, yet admits to being difficult. But he defends himself by saying, "I think difficult is good, especially if you're dealing with the 'creative process,' in which you have to make editorial choices . . . . All you really have to contribute is what you think. There is no rightness involved only being true to oneself."

Diller's words yet again eerily evoke the ghost of Irving Thalberg. In his notes for *The Last Tycoon*, Scott Fitzgerald recalled a chance conversation he had with Thalberg in the MGM commissary in 1927, during which Thalberg eloquently described his decision-making process. Fitzgerald was so struck by his comments that he later paraphrased them in a speech made by his hero, Monroe Stahr.

"Suppose there's got to be a road through a mountain," Thalberg told Fitzgerald. ". . . there seem to be half a dozen possible roads through those mountains . . . . [S]uppose you happen to be the top man . . . . You say, 'Well, I think we will put the road there,' and . . . and you've got to pretend . . . that you did it for specific reasons, even though you're utterly assailed by doubts at times as to the wisdom of your decision, because all those other possible decisions keep echoing in your ear. But when you're planning a new enterprise on a grand scale, the people under you . . . mustn't ever dream that you're in any doubt about any decision."

Surely, Barry Diller, like Irving Thalberg, the wunderkind of an earlier moviemaking generation, must also have private doubts about the wisdom of some of his decisions. Silver King, a collection of 12 television stations that feature home shopping programs, is a far cry from the boardroom seats of power and influence he once occupied. Still, he professes to be as convinced today of his choice of a road through the mountains as he was 10 and 20 years ago when the entertainment world was his for the asking.

Nevertheless, the questions inevitably arise: How did he come to wear the mantle of power so early and so comfortably, and how did he manage to let it slip from his grasp? Why have his recent efforts to reclaim his position so conspicuously and spectacularly failed? What forces drive Barry Diller to chase what some might call an impossible dream? Does he suffer from some fatal character flaw that will ultimately prevent him from achieving his fantasy of running his own show?

These are questions best answered by people close to Diller— people he respects—but they were unwilling to share their insights. Some spoke anonymously, others of lesser note were reluctant to talk because of Diller's power and status. Perhaps the day will come that Diller will choose to write his autobiography. Until such time, however, this exploration of Diller's much discussed public persona, as well as his private life, shrouded in secrecy, will shed some light on this extraordinarily complex human being—the once and perhaps future mogul, still in search of his empire.

An Issue of Privacy

Barry Diller is often described as a man of passion. Most of all, he has a passion for privacy. "I care a lot about privacy," he has said flat out.

He rarely gives interviews, and when he does, he quickly retreats from the personal, preferring to talk about business issues, creative and technological concepts, ideas rather than emotions. His discomfort, when queried about his inner life, is palpable. He avoids introspection, at least in a public forum, and claims to "have no powers of self-observation." Caught in the act of self-analysis on the subject of how he makes his hiring decisions, he has said, "I really don't know anything about anything. . . . This is all babble. It's pure pretentiousness."

"I have never given a personal interview in my life," he has boasted, and it's the rare and exceptionally secure friend or colleague who will make a statement about him on the record.

Unlike most of his peers, Diller has no press agent. And yet, for all of his detractors, he consistently gets great press, because his accomplishments stand on their own merits. "He really is the brightest of the bunch," says Julia Phillips, one of the few in Hollywood who will speak for attribution. (The successful producer and author of *You'll Never Have Lunch in This Town Again* truly has nothing to lose.) "He really did do all those things his admirers say about him."

Diller's profound sense of privacy extends to those selected few who share his personal life, about which he admits to being shy. "I respect privacy in other people, and I expect them to respect it in me," he once told a journalist who tried, with little success, to probe the recesses of Diller's psyche. Asked to comment on some of the people who make up his most intimate circle, he replied, "I wouldn't ever talk about a friend."

Yet some facts are a matter of public record.

Michael Diller, Barry Diller's father, was the youngest of seven children born to Bernard Diller, an Austrian-Jewish immigrant who arrived in San Francisco in 1902, at the age of 37. It took Bernard, a butcher and grocer, only three years to save enough money to send for his wife, Ida and their children: Charlie (born 1891), Minnie (born 1895), Fanny (born 1899), and Sammie, who would later be known as Richard (born 1902, according to some records, or 1905, on the boat to America, according to others).

The year after Ida and the children arrived in America, the Dillers, along with thousands of other San Francisco residents, lived through the worst earthquake and fire in the city's history. Nevertheless, they remained in their newly adopted hometown, where they worked hard to establish themselves, eventually buying a house at 1081 McAllister Street to raise their family. Bernard, a deeply religious man, opened a market where he sold kosher meat (slaughtered according to Jewish law) and groceries in the heart of San Francisco's Orthodox Jewish community, while Ida took care of their ever-growing family. In all, she was pregnant 11 times; four babies died in infancy, and three more were born in

San Francisco: Esther (1905), Morris (1908), and Meyer Diller (1909), who would later change his name to Michael.

The patriarch of the Diller family was also the dean of the city's orthodox Jews. Greatly respected and admired within his circle, he was noted for his generosity to various charities. He was also a member of several Jewish communal organizations, including the Hebrew Free Loan Association and the Jewish Education Society. He was a charter member—and later served as president—of the Chevra Kadisha, founded in 1905 to ensure that indigent Jews would be given a proper Jewish burial.

By the time Michael met Reva Addison, a pretty young receptionist who was originally from Massachusetts, the Diller family had several well-established stores, including Diller Meats and Diller's Market, where Michael worked. (A third store, Diller Deli in the Financial District, survives to this day and is considered by many guidebooks as one of the city's 10 best breakfast places.) Reva was not Jewish, which most likely posed a problem for her orthodox future father-in-law, who would have preferred that his son marry within the Jewish faith. Nevertheless, the couple was wed on February 14, 1932.

Reva gave birth to their first child, Donald Addison, on November 6, 1938. Their second son, Barry Charles, was born almost four years later on February 2, 1942, in Mount Zion Hospital. Sadly, the boy would never know his dynamic and highly regarded grandfather, who had died seven months earlier from cancer, but in keeping with Jewish tradition, the new baby was given the name Barry, in memory of Bernard.

Barry spent his early childhood at 206 Willard Street, surrounded by his many uncles, aunts, and cousins. At the age of seven, he experienced the first major upheaval of his life when his father and his Uncle Richard relocated their families down the coast to Los Angeles. The reason for the move was financial. The postwar economy was booming, and Richard Diller wanted a piece of the action. Returning World War II veterans desperately needed mid-priced housing, which they were able to pay for with the newly enacted guaranteed government loans.

He and Michael set up their home construction business, which eventually spun off into a multitude of construction and real estate development companies that included Diller Building Corporation, Denlo Corporation, Diller Beverlywood, Diller Encino, Lassie Corporation, Dilworth, Jowett, and Joyce Properties—at 8549 Wilshire Boulevard, between a Midas Muffler shop and a Mobil gas station. Richard was the head and brains of the operation, while younger brother Michael, who identified himself for most of his career as a construction worker, was the expediter, salesperson, and general go-fer.

Both Diller families bought houses not far from their office in Beverly Hills, which even then was home to many movie stars and industry executives. The fabled enclave got its start in the mid-1920's, after the three highly publicized trials of comedian Fatty Arbuckle for the murder of model Virginia Rappe at a marathon drunken orgy attended by several well-known Hollywood figures. Arbuckle was ultimately acquitted, but the industry's reputation was badly tarnished, and the studios felt the need for damage control.

They therefore invited William Hays, chairman of the Republican National Committee and a member of President Warren G. Harding's Cabinet, to become Hollywood's morality czar. Hays, who was charged with bringing decency to Hollywood, judged the movie community to be a modern-day Sodom and Gomorrah. He urged its residents to move to Beverly Hills, just to the west. Real estate development soared, as actors and actresses, directors, and producers built their new homes in the far more sedate, family-oriented town where Will Rogers was mayor.

Future indiscretions were to be kept very, very private; Hays and the studio heads demanded that the industry promote a public image of virtue and rectitude. The studio publicity departments worked overtime to maintain and polish Hollywood's squeaky-clean facade. This was the environment in which Barry Diller grew up—an atmosphere where drug and alcohol abuse, beatings and rapes, homosexuality, and unhappy marriages had no place—unless they happened behind locked doors and were kept a well-guarded secret from the moviegoing public.

By Diller's own description, Beverly Hills in the 1950s was very much a small town, with a population of only 30,000 people. Everybody knew one another, and the hordes of tourists who today come to sightsee on Rodeo Drive had yet to arrive.

Three major boulevards—Sunset, Santa Monica, and Wilshire—divide Beverly Hills into four, economically defined neighborhoods. The lower priced housing and apartment buildings are located south of Wilshire. Moving northward, the commercial district lies between Wilshire and Santa Monica. The homes of the well-to-do and moderately rich are situated between Santa Monica and Sunset, while the estates of the super-rich are tucked away north of Sunset, stretching up into the canyons of the Santa Monica Mountains above the Beverly Hills Hotel.

Reva and Michael Diller, who lived between Santa Monica and Sunset Boulevards, had hardly arrived in Los Angeles before they were having marital problems severe enough that they separated on August 14, 1949. Soon thereafter, the couple signed a property settlement agreement that gave Reva custody of the two children, as well as the furniture, alimony of five hundred dollars a month, and one hundred dollars monthly for child support. Reva filed for divorce on September 13, 1949, on the grounds of extreme cruelty, but the next day, Michael filed an answer denying the cruelty charges.

Whatever the truth to Reva's assertions, by May 1950, the Dillers had apparently patched up their differences. The divorce action was dismissed at Reva's request.

Although the Dillers were a large family, they didn't seem to be particularly close. Frances Anderson, Richard Diller's long-time secretary, remembers that her boss often mentioned to her that the Dillers didn't get together on holidays. There was no love in their family, he told her, and he missed that. Anderson says that the lack of warmth and intimacy seemed to greatly trouble him.

Those who knew the Diller clan in San Francisco talk about the "Diller drive," referring to the family's work ethic, sense of ambition, and philanthropic spirit. Richard Diller was responsible for bringing many Jews over from eastern Europe, including a young man who had just been released from a concentration camp. His daughter, Joyce, who was six years older than Barry, helped to establish the largest Jewish day school in the United States, located on Mulholland Drive in Los Angeles.

Barry Diller was exposed early to the insider realities of business, real estate development, and the glamorous entertainment world. He already showed signs of the Diller drive when at age eight, while visiting his family's modestly furnished business office, he wrote out a check for one million dollars. He showed the check to Frances Anderson declaring, "One of these days I'll be writing these checks for real."

Barry attended Beverly Hills High School, along with the children of such stars as Doris Day, Danny Thomas, and Frank Lovejoy. For the most part, Barry was bored by his schoolwork. He found the reading he did on his own far more rewarding than what was being taught in the classroom, and regularly buried himself in books on subjects that intrigued him.

"Everything I ever learned, I learned because I was curious, not because someone asked me to learn something," he said years later. "When anyone did, I would resent it and rebel against it. But I read an immense amount of stuff for a little person."

He didn't see much point in attending classes, demanding of his father, "Why should I go to school or work in real estate?" He had made other plans for his future: Danny Thomas, the father of his close friend and schoolmate, Marlo, would help him get a job at William Morris, the preeminent talent agency that represented Thomas. "I want to work in the movies," he told Michael Diller.

He was already showing signs of the articulate and assertive adult he was to become, eagerly engaging in discussions and argument with adults—particularly his father. "From a very early age, I loved to incite him and then do battle," he once said. "It drove my mother crazy."

By then, his older brother had left home and was pursuing a different lifestyle. According to police records, Donald Diller had been smoking marijuana from the time he was 15. At 17, when he had his first encounter with the police, he had moved on to heroin and was using approximately three grams a day.

Donald was arrested again when he was eighteen for bouncing a check, not the first time he'd done so, according to Reva. Indicted for passing bad checks, he was sentenced to prison and served six months there. In 1959, he voluntarily committed himself for treatment at a narcotics hospital in Fort Worth, Texas, where he remained for seven months, trying to break his drug habit.

Barry, meanwhile, was in his senior year at Beverly Hills High School. He had joined the staff of the *Cub*, the student newspaper, but his interest in journalism apparently didn't last long. He also played on the varsity football team, which gave him a certain amount of status among his schoolmates, even though the team couldn't seem to win many games. Despite new head and line coaches, and an offense strategy copied from the one used by legendary Vanderbilt University coach Red Sanders, who had recently moved to UCLA, the Beverly Hills High Normans lost to Lennox, Burbank, Hawthorne, Culver City, El Segundo, Morningside, and North Torrance High Schools. It would be the last time for 30 years that Barry Diller would play on a losing team.

2

The Mailroom
and Beyond

William Morris was a pale young man of 25 when he established his own theatrical booking agency in 1898 on 103 East 14th Street in New York City. Eschewing modesty, he named the agency after himself and proceeded to handle the talent for vaudeville houses across the country. Boston financier Joseph P. Kennedy was one of Morris's early backers, and among his first big acts was Harry Lauder, a former coal miner turned Scottish minstrel who appeared on stage in kilts with a routine that featured Scottish songs and clever patter. Morris got Lauder the unheard-of sum of three thousand dollars a week on the condition that from then on, Lauder would always wear kilts in public.

Four years later, in 1912, William Morris hired a 14-year-old office boy named Abe Lastfogel, who chose the job at the booking office over one he'd been offered by a tailor. The agency continued to grow surviving the 1931 death of its founder, who suffered a heart attack while playing pinochle at the Friars Club. Morris's son,

William, Jr., took over the business until the end of World War II, when the former office boy, Abe Lastfogel, became head of the company.

Under Lastfogel's leadership, the agency prospered, in part because it was the principal supplier of talent for the Las Vegas hotels. In the early 1950s, however, a major change was taking place in the entertainment industry, in response to the growing new medium of television and its seemingly insatiable demand for talent. Manufacturers and the business community, discovering the impact television could have on consumer consumption, lavished it with their advertising dollars. The competing networks, in turn, initiated a frenzied search for shows and personalities that would attract the greatest share of viewers and, thereby, more advertising. Abe Lastfogel and his colleagues were swamped with demands for shows, which made William Morris the richest and most powerful agency in Hollywood, and turned its clients into wealthy stars.

Leonard Goldenson, president of United Paramount Theatres, a federally ordered spin-off of Paramount Pictures, had just purchased the upstart American Broadcasting Company, and suddenly he needed talent to fill his airtime. Goldenson knew he couldn't afford the expensive and nerve-racking live performances that aired on NBC and CBS, the two major networks. He brought his problem to Abe Lastfogel, who over the years had provided him with the vaudeville acts that had played alongside the movies in his theaters.

Goldenson wanted to tape shows on film, which not only allowed for cheaper production, but also permitted the option of rebroadcasting the same show any number of times for the same price as one live performance. Lastfogel had plenty of talent to offer, but he insisted on creating package deals: If Goldenson—or any of the networks for that matter—wanted a particular client, he also had to hire another William Morris client.

Shows were thus created around comedians and song-and-dance men like Ray Bolger (*Where's Raymond?*) and George Jessel

(George Jessel's Show Business). It took longer to develop the right vehicle for comedian Danny Thomas, who was then earning ten thousand dollars a week at the Sands and other Vegas nightspots. But finally the agency came up with a show taken straight out of Thomas's life. *Make Room for Daddy* was about a nightclub comic, always away doing his act, who was trying to be a good father; it became a huge, long-run hit, and one of William Morris's biggest moneymakers.

During this period, as Frank Rose described in his book, *The Agency,* William Morris also connected with a young, wide-eyed comedian from North Carolina named Andy Griffith, who quickly became a national sensation, as well as another young Southerner, an aspiring singer who had been driving a truck out of Memphis. Harry Kalcheim, the agent who discovered him, thought he had seen it all, but the "baby-faced greaser with sideburns and a sneer who came out onstage in red pants and a pink shirt and a green jacket" was a revelation to Kalcheim. The most amazing part, Kalcheim told his coagents when he got back to the office, was that the respectable Southern girls in the audience were screaming and ripping their panties off and flinging them at the stage.

The greaser was Elvis Presley. The agency grabbed Presley as a client, and within months secured him a seven-year movie deal at Paramount and a number of television appearances.

The 1960s began with the stunning revelation that such big-bucks quiz shows as *The $64,000 Question* and *Twenty-One* were rigged. One of the former contestants involved in the deception was Charles Van Doren, himself a college professor and the son of a famous academician. William Morris rode out the scandal as well as several Justice Department investigations of it and other entertainment agencies.

In 1961, Barry Diller had dropped out of UCLA ("I sort of slid away," was how he described his very brief college experience). He had long coveted a job at William Morris, and now he turned to

Danny Thomas for help. Thomas's importance to the agency was such that Diller was hired to work in the mail room, the classic entry level slot, even though he lacked one of their basic requirements, a college degree.

Technically, Diller was supposed to copy contracts, memos, correspondence, and every other imaginable document relevant to the business, then return them to the various agents. He and his mail room co-workers, wrote Frank Rose in *The Agency,* a history of William Morris, "got to learn who was who, to deliver scripts and contracts and checks to people around town, to read the confirmation memos that went out setting forth the terms for deals that had just been struck."

Barry Diller set himself the task of reading every document that passed through his hands. Years later, he recalled the education he got at William Morris.

"I was nineteen years old, and I thought that was a great place to go and learn about the business. I wanted to learn everything that was going on. I'd take these huge stacks of files and read every detail in them. I mean, you go to college to read; that what I was doing at William Morris. I read their entire file room. It took me three years, but I did it.

"You know how people say they read at Oxford? Well, I read at William Morris. It may sound pretentious, but it is an accurate analogy, because for me William Morris was the best library in the world. They always talk about people being anxious to get out of the mail room. Well, I kept fighting to stay in it."

It took him a week and a half to go through Elvis Presley's six-foot-high file. "I was interested in the process of what Elvis was doing. I was like a sponge."

During his apprenticeship in the mail room, Diller made a key connection with another employee who had also avoided the college degree requirement. David Geffen, a slightly built and energetic young music maven, was to become one of his best friends. Geffen had been raised in Brooklyn by a single mother who supported the family by running her own corset-making business out of her home. Although Geffen was putting himself through the William Morris drill, he had no intention of staying on as an agent. He, too, was determined to run his own operation, to be his own boss.

By Diller's own account, by the time he was finished with his reading course, he knew more about the agency than anyone else at William Morris. The files had taught him about life, about personal relationships, about the inner workings of a company. He had absorbed the informational equivalent of a business degree.

For a time, Diller was assigned the job of chauffering Abe Lastfogel around Los Angeles. But it quickly became clear that Diller was a maniac behind the wheel and he was soon relieved of the responsibility. He stayed in the mail room until 1964, when he was chosen to be secretary to Phil Weltman, one of the agency's top executives and a close friend of Sammy Weisbord, head of television for the agency when television was bringing in 60 percent of William Morris's profits.

According to Frank Rose, Weltman had assigned himself the mission of "developing manpower, taking green but ambitious kids like Barry Diller and turning them into sellers. Those who made it out of the mail room (like Barry Diller) went to work as secretaries for whoever happened to have an opening. They typed up memos, fielded incoming phone calls, listened in on phone calls to take notes and fed figures to the agent when he needed them. In the process, they learned how to talk to the buyers, how to make a deal, what to go for and what to leave behind. By the time they graduated to junior agent status, they were expected to have picked up a thorough understanding of the business. Weltman rode herd on the new guys. The core of his message was follow-through and integrity."

Weltman deeply admired Abe Lastfogel, whom he considered to be the ideal agent. Lastfogel was quiet, modest, and dedicated to the best interests of his client. Also, as Frank Rose tells it, Weltman saw Lastfogel as "a man motivated by incredible passion. Weltman wanted to instill that passion in his boys."

Barry Diller came to share Weltman's feelings about Lastfogel, and his example of passion helped to shape Diller's management style. (Diller, the former mail room kid, would be one of three people chosen to eulogize Lastfogel, the ex-office boy, at his funeral when he died of a heart attack in the summer of 1984.) He was also absorbing Weltman's lessons about the need to follow up on details, no matter how seemingly unimportant, and the importance of conducting oneself with integrity, which Diller understood to mean keeping one's word and being true to one's inner convictions.

Weltman eventually promoted Diller up the next rung of the William Morris ladder to junior agent. But Diller, by his own admission, had little interest in representing talent. He wanted to do *something* in the entertainment industry; that had been his goal for years. What that something might be was not altogether clear. His experience at William Morris—the thousands of documents he'd read, the training he'd received from Weltman and others—had shown him a dizzying array of options that he could pursue. The question was, where to go next? What would best suit his temperament and talents?

He was smart, a quick study, a hard worker. He was good at numbers and could hold his own in an argument. At a party given in 1966 by his friend Marlo Thomas, he met ABC-TV executive Len Goldberg, whom Marlo was dating at the time. Diller was only 24, but that didn't stop him from getting into a lengthy and heated argument with Goldberg, ". . . a tremendous fight," as Goldberg described it. "Not with fists. A verbal battle. I started it purposely. I wanted to provoke him, see what he was really like. I was very impressed with Barry's knowledge—being such a young man."

Goldberg decided to offer the knowledgeable young man a job at his earliest opportunity, which came soon thereafter, when he asked Diller to become his assistant. Although it was a demotion of sorts, Diller accepted the position. And then came a sudden stroke of luck, which Diller remembers thusly: "In some ways, my career has been a series of little surprises. The first surprise came as a result of getting to know the boyfriend of my friend Marlo Thomas, Leonard Goldberg. Anyway, the day I quit William Morris, the guy Goldberg worked for—the head of all programming for ABC in New York—left the network. And they reached down and picked Leonard Goldberg to replace him. So suddenly, instead of being the assistant to a middle-level vice-president at a West Coast outpost, I was the assistant to the overall head of programming for the entire network. And, that, as they say, was that."

His new position meant leaving the West Coast for New York, where he knew no one and had neither friends nor family. Manhattan was a very long distance, psychologically and geographically, from the "small town" of Beverly Hills. Officially, Diller was Goldberg's assistant, but that didn't stop people from teasing him about being a secretary. And ABC itself was in the midst of an attempted merger with International Telephone and Telegraph (ITT) to save its corporate identity.

ABC, originally known as the Blue Network, got its start as an offshoot of NBC. When Leonard Goldenson purchased it in 1951 (the actual deal wasn't confirmed until 1953 after 19 months of government hearings), ABC was the perennial weak sister among the triumvirate of networks. (A favorite joke among media followers at the time was that the television marketplace had room for only two-and-a-half networks—and ABC was the half. A fourth network, pioneered by Allen B. DuMont who manufactured TV sets, had begun broadcasting in 1946, but collapsed in 1955 when it ran out of money.)

The television industry as a whole was struggling to find itself in that first postwar decade. Then, as now, the biggest problem facing all the networks was finding product. The networks were committed to provide their affiliates around the country with 28 hours a week of prime-time programming. But where to find the programs to fill all those hours? For CBS's William Paley and NBC's David Sarnoff, the easy answer was to move the stars of their radio shows—Bob Hope, Edgar Bergen, Jack Benny, Bing Crosby, and George Burns and Gracie Allen—over to television.

Leonard Goldenson, coming from Paramount, saw another obvious source of programming material—licensing the rights to broadcast movies. Motion pictures were still the most popular form of entertainment in the country, and one movie could fill two hours of programming time. But a major barrier existed to this solution: Hollywood regarded television as its deadly enemy. Movie executives were notorious for battling every technological advance that required them to make an adaptive response. They had fought sound, resisted color film, and railed against radio. Now they saw television as an invention of the devil, created to destroy their industry. The studios therefore declared war on the box in the living room. They forbade their stars to appear on television and refused to provide movies to their upstart competitor.

As the pressure of demands by the networks and their viewers increased, however, the studios decided to release old movies that no longer had significant box-office appeal. Eventually, that too changed, as the studios began to calculate the profits they could reap from licensing to and producing for their television rivals.

Although some people in Hollywood regarded Goldenson as a traitor for buying ABC, he still had a lot of friends in the movie industry. Nevertheless, it took him a long time, and many conversations, to find a studio head who would take the lead in making a deal with the TV devil. Finally, in 1953, at dinner with Jack Warner, Goldenson succeeded in convincing the elderly studio head that he should create movies explicitly for television.

The next big step for ABC came in 1954 on the wings of a fantasy envisioned by one of Hollywood's greatest artistic geniuses, Walt Disney. Disney dreamed of building a giant amusement park unlike anything that existed in America. His chosen site was on 160 acres of farmland in Anaheim, an area southeast of Los Angeles settled by German immigrants.

The problem was how to find financing for his project. His brother Roy didn't support the idea. and the banks scoffed at Disney's projection of a million visitors a year going through the turnstiles of the Magic Kingdom. William Paley and David Sarnoff both turned him down because they imagined a park that looked something like the tawdry sideshows and daredevil rides at Coney Island.

Disney turned in desperation to Leonard Goldenson, who agreed to buy 35 percent of Disneyland for $500,000 and guaranteed the bank loans for several million more. In addition, ABC got first crack at Disney movies and the rights to the weekly Disney show that aired on Sunday evenings, as well as to the *The Mickey Mouse Club,* which ran five afternoons a week. (Disney far underestimated the annual attendance at Disneyland. The first year he opened the gates to the Magic Kingdom, six million visitors showed up.)

ABC continued to be the financially struggling underdog into the early 1960s, when Goldenson had to confront the need for an infusion of serious money to enable his network to survive the competition with CBS and NBC. RCA, NBC's parent company, had created a government-approved system of color television, and both Madison Avenue and the public were demanding that television transmission and reception be converted into color. Switching from black-and-white equipment and programming would cost ABC an enormous amount of money that it didn't have. But without color, the network would lose viewers and advertisers in droves.

ABC was further hurt by the fact that once Hollywood had discovered the money to be made from peddling its films—already produced in color—to the networks, it began to boost its fees. And Goldenson, who had helped them find their way into television, was given no price breaks for his efforts.

By 1964, ABC found itself in desperate need of $134 million in new capital to convert to color. Beyond that, most of its stock was not closely held by a few people, as was the case with NBC and CBS. This set the scene for Norton Simon, a 1960s style corporate raider, to begin buying up ABC in little chunks and pieces. Goldenson saw Simon as a serious threat to his control of the company. In December 1965, he called for help from his friend Laurence Tisch, the chairman of the Loews Corporation.

Tisch put Goldenson together with an oddball corporate financial guru, Harold Geneen, who ran International Telephone and Telegraph, a multibillion dollar giant that few people knew much about. The two men each had something the other wanted: Goldenson needed a massive cash infusion for ABC, and Geneen was convinced that affiliation with ABC would give ITT greater public name recognition, which would thus increase the value of its stock.

But could the two of them work together? Goldenson and his key executives were dubious because Geneen had a reputation as an inquisitorial number cruncher who required detailed reports, which the ABC people had always avoided. Nevertheless, there seemed to be no other choice, and ABC's board approved what newspapers heralded as the largest merger in the history of communications.

The deal still had to pass the scrutiny of the Federal Communications Commission and the Justice Department; how long their investigations might take would depend on the political winds blowing in Washington. In the meantime, ITT was advancing money to ABC in anticipation of a favorable ruling. The network was scrambling to catch up with its more affluent sisters when Barry Diller arrived there in April, 1966.

Television as a mass medium had developed by that time to the point that almost every home in America had a set, and TV viewing dominated five to six hours a day of everyone's life. Programming was dominated by the three networks, a much different configuration than the current 36-plus channels and the promise of 500 more. Network-affiliated programming accounted for 93 percent of all shows on all television channels. These shows would be repeated several times on whichever of the three networks had underwritten their production. They would then be given a second life when they were recycled again and again in syndicated reruns on independent stations, much as they are to this day.

Control of the networks had shifted away from the technicians and engineers who had ruled in the early days of television development, and into the hands of the programmers who had to meet the demands of Madison Avenue. Television was evolving into a very profitable enterprise. As broadcast pioneer and former head of CBS News, Fred W. Friendly, characterized it, "The people from Harvard Business School taught the networks how to institutionalize their greed."

During his early years at ABC, headquartered on West 66th Street in a building that formerly had housed a riding stable, Diller was aware that there was turmoil in the executive suite as Goldenson and his team tried to solve the financial problems of a network whose profits plummeted 25 percent in 1967. But the more immediate problem faced by Leonard Goldberg, and therefore Diller, was to create programming and feed it to the affiliate. He had brought with him from William Morris a deep understanding of the movie business beyond his years, as well as the contacts he had made there, both of which would greatly benefit his new employer. It certainly didn't hurt that through Phil Weltman, he had gotten to know Sammy Weisbord, the head of the agency's television department.

Diller was excited about getting involved in what he recognized as an enormous opportunity. "The wonderful thing about ABC was that it allowed people to take all the responsibility we wanted," he recalled. "It was never a question of waiting for somebody to *give* us responsibility. With the responsibility came authority."

The essence of his management style began to emerge during this period. Goldberg would later say of his former assistant, "The best thing about Barry was that you told him to get something done and you could blank it from your mind. You never asked how it got done. Command came easily to him. He was always comfortable with power."

He was also very ambitious, highly focused, and fearless. In situations where others, even those with more experience, might second-guess themselves, Diller saw a challenge to be met, rather than a problem to be concerned about. He enjoyed taking risks, and the atmosphere at ABC encouraged that facet of his personality.

For all of that, his first two years were difficult ones. He was having to learn his way around network television at a time when the whole ABC organization was lurching from one crisis to the next. Confusing rumors were constantly circulating about the pending ABC-ITT merger. Meanwhile, Tom Moore, president of the network, was trying to elevate the level of ABC programming and upgrade the company's image. He won praise from the critics for his efforts, but the all-important ratings fell.

ABC had long been the butt of jokes in the television industry, largely because of its second-rate programming and lack of clear goals and style. Unlike CBS—the "Tiffany network"—noted for its high-class programming and top-notch news department, or NBC, whose technicians oversaw the most advanced equipment in the industry, ABC was in the middle of an identity crisis. The network simply could not create shows that would become long-term hits.

As one joke put it in the late 1960s: "Want to end the war in Vietnam? Put it on ABC-TV and it will be over in thirteen weeks."

The prolonged government investigation into ITT's foreign connections, which Washington feared might try to influence news broadcasts if the corporation were to acquire ABC, ultimately killed Harold Geneen's interest in the deal. On New Year's Day, 1968, Goldenson received word that the ITT board had voted to rescind its offer. The sighs of relief could be heard on both sides.

Reinventing the Wheel

The same year that ABC was set loose from ITT, Barry Diller received a promotion. At age 26, he was made vice-president of prime-time programming, in charge of buying feature films for the weeknight time slots when the network ran movies. He was entering into deals for ABC that involved millions of dollars.

In this new role, Diller theoretically held the weaker negotiating position, because ABC needed the product far more than the movie producers needed ABC. Diller, however, handled the negotiations as if he had the upper hand. Leonard Goldenson recognized and appreciated his young employee's talents. "Barry Diller had quickly evolved into a tough, capable businessman and a hard-nosed negotiator," he later remarked. "His forte was negotiating the purchase of rights to feature pictures from the major companies."

Diller was given almost free rein and a tremendous amount of power for someone so young. He was dealing with top movie executives, talking terms and numbers with men like Lew Wasserman of

MCA, Arthur Krim of United Artists, and Charles Bluhdorn, the chairman of Gulf & Western, which owned Paramount Pictures.

Thanks to his William Morris background, Diller not only talked the same language as the movie pitchmen, he also understood that the studios were always hungry for more money to produce their films. He listened to hundreds of film ideas and quickly learned how to separate the garbage from the worthwhile project, training that would be worth millions to him later in his studio career.

At this point, the networks still thought of themselves as electronic movie houses sans popcorn. They were all three purchasing mostly older films from the studio archives. Diller's exposure to movie pitches by executives from the major studios soon had him brainstorming about other possibilities, asking himself "what if" ABC-TV could move in a somewhat different direction.

From thinking about "what if," Diller realized that ABC-TV was in the *entertainment business.* Buying and exhibiting product were only two aspects of that business. The key would be to come up with other concepts that could stretch the existing boundaries of how the network defined itself. He was still considering this question when Leonard Goldenson picked up the March 21, 1968, issue of *Variety,* which featured an article by a producer named Roy Huggins, who five years earlier had dreamed up the idea for *The Fugitive,* which became a four-year hit series for ABC. Now Huggins was suggesting that the industry create weekly 90-minute movies just for television. Huggins had already presented his idea to, and been dismissed by, Universal Studios, with whom he was under contract, CBS, and NBC. One CBS executive called the idea the worst he'd ever heard in his life.

Goldenson invited Huggins to come meet with Len Goldberg and Barry Diller. ABC in the 1960s was "a hip-shooting place," as Diller put it. And it was precisely because ABC habitually ran third in the network ratings that revolutionary ideas, which today seem perfectly obvious and commonplace, were welcomed and explored.

The two men saw possibilities in Huggins's concept of "hard-hitting melodramas and mysteries" that the other networks had missed. They also realized they didn't need Huggins to make it happen, although they did offer him control over 8 of the 26 shows they had decided to produce exclusively for television. Huggins wanted to make all 26 for ABC. Angry that his concept had been stolen from under him, he declined their offer. Diller was put in charge of translating the idea into reality. In short order, the job took over his life.

He and Marty Starger, who was later to succeed Len Golderg as head of programming, presented the idea to the ABC board; they requested a budget of $14 million for the series, and a commitment for a series. Despite the board's misgivings—there was neither pilot nor script at this point—they were given the go-ahead.

Diller typically wanted to produce the movie himself, rather than give over control of the project to the Hollywood studios. His superiors at ABC were dubious: what did Diller, or anyone at ABC, for that matter, know about moviemaking? Universal had been producing two-hour movies for television since 1962, and Diller was in charge of negotiating with them for movie rights. Now, he approached Universal about working out a deal for ABC's new concept. Universal was willing to produce *Movie of the Week* at a cost $400,000 per show; they also wanted a guarantee that any and all future movies to be aired on ABC would be made with Universal.

ABC, understandably, did not want to be tied to such a contract, and Diller insisted that he could make the 90-minute films for $350,000 apiece. Although Lew Wasserman soon regretted the demands his company had made of ABC and attempted to restructure the deal, Diller prevailed. ABC formed its own production company and assigned the various movies to hungry young producers who established their own independent companies on the basis of their new relationships with ABC.

The first *Movie of the Week,* which aired in the fall of 1969, was about a returning war veteran. Entitled *Corporate Cracker,* it was produced by Aaron Spelling, who was eventually credited by the *Guinness Book of Records* as the most productive television producer of all time. Steven Spielberg made his debut film feature for Diller, with *Duel.* The series' ratings were remarkable. The weekly movies drew 33 percent of the total TV audience the first year, and 38 percent after that.

Beyond inaugurating the *Movie of the Week,* Diller had complete control of the advertising, promotion, and direction of the project. He was, in effect, supervising a new, small-scale movie studio.

"We did it with a tiny staff, just five people in the beginning," he said. "At first, every detail of every production, from idea to script to finished movie, was supervised by me and Jerry Eisenberg. Then Michael Eisner, who was working in another part of ABC, joined us along with one or two other people and that was it. It's amazing what you can do with very few people if you know what you're trying to do."

"A scrappy group of guys," was how Michael Eisner described the team that worked with Diller.

In 1966, Eisner had been laboring at CBS at a tedious, low-level position when he sent out his resume to television executives all over New York. Diller, the only one who responded, met with him and liked what he saw. Diller was proven to be a sharp judge of talent when his protégé, who was just a month younger than he, proceeded to become an integral part of ABC's programming success.

Eisner had grown up in luxury on Park Avenue, the son of a Harvard-educated lawyer who founded the American Safety Razor Company, later sold it out for a fortune to the Phillip Morris company, and then invested in lucrative New York real estate. Michael and his sister had a strictly disciplined childhood that included two hours of reading a day before they could watch one hour of television, ballroom dancing school, and a chauffeur-driven family station wagon.

Eisner attended the exclusive Lawrenceville School where he was unsuccessful at sports, but enjoyed dabbling in theater. He failed to develop into the outstanding student his parents had hoped he would become, and instead of following his father to Princeton University, Eisner enrolled at Denison University, a smaller, far less prestigious school in Granville, Ohio. At Denison, he was a shy premed student who fell in love with writing plays. His first job in the entertainment industry was during the summer of his junior year, when he worked as a page at NBC. After graduation, and a trip to France where he briefly indulged his fantasy of writing the great American novel in Paris, he returned to New York and found an entry-level job at NBC.

Two years later, having moved on to CBS, he was interviewed by Diller, then still Len Goldberg's assistant, who sold his boss on hiring the tall, boyish-faced Eisner. (Goldberg's first thought on meeting Eisner was that he should comb his hair.) Eisner's initial job at ABC was in the programming department where he soon became assistant to Gary Pudney, the newly hired director of specials and talents. "Take this kid and see what you can do with him," Goldberg told Pudney. "If he works out, we'll find a place for him. If he doesn't, fire him."

Eisner, who looked like a big, rumpled kid, often showed up at the office toting his motorcycle helmet. But he was smart, charming, enthusiastic, and indefatigable in his search for new talent in the city's theaters, clubs, and coffeehouses. He soon became manager of specials and talents.

Diller recognized Eisner's childlike sensibility which enabled him to intuit the kind of programs that would appeal to younger audiences. By 1970, he had arranged to have Eisner, then all of 28, put in charge of ABC's Saturday morning children's programming, material designed to keep the kids occupied while mom and dad slept late.

Before long, Eisner managed to steal *Bugs Bunny* away from CBS—no small coup. But Bugs was just the beginning of Eisner's triumphs at ABC. He decided it made sense to create animated versions of real-life teenage idols and sold his bosses on producing cartoons based on the Jackson Five, the Osmond Brothers, and Super Friends. The shows made ABC the number one network with children on Saturday morning. Within five years, Eisner would be in charge of all children's and daytime programming, and would help develop ABC's hit soap operas, *All My Children, One Life to Live,* and *General Hospital.*

On the business side, Leonard Goldenson was able to arrange, finally, for a fifty-million-dollar convertible debenture to be floated and used to pay off the twenty-five million dollars borrowed from ITT. That left enough money to help ease the network into color television and theatrical movies. In this last, he had the help of Diller, who was a tough and careful buyer of what the market had to offer.

The image of Barry Diller as boy wonder was starting to take shape. People had begun to notice him. "'All right, how did you do it?'" he recalls them asking. "'Where do I sign up for a job like yours?' And I'd look at them, these well-balanced, relatively calm people who had these normalish lives and I'd say, 'I can tell you, but you won't be able to imagine the level of energy and commitment and the things that you have to give up if you really want to do something like this.'"

Diller's life was consumed by his work. While others left the office at five o'clock or five-thirty to go home to their families or out to dinner, he was still at his desk, "thinking and worrying and talking and doing." His day would last another five or six hours, particularly after he was given responsibility for producing and scheduling original movies for three nights a week. (Within three years, he would be making 75 movies a year.) He was also still in charge of buying feature films from other producers to run on Sunday and Monday evenings.

As if he weren't already juggling enough creative and administrative balls, Diller was given responsibility for yet another programming innovation. The *Movie of the Week* had proved to him that people loved a good story and would stay with it even if the film ran longer than the traditional one-hour time frame into which most TV dramas were bracketed. On a trip to England, Marty Starger, who in 1972 had become president of the newly structured ABC Entertainment department, had discovered a new format created by BBC—the *miniseries:* Well-known novels and stage plays were broken up into episodes to be shown on television over three or more nights. Starger suggested that ABC create what he called *Novels for Television* and adapt the concept for American television.

Diller immediately grasped the possibilities of the concept. The miniseries was bursting with positive payoffs. Always an avid reader, he understood that some wonderful, dramatic novels were too long or complicated to be captured in a 90-minute movie. A six- or eight-hour format, spread over three or four nights, could accommodate even a sprawling, epic story. The additional time would allow for plot and character development that would pull in and hold a large audience.

Beyond the artistic considerations were the financial advantages. Generally, it would cost less per minute to produce one six-hour program than to produce six one-hour programs. Each program had its basic start-up expense, and having to do it once for six hours of programming was cheaper than doing it six times for six hours of programming. Longer scenes on the same sets with the same actors also provided a less expensive way of filling programming time. Most importantly, Diller could sell bigger blocks of commercials for the longer programs.

There was yet another benefit that Diller was quick to recognize. He was well aware that, with a few notable exceptions, people do not watch a particular television show at a particular hour. Instead, people tend simply *to watch television,* staying tuned to whatever channel they happen to be on.

For this reason lead-ins and tune-ins are important to local television stations. Thus, many stations today buy syndicated shows like *The Oprah Winfrey Show* or *The Ricki Lake Show* to run in the afternoon just before their local news programs because the talk shows attract big audiences with the demographics that advertisers want. Once the audience turns to the station at three or four in the afternoon, it tends to stay on that channel for the local news. Even if the local station loses money buying an expensive syndicated talk show, it can make up the loss by selling commercials in the local news programs that follow the strong lead-in.

Diller saw the miniseries as a way to capture an audience and have it tune in to ABC for several nights running. Not content to take the safe or easy path, he chose to launch the format with *QB VII* by Leon Uris, a story about a slander trial in England that also dealt with the Holocaust and castration. The show was produced by Douglas Cramer, who went on to become the co-executive producer of *Dynasty,* and starred Anthony Hopkins as the plaintiff.

"That's a very tough subject for television," he later acknowledged, "but I wanted to test this form against something tough, not something easy. We got remarkable results."

He followed up with *Rich Man, Poor Man,* by Irwin Shaw, "simply because I thought it was a good, good read."

Fred Pierce, the president of ABC Television, would observe, "We looked like geniuses, but we really were not. We simply had that product ready and that was the place to put it." The reason that they had that product ready was because Diller had pursued it and got it made in the hope that a miniseries format would catch on as it did.

Expanding on the miniseries concept, in 1972 Diller boldly chose a saga about black heritage and slavery called *Roots,* by Alex Haley. It was a daring and risky decision, with several negative points working against it.

Roots was a sympathetic, moving saga of a black family brought to America as slaves and abused through several generations. Although the story ended on a high note of freedom and reconciliation, more than a few of the white characters and white institutions were depicted as despicable and cruel, which could well alienate large segments of the viewing audience. The story was long and complex, as any multigenerational saga is. Unless the writers could keep the script fairly direct and simple, the series ran the risk of losing the average viewer who might have trouble remembering previous episodes from one night to the next.

Finally, since the show would be spread over several nights—five in fact—there was concern among some ABC executives as to whether it could hold the audience. Would viewers turn to another network where some of them would inevitably stay? To minimize this possibility, Diller and his colleagues decided to schedule the show to begin at 9:00 P.M., at the end of each evening's prime-time schedule.

Like many classic Hollywood production stories, *Roots,* the miniseries, almost didn't happen. Indeed, it might not have been made at all but for the determination of a filmmaker who had Diller's enthusiastic support. David Wolper, a seasoned producer of documentaries, had heard from Ossie Davis and Ruby Dee that black writer Alex Haley was working on a sweeping account of his family's history that spanned seven generations from his African ancestors up to the contemporary generation.

Intrigued by their description, Wolper investigated and found that Haley was some time away from being finished, and that Columbia Pictures already had the story under option. The Hollywood-savvy Wolper knew, however, that the big studios routinely optioned any number of books, articles, and proposals for relatively few dollars and then allowed the project to die, rather than spend the money to make the movie or let it fall into the hands of their competitors.

Wolper suspected that Columbia would never produce so controversial a film. It had taken 50 years after D. W. Griffith's *The Birth of a Nation* for Hollywood to make another movie—*Cabin in the Sky,* by Vincente Minnelli—that featured black actors in starring roles. He thought it highly unlikely that the studio would produce as controversial and dramatic a story as *Roots,* and that the option would most probably lapse.

Soon thereafter, Wolper went to have lunch at the Russian Tea Room on New York's West 57th Street. He noticed a friend of his seated at a table with two other women. When he went to say hello to his friend, she introduced him to her companions, one of whom happened to be Alex Haley's secretary. Of course, Wolper mentioned his interest in buying the book for television. As it turned out, Columbia's option had just expired. Wolper immediately called Haley's agent, and a deal was made.

Wolper went to Brandon Stoddard at ABC to sell him on producing the story for television. Stoddard and Diller both liked the idea, and Diller took it over, to do as a miniseries, even though it would be an immense undertaking because of all the sets and costumes that would be involved. It was just his sort of project—controversial, daring, a landmark. What none of them knew as they discussed the enormity of the project was that Alex Haley had not yet written one word of his book.

By the time the miniseries aired at the end of January 1977, Barry Diller was ensconced in Hollywood as chairman of Paramount Pictures, Wolper had been sidelined with a serious heart attack, and production had gone more than a million dollars over budget. *Roots* scored the highest collective ratings of any such program in television history. Its success was a more than fitting tribute to Diller's vision, tenacity, and commitment to quality, all of which had greatly burnished ABC's image and enriched its coffers.

Long before *Roots* captured America's imagination, Diller was becoming restless and dissatisfied. He was 32, ABC's senior programming executive, and he hated his job. He was spending too much of his time working on prime-time series, an area of television he was not familiar with and did not understand. Indeed, the prime-time lineup for the 1974–1975 season, his last at ABC, was very weak. "Lousy," is how one of his ABC colleagues later described it in an article that appeared in *Los Angeles* magazine in December, 1993. Another television executive who arrived at ABC shortly after Diller left says, "The shows were all terrible. The whole thing was a mess." Diller's legacy of shows for that final season included, among other long-forgotten series, *The Sonny Comedy Revue.*

Diller had been pursued for some time by Charles Bluhdorn, chairman of Gulf & Western, to work for him at Paramount. Bluhdorn, like Diller, relished the heated back-and-forth of a high-stakes negotiation and thrived on making deals. Bluhdorn had gotten to know Diller over the course of their discussions about movie rights. He was impressed by the young executive's style, his knowledge of the movie business, and his cold-blooded ability to flatly turn down a deal that didn't suit him, no matter that it was being offered by the chairman of the board of a major corporation.

Early in their relationship, Bluhdorn, who loved negotiating so much that he refused to delegate the responsibility to any of his underlings, telephoned Diller to give him a list of Paramount movie titles that were available for television and how much they would cost ABC. Diller was sunning himself by the pool at the exclusive Bel-Air Hotel in Los Angeles when Bluhdorn's call came through. He listened in silence to Bluhdorn's proposal. Then, oblivious to the other people seated around the pool, he yelled into the phone, "Over my dead body!" and hung up on Gulf & Western's chief executive.

Rather than take offense at Diller's brash response, Bluhdorn gave him credit for rejecting movies that were old and tired. By torpedoing the sale, Diller had saved ABC from a major embarrassment. Bluhdorn was new to the movie business, and Paramount, which represented one of his biggest investments, was floundering. As Bluhdorn got to know and admire Diller during several years of dealmaking, he came to see him as the person to help him right Paramount's course. Finally he put in a call to Diller's boss, Fred Pierce, who was president of ABC Television.

Pierce remembers their conversation. "Charlie called me in 1974 and asked if I'd let Barry out of his contract. He wanted to make him chairman of Paramount, but before he spoke to Barry, he wanted our approval."

Pierce, and his immediate superior, Elton Rule, ABC's president, agreed they couldn't legitimately stand in the way of Diller's accepting Bluhdorn's offer, which would be a wonderful career opportunity. Besides, they agreed it could only be to ABC's benefit to have one of their former employees at the helm of a Hollywood studio.

With their approval, Bluhdorn next called Diller and invited him to dinner. He wasted little time in offering him the job of heading Paramount Pictures. It was a no-lose situation for Diller, whose stature within ABC was enhanced by having been asked, whether he went or not.

According to Diller, until Bluhdorn offered him the position, he had never considered being in charge of Paramount, at least not consciously. "It was only Bluhdorn's desperation over the situation at Paramount—and certainly his genuine, long-term interest in me—that made it happen.

"I think he respected me not because I was so young, but that I wanted to prevail. Winning requires an act of will. There are moments and times when the exercise of my will is strong. And this business is all about will."

"I can't say no to him," he told himself. Seeking advice, he went to Berry Gordy, the founder of Motown Records. Gordy, a successful businessperson and close friend, could be objective because he was involved in a totally different arm of the entertainment industry.

"You're thirty-two years old, you've been offered the chairmanship of Paramount, and your response is that you *can't* say no?" said Gordy. "You're crazy!"

When Diller reported Bluhdorn's offer to Leonard Goldenson, the ABC chairman was equally unequivocal. His response to Diller's news was, "You have to take this opportunity."

4

At the Movies

When Barry Diller assumed the chairmanship of Paramount Pictures on October 1, 1974, he became part of a creative and business tradition that stretched back three-quarters of a century. He had grown up in the movie universe of Beverly Hills, which is actually the real locus of power in what is commonly and inaccurately called "Hollywood"—a sprawl of movie plants stretching from Culver City to Burbank with the actual community of Hollywood lying in between.

Sixty/sixty is the magic figure for the American entertainment world. Each year, Americans lavish 60 million hours and $60 billion on entertainment in its various forms, including American-made movies, TV programs, and popular music. Worldwide, 75 percent of all television revenues, 55 percent of all movie and videotape revenues, and 50 percent of recorded music revenues are spent on American artists and companies. The movie and television industry employs tens of thousands of people. Thus, the people who control movies, television, and music have enormous control over our lives and our culture. And America is still the unchallenged leader of the entertainment business.

The first working motion picture camera was invented by W.K.L. Dickson, an employee of Thomas Edison. The two men applied for a patent for a Kinetoscope camera in 1891, and Edison came up with a primitive system in which the earliest moviegoers put their eyes to a hole in order to view the filmstrip. In 1902, Edwin S. Porter produced *The Life of an American Fireman,* the first dramatic film with a plot. Porter, who for some years had been touring fairgrounds showing short films, followed up a year later with *The Great Train Robbery.*

Movies swept the country like a prairie brushfire and, within four years, thousands of small movie houses had been set up all over America, many of them only storefronts with folding chairs. The movie-hungry public, enthralled by the fascinating new medium, demanded as many new movies as could be produced. Southern California, with its mild climate, abundant sunshine, cheap labor, and the variety of diverse landscapes, provided an ideal environment for the small but burgeoning movie industry. In 1911, David Horsley leased a plot of land in Hollywood at the corner of Gower Street and Sunset Boulevard and established the Nestor film studio. By year's end, 15 more moviemakers had followed him there, and Hollywood and a mighty industry had been born.

The first movie mogul was Carl Laemmle, a German immigrant and former men's clothing retailer. Laemmle set up a nationwide distribution system, invented the star system, and made a hundred movies in the initial year of his Independent Moving Picture Company, which ultimately became Universal Studios. Other Hollywood pioneers included Jesse L. Lasky; Cecil B. De Mille; D. W. Griffith; two immigrant furriers, Adolph Zukor and Marcus Loew; and William Fox, a German immigrant who founded the studio that Barry Diller would someday run.

The world of the movies—the creative talent and their stars—became a special universe unto itself, remote from the concerns and realities of the majority of Americans. When Hollywood of the movies was coming into existence, most of the population centers of the United States were a three-day train ride away from southern California. Moviemakers and their stars lived a relatively isolated life of glamour in an idyllic climate. The moneymen, on the other hand, stayed in New York, far away from the fabled lots where legends were being made and stars were being born. This sense of distance generated a mystique about and a fascination with moviemaking that have endured to the present day; the myths infected Hollywood itself, which created its own unique subculture of heroes and icons.

Samuel Goldfish changed his name to Goldwyn when he joined with the Selwyn Brothers in 1916 to create Goldwyn Pictures. Marcus Loew bought Metro Pictures, then Goldwyn Pictures, and finally the studio founded by a former scrap metal trader, Louis B. Mayer, to create the biggest production company in Hollywood, Metro-Goldwyn-Mayer (M-G-M). Other companies formed in this era included Columbia, RKO, Twentieth Century-Fox, Paramount, and Warner Bros.

While other studios turned up their noses at the notion of adding sound to moving pictures, Warner Bros. embraced the concept with *The Jazz Singer*, which opened on October 6, 1927, starring Al Jolson. The movie was a huge hit and created an instant demand for "talkies."

William Fox, meanwhile, was expanding his company's ownership of movie theaters; he also launched the weekly Fox Movietone newsreels and made a bold try at taking over M-G-M. Fate knocked him out of action in a serious car accident just before the 1929 stock market crash. His empire collapsed around him, and the feisty German immigrant lost control of his studio. (In a sad footnote to his golden days in Hollywood, in 1941 William Fox ended up in jail for trying to bribe a judge. After he was released, and until his death in 1952, the Hollywood community—which traditionally loves only winners and is terrified of losers—turned its back on him.)

The Great Depression affected the movie industry as it did the rest of the country. Movie attendance dropped sharply as a new form of entertainment—radio—penetrated homes across America. Thanks to the genius of Irving Thalberg, M-G-M survived the period better than any of the other studios. Thalberg, who died tragically young in 1936 at age 37, served as production supervisor under Louis B. Mayer, the most feared and hated man in Hollywood.

Strong-willed and opinionated, Mayer totally controlled his studio, the pictures it made, and every aspect of the lives of the stars who made them. He was so dreaded and despised that at his funeral, which was attended by thousands of spectators if not mourners, comedian Red Skelton reportedly said, "See, if you give the people what they want, they'll come."

Despite the constant feuding between its two principals, Harry and Jack Cohn, Columbia weathered the Depression through its production of low-cost Westerns and an occasional star turn, such as the 1934 *It Happened One Night,* starring Clark Gable and Claudette Colbert, and directed by Frank Capra.

A year later, Fox merged with Twentieth Century Pictures to become Twentieth Century-Fox, which—like Columbia—turned out a series of low-cost, routine plot films mixed in with the occasional masterpiece, such as *The Grapes of Wrath,* released in 1940 and starring Henry Fonda.

The war years of the 1940s were golden years for Hollywood as movie attendance soared. But after World War II, Americans began discovering new forms of recreation such as miniature golf, bowling, and, most of all, television. By 1948, 200,000 TV sets a month were being sold; it was an electronic miracle that would affect American life more than almost anything else invented in the twentieth century. Hollywood moguls at first attacked and boycotted the television industry, then ultimately and inevitably embraced it, reaping millions of dollars through their partnership with the infant medium.

Worse troubles were to come. The federal government won a complicated antitrust case in 1948 that forced studios out of the distribution and exhibition business. They weathered the blow, regrouped, and fostered the "independent" production companies to which the studios rented costumes, sets, props, soundstages, back lots, and so on.

Nevertheless, the mid-1950s represented a period of decline for the studios, which continued to follow the old "studio system"— a handful of moguls retained control of the entire industry. With more people watching television in the comfort of their living rooms than filling the movie theaters, M-G-M survived by selling off some of its assets, starting with its back lots.

With the 1960s came the bottom-line mentality of the financial investors who, in the tradition of Joe Kennedy, were lured by Hollywood's charms. Charles Bluhdorn and Gulf & Western bought up Paramount; insurance giant Transamerica took over United Artists; Kinney National—a conglomerate that owned funeral parlors, parking lots, and janitorial services—assumed control of Warner Bros.; and oil wildcatter Marvin Davis won his fight with Herbert Siegel of Chris-Craft for ownership of Twentieth Century-Fox. Davis defeated Siegel's efforts with the help of a partner, Marc Rich, who was a criminal fugitive wanted by the U.S. government for tax evasion, fraud, and racketeering.

During Hollywood's heyday, from the 1920s through the 1940s, there were eight major studios: Columbia, Fox, M-G-M, Paramount, RKO, United Artists, Universal, and Warner Bros. Today, RKO is gone; its last owner was the reclusive and idiosyncratic millionaire, Howard Hughes. United Artists—after almost being destroyed by *Heaven's Gate,* one of the most expensive bad movies ever made—merged with M-G-M and is being kept afloat by a French bank.

Two companies that successfully survived the 1960s were Universal Studios and Walt Disney Productions, which was founded in the early 1930s on the backs of animated cartoon characters Mickey Mouse, Donald Duck, and Goofy. Disney did well because of the balance, and tension, between Walt and Roy Disney, until Walt's death in 1966, and the subsequent power struggle that ensued within the family through the early 1980s.

At the helm of Universal was MCA's Lew Wasserman, the Grand Old Man of Hollywood who knew how to flex the entertainment industry's financial and political muscle when and where it counted. Wasserman is a mysterious figure who doesn't leave the fingerprints of his influence. He hardly ever puts anything in writing, preferring to communicate through telephone calls and face-to-face conversations. Called by one observer "the Lamont Cranston of Hollywood" after the mythical radio hero, he is both feared and feted.

Once the agent of Ronald Reagan, confidant of presidents and kingmakers, Wasserman is said to be the largest individual contributer to the Democratic Party; he has also raised money for such diverse causes as the Jet Propulsion Lab, Cal Tech, and the Los Angeles Music Center. His ability to direct the enormous success of the MCA/Universal empire has earned him the sobriquet "the most powerful man in Hollywood."

Although he never went to college, Wasserman has a superb, insightful intellect that is able to grasp the intricacies of complex deals and the significance of events that leave others bewildered. He is not a creative artist, but rather a calculating, smart business executive who has mastered the art of finessing deals. To those who don't know him, Wasserman often seems imperial and impervious and unflappable—a man totally in control of himself and the situation. But behind closed doors, when angered, Wasserman has been known to rant and rage, leaving the target of his wrath shaking with fear.

Wasserman guided Universal Studios to safety until he finally sold it to the Japanese company, Matsushita, in the early 1990s for $6.5 billion. The deal infused Universal with the money it needed for its increasingly expensive competition with Disney. Matsushita later discovered that its corporate culture clashed irreconcilably with Hollywood's quirky business ethos, and it finally sold the company to whiskey heir Edgar Bronfman, Jr.

In spite of a string of hits in the mid-1950s and early 1960s that included *Shane, Rear Window, The Ten Commandments, Psycho,* and *The Carpetbaggers,* Paramount Pictures in the late 1960s was a company with big financial problems. Production was down, and the market value of its stock was dropping. By 1966, the studio was ripe for a corporate raider like Herb Siegel to swoop down and gobble it up. Siegel, a former talent agent enamored with the idea of being a movie mogul, didn't seem to have the grit to close the big deals by himself, so he teamed up with a couple of Broadway producers, Cy Feuer and Ernest Martin, to make a run at acquiring Paramount.

When Paramount's management, under its president George Weltner, got wind of Siegel's planned takeover, it set out to find a "white knight" who would buy the company and allow the reigning executives to remain in place. White knights rarely turned out to be either benign or benevolent. But Paramount's executives, like so many other corporate managers, preferred to ignore the possibility that the new owners might replace them in the interests of improving the company's bottom line and pleasing the shareholders.

Weltner sent his chief operating officer, Martin Davis, in search of a corporate titan who was both wealthy enough and willing to rescue Paramount from Siegel's unwanted advances. Davis came back with an improbable savior whose business was cotton, sugar, and car bumpers—Charles Bluhdorn.

Bluhdorn had arrived in America in 1942 from Austria as a 16-year-old refugee from the Nazis. He very shortly went to work on Wall Street. But the young immigrant was never comfortable with the traditional stock market trading establishment and used to rail at "those goddamn bluebloods," as he called them. He began his business career as a commodities trader, dealing mostly in cotton and coffee and earning a reputation as a man with incredible nerve and daring. He had earned his first million by the time he reached his mid-20s, in what was described by market analyst John Brooks as "a series of breathtaking deals in the commodities market."

His disdain for most of the Wall Street establishment was mutual. The old-line WASP snobs who ruled the Street considered his personality "too European," a euphemism for "too Jewish." Moreover, they complained, he lacked good taste in his acquisitions, going in for companies that made underwear, auto parts, and bowling balls, and published men's magazines.

Bluhdorn also talked too fast, alternately shouting and whispering at his audience. He was very emotional, and he spoke with a pronounced Viennese accent. One financier criticized his sputtering, grandiose speech as inappropriate for the exalted world of high finance.

By 1957, Bluhdorn had begun buying up overlooked or ailing companies with a view to creating a "conglomerate"—a developing business trend that was gaining popularity among stock traders. The concept actually got its start in the 1920s, when a number of large companies were flush with cash and casting about for profitable places to invest it. Most American companies had traditionally stayed within their own fields of manufacturing. But the entrepreneurial head of a conglomerate might use the springboard of one company to begin adding others from totally unrelated fields of manufacturing or enterprise, so long as the new companies could be purchased economically and make a profit. This new breed of corporate executives had decided that the principles of management were essentially the same from one enterprise to the next, even if the technical processes they employed were different.

Determined to imitate the damn bluebloods, Bluhdorn bought Michigan Bumper, a small, troubled company that made bumpers for Studebaker, a large, troubled company. Building on his base of Michigan Bumper, Bluhdorn continued to acquire other companies, until finally he fell in love with the idea of owning a movie studio. In 1967, he dramatically outbid Herbert Siegel for Paramount with an offer of 83 dollars a share.

His investment in Paramount suddenly thrust him into the magic of the movies—the glamorous world of beautiful young women, dashing men, and fantasy settings. One former Paramount official recalled Bluhdorn's visit to a location filming: "I'll never forget how Charlie came flying in by helicopter to the location of his first project, *Paint Your Wagon.* He had a kid's grin on his face. You just know he absolutely loved it."

By the time Bluhdorn purchased Paramount, he had renamed his conglomerate Gulf & Western. It included Kayser-Roth clothing manufacturers, Simmons mattresses, South Puerto Rican Sugar, Consolidated Cigar, Munsingwear, Bank of New York, Libbey-Owens-Ford, Brunswick, General Tire, Hollywood Park Race Track, and *Esquire* magazine.

Paramount was then at a low point in its history, a sagging, sinking film operation with a glorious past and a shaky future. It was suffering from money-losing films and a reluctance to get into television production. Bluhdorn moved to heal the ailing film company by selling off some of its assets and by overcoming management's resistance to dealing with television. He took over much of the negotiations himself, and when he still wasn't getting the rate of return he wanted on his investment, he took the more aggressive step of hiring the television-wise Barry Diller to head the studio.

Diller liked working for Bluhdorn because he respected the man's intelligence and guts, which Diller thought matched his own. Diller's assessment of the feisty trader was, "The sheer force of the man was just remarkable to watch . . . you could see he had a brain that was better than yours. . . . Yet, he was also the only businessman I would describe as a true romantic."

"The news hit Hollywood like a tomahawk through the skull," one observer noted when Diller became chairman and CEO of Paramount effective October 1, 1974. He was not only one of the youngest CEOs in studio history, he was one of the first to have come out of television. *Daily Variety* characterized Diller's appointment as a bombshell. Hollywood did not offer the returning Californian a warm or hearty reception.

Of his first days and weeks back in Hollywood, Diller has said, "I was the very first television person to go into the movie business. I was treated poorly. I was treated as less than scum. I remember being hurt a lot."

Although Diller had never before headed up a company, he quickly established that he understood the reality of his new domain. Executives at the other movie studios might fantasize that they were in the movie business, but what they were really about was banking and equipment rental. They had more in common with the Bank of America and Hertz than the M-G-M, Universal, Paramount, and 20th Century-Fox studios of the past.

In contrast to the first generation of movie moguls such as Louis B. Mayer and Sam Goldwyn, who ruled every aspect of the moviemaking process from reading scripts to supervising the personal lives of the stars, modern studio executives were preoccupied with the financing and distribution of films made by independent producers who rented costumes, soundstages, technicians, and equipment. The studios bankrolled and packaged other people's movies and had relatively little to do with the creative process. In many cases, the present studio heads weren't even headquartered on the studio movie lots.

At ABC, producing the *Movie of the Week* and miniseries, Diller had, in effect, run his own small studio. He had learned firsthand the cause-and-effect relationship between hands-on control and quality and profit. While he had little experience in corporate finance, he did know how to buy and sell movies, which was what he set about doing immediately on arriving at Paramount. In spite of the huge success of *The Godfather* two years earlier, the company needed an infusion of cash, so Diller pulled off a $76 million deal with the three networks that provided television with programs.

He also proceeded to educate himself in the economics of the movie business. If Diller was going to resuscitate Paramount's failing bottom line, he would have to understand the new, rapidly evolving Hollywood. The industry had changed significantly from what it had been in the studio-dominated era prior to World War II. The Paramount that Diller inherited was the child of major economic shifts that had taken place during World War II and directly afterward.

In the years that Diller was at ABC-TV television replaced movies as the mass medium. When he arrived there in 1966, 92.6 percent of all American homes had television. Eight years later, when he made the move to Paramount, almost 100 percent of Americans owned one set, and a high percentage had two or more. Television had not only became the mass medium of American culture, it had also become the best sales vehicle of merchandise in the history of the world.

The studios' reaction, as mentioned earlier, was to boycott television in the hope that it would somehow disappear. Their other strategy was to create an aura about the movies that made people believe they were getting a special experience on the big screen that they couldn't get on television. Studio stars were forbidden to appear on TV. Seeking to win back the adult audiences they had catered to in the past, studios began to make big movies with big stars—larger-than-life presentations that were not to be found on television. But the film executives of the 1960s had lost touch with their audience. They were still catering to the adults who had traditionally comprised the mainstay of their viewers; they were ignoring the teenage market, the group that *really* wanted to get out of the house and away from their parents.

A spate of spectacular blockbuster films, including M-G-M's *Mutiny on the Bounty* (1962), Fox's *Cleopatra* (1963), and *The Sound of Music* (1965), also from Fox, failed to attract the viewers the studios were hoping to pull in. Alfred Hitchcock pinpointed the financial disaster that these high-budget movies precipitated when he observed, "The worst thing that ever happened to this business was *The Sound of Music.* That film stimulated everybody into making expensive films."

Up until the end of World War II, the standard cost of making a successful commercial movie was half a million dollars. As the big-budget films became the norm rather than the exception, the costs rose dramatically. By 1952, the average film took a million dollars to make and by 1961, a million and a half. In 1972, the cost was up to two million dollars.

By the time Diller arrived at Paramount, the average cost of a film was in the $6 to $7 million range; the per-movie budget would soar to $12 million for production plus another $7 million for marketing and promotion during his years at the studio. Diller understood the simple principle of profits that had curiously eluded many people in the industry. There were only two ways to make a profit: by cutting costs and by raising income. Diller could strive to keep the lid on cost increases, but he also needed to better promote, exploit, and merchandise Paramount's movies.

One of the first formulations he grasped was the basic arithmetic of moviemaking. Approximately 15 percent of a movie's box office grosses, a relatively small slice of the pie, technically ended up in the pockets of the moviemaker. The rest belonged to the exhibitor, the distributor, the financier, and other nonartistic elements of the equation. Movie studios therefore also wanted a piece of a movie's financing as well as its distribution rights, in order to garner a greater share of the profits.

Diller also had to adjust to a crucial difference between television and movie economics. A television network buys or rents a program that it sends out to its affiliates. The network makes money from selling national commercials in the program which the local stations are required to air; the local stations either share in the income of selling those national commercials or are allowed to run local commercials or both. Thus, the network has to sell to a half-dozen media buyers at a New York advertising agency, whereas a moviemaker has to market its product via promotional campaigns and distribution to millions of moviegoers all around the country or, for that matter, the world.

Another issue that Diller faced when he arrived at Paramount was the perception people within the movie industry had of him. Charles Bluhdorn had taken a great risk in hiring a television executive who, despite his Beverly Hills upbringing, was essentially an outsider to Hollywood. His tremendous talents and drive would mean nothing if Diller could not find his way into the close-knit creative community that held the key to his future. Without their acceptance, he would have access neither to scripts nor to directors, without whom he would not be able to make movies.

Hollywood was—and continues to be—an incestuous, conservative, close-minded society that equates newcomers with intruders. Its worst fears about outsiders had only recently been realized by James Aubrey, who had been brought in from CBS-Television by Kirk Kerkorian in 1969 to run M-G-M. For the next four years, Aubrey slashed his way through the studio operation, selling off old movie props and what he deemed unnecessary real estate in order to make a profit on Kerkorian's investment of $80 million. The $62 million he raised was sunk not into making more movies, but into the concrete and steel of the M-G-M Grand Hotel in Las Vegas. Aubrey also instituted draconian cost-cutting measures that included firing 5,000 of the 6,200 M-G-M employees and usurping the traditional perks of directors and producers.

Film critic Vincent Canby wrote, "The Kerkorian-Aubrey management of M-G-M was the realization of everybody's worst fears of what would happen to Hollywood when the money men take over." Soon after Aubrey left M-G-M, Charles Bluhdorn hired Barry Diller to take over Paramount. Given the paranoia Aubrey had created in town, it is not hard to understand the chilly reception Diller received because his mission appeared to be the same, namely, to turn a losing movie studio into a profitable business asset. But Kerkorian and Aubrey had sought not to make movies, but to make money even if they had to dismantle the studio to achieve their goal. In contrast, although Bluhdorn had at one point considered selling the studio's 55-acre lot in Hollywood, he had scrapped the idea after the amazing and unexpected success of *The Godfather, Part II.* The mandate he gave Diller was to produce moneymaking movies.

Diller launched a complete reorganization of the Paramount structure. Paramount's executive offices had long since been removed to the posh environs of Beverly Hills, Diller's old stomping grounds. With its manicured streets, elegant homes, fine restaurants, and expensive shops, Beverly Hills was obviously a far more pleasant environment for the moguls than the tacky, rundown Hollywood neighborhood where the actual Paramount studios were located at Gower and Melrose.

Diller sent the executives back to the studio lot and put them in daily contact with their production people. He ordered that instead of sitting back and waiting for scripts to be offered, these executives must work the phones, connect with independent producers, scout around for good movie projects. The budget for new scripts and converting movie rights to books and plays was quadrupled.

He brought the sense of urgency and market sensitivity to movie production that was common in television, but rare in films. He also revamped the studio's concept of marketing and distribution. Hollywood traditionally favored the gradual advertising and release of a movie in selected areas over blanketing the market, as was the case in television. The old approach made no sense to Diller, who understood that gradual release allowed for bad word of mouth to circulate about mediocre or difficult films, while wide release meant that more people could see the movie in the first week and make up their own minds as to its merits.

Thus, for example, instead of initially releasing the 1976 *King Kong* in a few selected markets, Diller released it in a thousand theaters across the country, all at the same time. His strategy worked, and a so-so film became a financial hit.

He took a similar risk with *Bad News Bears,* also a 1976 release, one of the first movies he bought at Paramount. The script was lying in a desk drawer when Diller happened upon it. Its price tag of $30,000 was easy on his budget, and the story appealed to him. At ABC, he had come to believe that a good story was the cornerstone of a successful property.

"This I understood," he said. "Three acts. A rotten little team gets better, falls apart, and then prevails. I said, 'My God. A story.' I bought the script in twenty-two minutes. It was the first time that it seemed possible that things might just work out."

But the movie, which featured Walter Matthau and Tatum O'Neal, opened to tepid reactions. Diller loved the film and couldn't understand the poor box office reaction. Against the advice of all the so-called experts, who declared the movie dead and buried, he took out a double-page ad in the *New York Times,* and the movie miraculously revived itself into a big hit.

His unconventional methods did not always have the support or approval of the man who had been so eager to bring him to Paramount. Bluhdorn furiously upbraided Diller when he saw the ad in the *Times,* but Diller held his ground. The two men enjoyed what Diller has called a "noisy relationship." He considers Bluhdorn a genius, "the only person I could ever call that," and he has described their encounters at Paramount as "battle as fun." It's safe to assume that those battles contributed greatly to Diller's philosophy of passionate advocacy—the willingness to protect and promote one's beliefs and projects.

In spite of—or perhaps because of—Bluhdorn's heckling and admonishments, Diller thrived at Paramount. As immersed as he was in his work, occasionally he would call his older brother Donald, who was then living in San Diego, a short car ride away from Los Angeles. Nevertheless, the brothers did not visit each other; they may as well have been a continent apart, for the emotional distance that lay between them.

Donald had been arrested several times in the mid-1960s for the possession and sale of heroin. He spent a brief period in prison before he was paroled in 1965 to a rehabilitation center, but he failed to break his habit and was repeatedly arrested and sentenced to parole before he was again given a prison term in 1971 for dealing in heroin.

Donald supported himself during the 1960s as a musician, performing in small clubs in California and Nevada. He was also employed at various times as a bookkeeper, factory worker, and piano player, earning between $120 and $175 a week, hardly enough to support his drug habit. In 1967, he married a woman named Teresa Mendoza, whom he had met at a party when he was 16; he was "the only white boy there," according to Mendoza.

Donald Diller seemed to be crying out for help when, in October 1969, he was arrested twice within two days for burglary. He was sentenced to 10 years in prison but was put on probation.

Then, in March 1971, he was arrested again in Van Nuys, California, for selling drugs.

Interviewed later by his probation officer, he admitted that he had been dealing heroin, but he said he "was only using [it] occasionally."

The probation officer was not persuaded by Donald Diller's explanation. "The defendant's compliance with the law was strictly on a superficial basis," he wrote in his report to the court. ". . . the defendant is not a fit subject for any type of program that would release him back to the community. Therefore, it would appear that the most therapeutic program at this time would be commitment to state prison."

Four years later, in August 1975, almost a year into his brother's tenure at Paramount, Donald Diller was released on parole from the Tehachapi State Prison with the understanding that he would live with Teresa Mendoza, from whom he had been divorced in 1971, in San Diego. That arrangement lasted only a week before Mendoza insisted that Donald move out because he was once again using and dealing drugs.

He rented a room for $38 a week at a motel in La Mesa, just east of San Diego, but he and Mendoza remained on speaking terms, perhaps because of their daughter. On October 9, he showed up at Mendoza's apartment to give her some money; his parents had just sent him a check for eight thousand dollars. He showed her a .25 caliber blue steel automatic pistol that he told her he had recently stolen from his parents' home in Beverly Hills. He drove her to the home of one of his friend, a man he called Joker, where he tried to buy some bullets for the gun. Later he dropped Mendoza off at her house, left for a short time, then returned and told her that he had gotten high. Before he left that day, Mendoza gave him some clothes. It would be the last time she would see Donald Diller alive.

Two days later, the police were called to the Moritz Motel, where Donald Diller had been staying. The manager at the Moritz had found a body covered with a sheet and bedspread on a bed in one of the rooms. The murder victim was Donald Diller, dead from "what appeared to be a gun shot wound in his upper forehead," as the investigating police officer wrote in his report. Several witnesses came forward with a description of the suspected killer, but the man had disappeared, and the police could find no trace of him.

Barry Diller paid for his brother's funeral expenses, which amounted to $555.94. He arranged for his body to be cremated and for his ashes to be scattered under a grove of oak trees in the countryside outside San Diego. Neither he nor his parents made any inquiries about the progress of the investigation into Donald's murder. According to Detective Art Haber, the homicide detective assigned to the case, the family's reaction when they were notified of Donald's death was sadness mixed with a sense of fatalism, as if they had come to expect that such a thing would happen. As Haber put it, "The victim was the black sheep of the family."

5

The "Killer Dillers"

Whatever Barry Diller's feelings may have been about his brother's tragic death, he typically kept them very much to himself. From an early age, he had been marked as the achiever in the family, the son who would make his parents proud. Just as it could not have been easy for Donald to go through life as Barry's older brother, Barry Diller must have carried a heavy burden as the brilliant and successful younger son who so out-shone his errant sibling.

His father, Michael, had lived his life in the shadow of his big brother, Richard. Barry reversed that pattern and far surpassed anything that Donald might ever have hoped to accomplish. Yet, according to Teresa Mendoza, although the two had little to do with each other, Donald loved his brother very much and was very proud of his accomplishments. Mendoza has also said that Barry tried to get Donald "back on track." Unhappily, however he might have sought to help Donald, his efforts failed, and it fell to him to provide for his brother's funeral.

How and why he and Donald chose to take such different paths cannot be known, but it's fair to wonder whether one reason Barry pushed himself as he did was to compensate for his brother's failures. Also interesting to note, and perhaps no coincidence, is that from early on Diller made a point of seeking out and fostering the careers of talented young men—and women—whose ambitions rivaled his own. By helping to put his talented protégés "on track," was he perhaps attempting to re-create with them the sibling relationship he could not have with his own brother?

First and foremost among Diller's siblings *qua* protégés was Michael Eisner, whom Diller had been trying to lure away from ABC ever since arriving at Paramount. In November 1976, he finally came up with bait juicy enough to hook the reluctant Eisner: president and chief operating officer of Paramount. Here at last was a position that Eisner, like Diller two years earlier, *had* to take.

Eisner, again like Diller, had left his mark on the network that had given him a chance to develop his talents. Eisner had middle-of-the-road American tastes that showed in the ideas he brought to fruition. After scoring with children's and daytime programming, he had proceeded to create such hits *Laverne and Shirley* and *Welcome Back, Kotter.*

One of his greatest successes was born when Eisner was snowbound at Newark Airport with his wife and three-month-old child. "I wrote a five-page paper called 'New Family In Town,' " he said. When he showed it to the ABC research department as company policy dictated, the idea bounced back to him with a list of reasons why the concept would fail. But Eisner, who shared Diller's aversion to market research, calling it voodoo, pushed ahead with the concept. He changed the name of the show to *Happy Days* and did a pilot with Henry Winkler playing a character called the Fonz, which became the highest rated pilot ever tested with ABC-TV affiliate stations. The show was launched in 1974 and had become a huge success by the time Eisner, who was then head of ABC's West Coast entertainment operation, joined Diller at Paramount.

The two men were in many respects very different. Diller was a bachelor who didn't attend many parties or premieres; when he did show up at Hollywood events, he was often accompanied by his old schoolmate Marlo Thomas, actress Debra Winger, or dress designer Diane von Furstenberg, whom he met in 1975 at a party hosted by agent Sue Mengers. During one of their first weekends together, Diller and von Furstenberg attended a screening of *Won Ton Ton, the Dog Who Saved Hollywood,* at a movie theater in a suburban New Jersey mall. not his usual milieu. Diller later described the experience as "just awful . . . the lowest. To watch that movie in that huge theater . . . was an awful experience." Fortunately, he could lay blame for the movie on Frank Yablan's administration.

Diller's crowd included certified members of Hollywood's celebrity "A" list: his old friend from William Morris, David Geffen, now a millionaire record producer; director Mike Nichols; Warren Beatty; and clothing designer Calvin Klein. He often seemed shy and ill at ease, projecting an intensity and single-mindedness that could be extremely intimidating.

Eisner, on the other hand, was likeable and charming. Happily married and the devoted father of three, he was much more inclined to spend his free time eating pizza with his family than socializing with Hollywood's movers and shakers. On his way home from the studio, he would often stop in at one or more movie houses in the Los Angeles suburbs to take an informal poll of the audiences' reactions. Unlike Diller, who was always impeccably dressed, Eisner's clothes were perpetually wrinkled and creased. Even with his new title and status, he maintained his casual approach, sometimes holding meetings at his beach house in Malibu, where shorts and sandals were acceptable attire among the California crowd.

The two men, however, shared several key traits that made them successful both individually and as a management team. As novelist-screenwriter William Goldman wrote in *Adventures in the Screen Trade,* moviemaking is a very complicated and mysterious process, and no one really knows what will succeed and what will fail. But Eisner, like Diller, believed that the story was more important than the star. He summed up their philosophy in a *New York* magazine interview:

"The one thing you cannot be bad at in this business is choosing material. Yes, it helps to keep your negative costs down, to keep away from the hype, and not to grab for stars and pay ridiculous prices."

Despite their privileged backgrounds, when it came to getting what they wanted, Diller and Eisner behaved like two scrappy streetfighters. They "wanted to make your film for you," recalled one movie executive. Sue Mengers described Michael Eisner as a person who "simply must win." Eisner said of himself, in *Prince of the Magic Kingdom* by Joe Flower, "I tend to want everything."

The same could be said for Diller, and together they made sure they got everything they wanted. They didn't hesitate to put pressure on writers, directors, and producers to get their movies made within their desired budget and time frame. A joke that made the Hollywood rounds had Paramount summing up its new philosophy in this warning to writers and directors: We'll okay the movie and then dare you to try and make it.

Diller insisted that his team become personally involved in the films that Paramount produced. He demanded that they track the progress of each movie to keep costs under control and production on schedule. He drummed into his associates that regard for detail promoted quality of product. No item could be too small, too routine for their attention. He would argue for hours with his staff over the specifics of a film premiere or the image on a movie poster. Often he would demand that one of the elements—the advertising copy, lettering, graphics—be changed at the last minute, no matter what the cost.

Diller also pressured his people to develop many of their own projects in-house, thereby avoiding the demands of agents who sought to create expensive preassembled package deals that involved screenwriters, actors, and directors, all of whom were their clients.

Dawn Steel, another of Diller's hired guns who became part of the team known in the industry as the "Killer Dillers," said of her boss and mentor, "Diller was our general. He was out to break the agents' hold on Hollywood. He refused to sit around waiting for agents to sell him packages. By and large, movies were much more expensive that way, to say nothing of the fact that you didn't get to choose the combination of talent you wanted to work with. Under Diller, Paramount developed its own movies. It was our responsibility to get our own ideas and develop them. At the time I didn't know how unique this way of doing things was. I thought all studio executives stood on tables and screamed."

And if they didn't like the results they were getting, Paramount executives wasted no time making changes. Ron Gover, in *The Disney Touch*, described how when director John Avildsen rewrote the screenplay for *Saturday Night Fever*, which the Paramount team very much liked in its original incarnation, Diller unceremoniously fired Avildsen, even though he had just been nominated for an Oscar for *Rocky*.

At ABC, Diller and Eisner had become proficient at developing shows whose basic story line could be reduced to one or two simple sentences. Indeed, Diller has been credited by some for creating this now familiar and often quoted formula, known in the industry as "high concept." He and Eisner instituted that policy at Paramount, where together they succeeded in creating one high-concept hit after another.

Eisner brought something to the table that Diller did not—the sense of popular taste that put lines around the block at theaters. He had a flair for producing films that appealed to families and young people. He was daring, demanding, and dedicated, as evidenced by the case of a strange adventure movie that was conceived by George Lucas and Steven Spielberg and directed by Spielberg. The movie, which had been turned down by every other studio in town because of its price tag, was called *Raiders of the Lost Ark;* its plot was rooted in Jewish religious mythology and was seasoned with references to Nazi ideology.

Raiders had a $17.5 million budget—astronomical by Diller's standards and therefore enough reason not to get involved. But Eisner envisioned it as a Saturday morning kids' cartoon done in real life on the big screen. He loved the concept, became its ardent backer, and kept pushing to get it made. The movie, which was released in 1981, netted Paramount $115 million and became the template for almost every other action-adventure film of the decade.

Reds, on the other hand, was a pet project of Diller's, who backed the historical film even though its budget far exceeded what was then typically allotted at Paramount. Its co-writer, director, producer, and star all happened to be Warren Beatty, Diller's close friend. Diller said he "cared a lot about the movie," which was "controversial in a lot of ways. Here was Gulf & Western, this big bastion of capitalism led by Bluhdorn, and we were making this romantic movie about communism."

A long and sprawling tale about the Russian Revolution, the movie was difficult to make, especially because the preproduction process was rushed and incomplete. One of Diller's ironclad commandments was that producers were to keep the costs and expenses down to a minimum; *Reds* turned out to be the most expensive film produced under Diller at Paramount. But because of a complicated financial deal with British banking interests, Paramount was assured of not losing money from the very start of the project.

The movie won three Oscars, including Best Director for Beatty. It also helped Diller earn a reputation for making "serious" films, a reputation he has denied, citing such Paramount hits as the 1977 *Saturday Night Fever* (the story of a Brooklyn boy with disco fever that made John Travolta a star), and the 1978 comedy, *Heaven Can Wait,* codirected by Warren Beatty (about a dead football player who comes back to earth in another man's body).

Many Hollywood cognoscenti would argue that it was Eisner who was responsible for bringing the latter two movies to Paramount. On the other hand, few would disagree that Diller demanded that all of Paramount's films be well crafted, no matter what the audience.

In fact, Diller pushed his executives to produce a healthy roster of what he called "tentpole" movies—blockbusters that provided a broad, sheltering canvas of financial success and allowed for the undertaking of smaller, less commercially viable projects. His tentpole theory harkened back to one of Irving Thalberg's prime tenets: A profitable company could choose to make a film that was not a huge moneymaker, so long as the movie bolstered the studio's prestige. Thus, the hugely successful *Star Trek* and *Raiders of the Lost Ark* became tentpoles for such critically acclaimed but lesser grossing films as *The Elephant Man, Ordinary People,* and *Reds.*

Another key member of Diller's team was a cocky 24-year-old named Jeffrey Katzenberg, whom Diller hired as his assistant shortly after he arrived at Paramount. A New Yorker who, like Eisner, had grown up on Park Avenue, Katzenberg spent a summer while still in his teens working on John Lindsay's 1965 mayoral campaign. Lindsay's army of volunteers was taught to "ask and thank, ask and thank," as they marched through the streets of New York, canvassing for votes and financial support. Katzenberg later dropped out of

New York University to work for Mayor Lindsay as an organizer and advance man. Sid Davidoff, a Lindsay aide who shared an apartment with Katzenberg, compared his former roommate to "a pit bull, tenacious as hell . . . . He didn't have to be center stage. He just wanted to be in the middle of everything."

Katzenberg left politics after Lindsay lost his bid for the Democratic presidential nomination. He briefly co-owned a restaurant, then just as briefly supported himself by making the rounds of gambling casinos from Las Vegas to the Bahamas where he consistently beat the house at blackjack. Eventually he got a job as an assistant to a movie producer who introduced him to Diller.

Katzenberg has said that when Diller interviewed him, he (Katzenberg) was "totally out of control, obnoxious . . . . But maybe being out of control was what made me hit a home run with him." Perhaps Diller saw mirrored in Katzenberg some of the same qualities that had pushed him to such early success. He was not afraid of hard work—in fact, just the opposite—he seemed to welcome it.

By all accounts, he was dedicated to getting what he wanted— or what Barry Diller wanted. And he kept in touch with people, regularly checking in with some two hundred of them a week—writers, directors, agents, journalists, financiers and producers—to find out what they were working on, a brief phone call to establish contact so that they would think of him the next time they had a project to pitch.

Katzenberg worked as Diller's assistant for only a year before Diller promoted him to the marketing department, where he continued to shine as a stubborn and conscientious go-getter. In short order, he became assistant to Don Simpson, who was then Paramount's head of production. One of the first tasks he chose for himself under Simpson was to transform a failed television movie of *Star Trek* into a big screen version. Simpson actually tried to dissuade Katzenberg from going forward with the project, but the young man persisted. He even managed to convince actor Leonard Nimoy to reprise the role of Mr. Spock which he had played some 10 years earlier. The movie opened in 1979. Thanks in no small part to its success, when Simpson left Paramount to become an independent producer in 1982, Diller chose Katzenberg to replace him as production chief.

Katzenberg's single-minded tenacity exemplified the one quality above all others that Diller demanded of his executives: a sense of passion for any idea or product they were trying to sell to him. Often Diller would initially seem to be negative about a project, offering probing, rigorous critiques to provoke a reaction from the person making the presentation. If the executive wasn't willing to kick and scream and demonstrate his or her passion, the project was as good as dead.

Dawn Steel calls this aspect of his management technique the "aggressive advocacy and yelling system." Steel came to Paramount after several years promoting such arcane items as the "Cock Sock" (which she says were all labeled extra large), and toilet paper printed with what appeared to be the intertwined GG trademark of the Gucci family but was really the letters "GC." She landed a job as Paramount's director of merchandising goods, selling items such as *Mork and Mindy* suspenders and shirts and assorted other products that were spin-offs of *Happy Days, Laverne and Shirley,* and *Urban Cowboy.*

She quickly absorbed the rules of survival and success at Paramount. From Diller, Steel learned that developing a movie project can often be a long-term process that may extend over several years. (*Forrest Gump,* for example, quite possibly one of the most financially successful films in the past quarter century, was in development for over 12 years.) Diller insisted that his executives be dedicated to and immersed in their projects, in order that their enthusiasm could see them through the process, no matter what stumbling blocks they might encounter along the way.

Steel emulated Diller by educating herself as he had done, poring over files, contracts, and deal memos. Exposed to his and Eisner's management messages, she became increasingly competitive and absorbed in her work, winning promotions within the studio hierarchy. In 1980, she was made vice-president of production for Paramount Pictures.

But she had yet to prove that she could handle the complex process of making a movie. Steel had heard about a story that was under consideration by another studio. She begged the writer's agent to let her take a look at the screenplay. Permission was granted, but only if she read the script in her car, then immediately return it so that no one would know she had seen it. She immediately fell in love with the story, which lived up to Diller's dictum that it be high concept. "It's a female Rocky," was how Steel summarized what she had read.

The story, called *Flashdance*, was about a woman welder who worked evenings as a nightclub dancer in order to achieve her dream of a better life. When Steel presented her project to Diller, he told her, "If you have enough passion to get up on top of this table and tell me why I should make this movie, then chances are I'm going to make this movie."

Whether or not she actually climbed the table, Steel did pull together the talent and support she needed, so that by October 1980, she had the go-ahead to produce *Flashdance*. Steel had been paying attention to the lessons of her mentors. Her co-workers began to think of her as a tank who ignored all obstacles, someone who put her head down and kept moving forward. The movie, a huge success, made Paramount $90 million gross against a $7 million production cost and sold five million copies of the soundtrack records.

At a meeting of Paramount executives, Diller pointed to Steel as an example of someone who, even though she was not at the top of the corporate ladder, had made a movie because she had wanted to do it badly enough. Furthermore, he said, *Flashdance* illustrated how movies could be made by people who were passionate and tenacious.

Steel, for her part, seemed to have elevated Diller to an almost godlike status; certainly, she sounded very much in awe of him when she said, "In the flesh, he was power incarnate. He was the sexiest man I'd ever met. He handled power differently from anyone I've ever known, in this very complex, sexual way. His voice boomed. You couldn't not look at him. He had fantastic personal power. Nothing anyone ever did was good enough for him. Consequently, he pushed you into finding out how good you were."

The darker side of Barry Diller's "fantastic personal power" manifested itself in the way he tyrannized his associates, often unleashing a fiery temper and a lacerating tongue. Former employees have described him as a completely self-absorbed man obsessed with the minutiae of his world. He has been labeled a bully and compared to a pit bull terrier, and the epithets are not without cause.

For years, colleagues and subordinates have lived in fear of his moods, nervously anticipating the next angry outburst, the next round of scorching criticism. They cite his unpredictable mood swings, which alternate between the extremes of ingratiating charm and furious intimidation.

His houseman would routinely telephone his office the minute that Diller, dressed in one of his hand-tailored white shirts and trademark beige suits, headed down the winding road from his home in fashionable Coldwater Canyon. His mission would be to alert the staff that Diller was on the way, as well as to give them a status report on his mood. The secretaries knew they had approximately 20 minutes before Diller arrived because he drove fast, with little regard for the speed limit. And there was always the concern that he might get stopped again for speeding and be given another ticket, in which case he would arrive at the office in a foul frame of mind.

While they awaited Diller's arrival, the secretaries double-checked to make sure all was in readiness for their exacting boss. Mail, messages, and reports had to be displayed on his desk in the precise and particular arrangement that Diller demanded. Secretaries were not permitted to enter his office unless he summoned them. Thus, whatever paperwork came in once Diller was present had to be similarly arranged on a secretary's desk until Diller left his very neat and uncluttered inner sanctum.

Among their other duties, the secretaries had to make sure that cups filled with Marlboro Red cigarettes as well as ashtrays were strategically placed around the office for their chain-smoking boss. Whenever Diller left his office for any reason, they would hurry into the room to replenish the cigarette cups, empty the ashtrays, and add to the carefully arranged piles of letters and messages on his desk.

Secretaries were summoned inside by a buzzer; one buzz meant Diller wanted a secretary to come in to take dictation, two buzzes meant he wanted a cup of hot tea, to be prepared with water at a certain temperature, his special brand of tea, and the teabag dunked exactly five times. If Diller had a guest in his office and he buzzed twice, the secretary was to prepare and bring in Diller's cup of tea first, then inquire whether the guest wanted something to drink.

It was not uncommon for Diller to emerge from his office and publicly berate a secretary in the most vicious terms for some trivial infraction of the office rules. Secretaries and other subordinates regularly fled sobbing to the restroom. In one instance, Diller scanned the telephone log kept by a secretary who was responsible for recording his incoming calls. When he saw that, contrary to office procedure, a call he had already returned had not been crossed off the list, he flew into a rage that lasted for 20 minutes, upbraiding the woman until she retreated from his presence in tears.

Top executives were not exempt from Diller's fits of fury or his slash-and-burn diatribes. His colleagues at Paramount recall witnessing the painful sight of Michael Eisner and Jeffrey Katzenberg, among others, standing in Diller's outer office like truant schoolboys, almost quivering with fear as they waited to see Diller.

Diller has said of himself, "I have never functioned in any environment of support." As Paramount's chief executive officer, and later at Fox, he had the freedom to create a climate that suited his temperament.

His frequent noisy interactions with Charles Bluhdorn reinforced his almost reverential regard for conflict. "That's one of the places I learned you'd better be up for a fight," he said in a 1989 *Playboy* interview. But in fact, Barry Diller had been a fighter since adolescence, when he had regularly indulged in verbal sparring sessions with his father.

With his low threshold for incompetence, he developed a reputation for driving his employees to the breaking point, then pulling them back from the abyss with assurances that he respected them. He was often loud and vulgar, taunting his subordinates, calling them names like "fuck-head" and "asshole." At some point in his development as a manager, he had formulated the belief that creative tension brought out the best in people and thereby benefited the company. A close colleague said of him, "He loves very strong executives . . . who will fight him tooth and nail if they feel passionately about something. He feels that out of that combat will come a better result or a better judgment."

Whether it was the "Diller drive" pushing him to succeed at all costs, or some unacknowledged, unresolved conflict with his father, Barry Diller initiated a reign of terror that shook up the moribund structure of Paramount's operation and remade it in his image. He surrounded himself with a small but elite circle of young moguls-in-the-making who adhered to and adopted his management philosophy. People who were not comfortable with his style quickly fled the company, but there were those who flourished in Paramount's pressure cooker atmosphere—and went on to head up some of Hollywood's most exciting ventures.

The track record he amassed with Michael Eisner was not unblemished: Eisner passed on both *Private Benjamin* and *The Big Chill,* and they had their fair share of failures. But the wins far outstripped the losses. Together they tripled Paramount's profits from $39 million in 1973 to $140 million in 1983. They pushed Paramount from last to first place among the six major studios, and in one 18-month period, they created 20 moneymaking movies. They brought to the screen a string of highly profitable movies: 1977—*Saturday Night Fever* ($260 million) and *Looking for Mr. Goodbar* ($45 million); 1978—*Grease* ($350 million) and *Heaven Can Wait* ($132 million); 1979—*Star Trek—The Motion Picture* ($150 million); 1980—*Airplane!* ($154 million), *Ordinary People* ($76 million), and *Urban Cowboy* ($60 million); 1981—*Raiders of the Lost Ark* ($340 million); 1982—*An Officer and a Gentleman* ($170 million); 1983—*Terms of Endearment* ($147 million); and 1984—*Beverly Hills Cop* ($286 million). The Indiana Jones series alone grossed $224.6 million against a combined cost of $49 million.

One experienced observer, Ron Grover of *BusinessWeek*'s Hollywood bureau, wrote of them, "Many people in Hollywood chose not to work with the Diller-Eisner team. But in the eight years that the two men worked together . . . Paramount became a leader not only in hit movies, but in network TV programs like *Cheers* and *Family Ties,* syndication and home video."

It was at Paramount that Diller established himself as a major player on the Hollywood scene. He would later say of that period, "Paramount was a big part of my life and it meant a lot to me in a lot of ways. I think about it only romantically. I never think about the struggle. And, God knows there was struggle."

An obvious symbol of the degree to which Diller succeeded in reversing Paramount's fortunes was that in 1980, of the five movies nominated for Academy Awards for Best Picture, two were Paramount productions. "I was driving to the studio when the radio announced the nominations," Diller said. "I almost ran into a wall."

Aboard the Twentieth-
Century Express

On February 19, 1983, people arriving at work at Gulf & Western's New York headquarters at Columbus Circle were greeted with shocking news about their 56-year-old chairman. They were stunned to learn that Charles Bluhdorn had died of a heart attack aboard the company's Gulfstream jet while returning from the Dominican Republic, where Gulf & Western owned a hotel along with vast sugar plantations. It had been an open secret for some time within the company that Bluhdorn was suffering from cancer, but no one had anticipated that he would die so suddenly and unexpectedly.

Bluhdorn, despite his blunt-spoken style and unpredictable temperament, was respected and well liked by workers at all levels of the corporation. Now, they huddled together in small groups throughout the office building, which towered above Central Park at the intersection of Broadway and Central Park South, mourning his death and wondering what the fallout would be—for themselves personally, as well as for Gulf & Western.

Many of them feared that the leadership void created by Bluhdorn's death would be filled by senior vice-president Martin Davis, Bluhdorn's trusted chief aide and "hatchet man." Davis was a 20-year-old high school dropout and army veteran when he was hired for an entry-level position at Samuel Goldwyn Productions' New York office in 1947. He rose quickly through the ranks in the eight years he worked at Goldwyn, eventually negotiating deals with writers and producers, as well as handling publicity.

After a short stint at Allied Artists Picture Corporation, Davis moved in 1958 to Paramount Pictures. He began in sales and marketing, but quickly moved on and up to become chief of advertising and publicity. Soon after that, he was promoted to vice president of distribution, as well as official spokesman for corporate affairs. By 1967, he had been appointed Paramount's chief operating officer.

Davis had adroitly engineered a move by Charles Bluhdorn to acquire Paramount as part of his growing Gulf & Western conglomerate. Bluhdorn repaid Davis by getting him elected to Paramount's board and executive committee. He also appointed Davis as head of the studio, which was then lagging far behind the other major studios in terms of box office hits, distribution, and television production. Davis, the tough guy, played hardball, cutting corporate costs and drastically thinning employee ranks years before downsizing became a favored euphemism of corporate America.

Three years later, he became senior vice president in charge of acquiring new companies, a position of enormous responsibility and power, given Bluhdorn's penchant for hustling in the corporate marketplace. Beginning in the mid-1970s, it also fell to Davis to protect Gulf & Western from exhaustive inquiries into its finances, including Bluhdorn's sugar-trading practices in the Dominican Republic, by both the Securities and Exchange Commission (SEC) and the Internal Revenue Service. He succeeded well enough that the investigation was dropped in 1981, a month before the case was due to go to trial. The SEC dropped its charges against Bluhdorn, and Gulf & Western was required only to pay a minor fine to the Dominican Republic.

Davis's leading rival for Bluhdorn's seat was David Judelson, Gulf & Western's president, although, according to Barry Diller, he was offered—and declined—the position. As he tells it, Diller threw his support behind Davis after Davis assured him that he would continue to follow Bluhdorn's policies in running the company. (Davis denies that he ever gave such assurances.) Bluhdorn's widow, Yvette, also backed Davis. Both she and Diller were soon greatly to regret their decisions.

The atmosphere within the company changed almost immediately—and not for the better, as far as most employees were concerned. Under Charles Bluhdorn, Gulf & Western had felt "like family," according to one long-time secretary. But not so under Chairman Davis. The secretary, along with hundreds of other employees, was soon to be laid off in the wake of Davis's reorganization of his newly inherited empire.

After all his years as second banana, Davis embraced the role of boss with a vengeance, earning a reputation as a brusque and tough leader, with a bare-fisted style that made for barbed relationships with his managers. He quickly froze out Yvette Bluhdorn, yanked her company-paid driver and limousine, withdrew corporate support from her favorite philanthropies, even—some say—cut off her benefits. Then he proceeded to reinvent the multinational conglomerate into the kind of company he felt comfortable running.

Charles Bluhdorn had been a wheeler-dealer trader and investor who picked up diverse businesses as if they were so many plates of food at a smorgasbord. (Mel Brooks poked fun at Bluhdorn in his 1976 comedy, *Silent Movie,* which featured a company named "Engulf & Devour.") He had wielded the phone like a weapon, rising at four in the morning to play the overseas markets, until the opening bell rang at the New York Stock Exchange. Nor had he been shy about calling Barry Diller and Michael Eisner, if the mood seized him, to discuss everything from cost-cutting measures to casting to movie ideas.

He had ceded to Martin Davis and his other top lieutenants what he considered the mundane, day-to-day details of running the corporation. Davis lacked Bluhdorn's fascination with stock trading; his obsession was with bottom-line profits, and he would stop at nothing to create a lean and profitable operation. He sold off what he considered extraneous companies and got rid of Bluhdorn's handpicked portfolio of stocks to diminish the corporate debt. He also named Barry Diller as head of the newly formed Gulf & Western leisure-time division. But the promotion soon proved to be a mixed blessing for Diller.

For one thing, it meant his involvement in areas for which he quickly discovered he had little interest. He knew how to run a studio, how to make movies, how to maneuver his way through Hollywood politics. But now he was also responsible for Madison Square Garden, home to the New York Knicks basketball team, and the publishing house of Simon and Schuster, which was run by another strong-willed, hard-driven executive, Richard E. Snyder. And although Diller had long maintained dual residences in Beverly Hills and Manhattan, now he had to spend more time in New York, which meant more frequent face-to-face dealings with Martin Davis.

He and Davis had gotten along just fine when each was running his own separate fiefdom and reporting separately to Bluhdorn. Bluhdorn, for his part, had respected and depended on both executives, whose styles were at the same time very similar and different. Both men were demanding and forthright to the point of being abusive. But while Diller was constantly in search of the next great idea, pushing himself and his people to stretch their minds, Davis was the consummate manager, the Elmer's Glue® of Gulf & Western, who had made order out of Bluhdorn's chaos.

He had headed up Paramount Pictures himself for a time, which no doubt gave him additional credibility—at least in his own mind—when he issued orders in the guise of suggestions about how to run the studio. Charles Bluhdorn had also been prone to making suggestions to Diller and Eisner. But he and Diller had a long-standing relationship based on mutual respect and deep affection. Bluhdorn, like Diller, was a bit of a wild-eyed visionary who respected the kind of creative thinking for which Diller and his team were famous. He and Diller fought often and loudly, but they always made up.

Diller and Davis, on the other hand, shared no such commonality of vision, and whatever warmth might have existed between them quickly evaporated as they got to know each other better. Diller soon came to believe that Davis was "executive-adverse . . . that he didn't believe in people . . . that he did nothing for them." Nor, says Diller, did he develop "an overarching strategy" for Gulf & Western. Eisner, too, lost faith in Davis; Diller remembers him listening to Davis and commenting under his breath, "God, this man is such an imbecile."

Paramount Pictures was having a banner financial year, but Davis—rather than appreciating Diller and Eisner's achievements—seemed downright resentful. He decreed that Eisner, who was accustomed to Bluhdorn's frequent phone calls, was not to communicate directly with him, insisting instead that Eisner report to him through Diller. To add to the insult, Frank Mancuso, Paramount's head of marketing and the only top studio executive who worked out of New York, had begun to bypass the chain of command by ignoring Eisner, who was officially his boss, and bringing his marketing plans directly to Diller—when he wasn't bypassing both of them and making his own marketing decisions.

In October 1983, Jeffrey Katzenberg had a meeting in New York with Davis, during which Davis criticized the top Paramount executives and accused them of working against him. Katzenberg reported Davis's outburst to Eisner, who brought his concerns to Diller. But Diller seemed unresponsive to his fears, calling Eisner "too sensitive."

Diller's already complicated relationship with Michael Eisner began to fray at the seams as Diller felt the pressure of simultaneously keeping Eisner happy and meeting Davis's demands. Davis was outraged that between the two of them, Diller and Eisner received more than 50 percent of the studio's annual bonus pool of profits. (Diller's share in 1983 was 31 percent, Eisner's 26 percent.) Despite the fact that Paramount would show a $150 million pretax profit for 1984, Davis vilified Diller for his high salary and executive perks. "He was acting like the goddamn protected species at the company," Davis was still complaining 10 years later in a 1994 interview with Bryan Burrough that ran in *Vanity Fair*. "I was sick of it. He was political, destructive, playing games, trying to undermine me."

One colleague at the time summarized Diller's feelings: "Diller came to loathe Davis. He basically wanted to rip out his eyes and piss in his skull. Barry didn't like working for anybody, let alone somebody he despised."

Diller's contract was due to expire on the last day of September 1984, and rumors of tension between him and Davis were circulating in the Hollywood business community. Early in 1984, Marvin Davis (no relation to Martin) had begun to court Diller to join him at Twentieth Century-Fox, which was hemorrhaging money under chairman Alan Hirschfield. Martin Davis heard talk that Diller was being wooed by the other Davis, but he "didn't give a damn."

It had come down to this: Neither Diller nor Davis suffered fools gladly, and now each was beginning to view the other as a fool.

That spring and summer, ironically, Paramount had a star turn as the print media darling. Within a three-month period, *News-*

week, BusinessWeek, and *New York* magazine all spotlighted the studio in a series of highly complimentary articles. Diller, Eisner, and Katzenberg were cited as the hottest team in Hollywood, consistent winners who ran the "best all-around movie studio," according to *Newsweek.* In April, Paramount's *Terms of Endearment* garnered five Academy Awards, including Best Picture.

The attention seemed only to increase Martin Davis's wrath. Also that spring, during one of Diller's visits to New York, Davis demanded that Diller fire Eisner because, said Davis, Eisner wasn't a team player. Although Diller had frequently bitched about Eisner to Davis, in the course of a heated discussion that lasted over some eight hours, Diller told his boss, "This is insane. And I can't figure out why you're doing this."

The meeting ended in a draw. Davis agreed to table his demands. Diller returned to Los Angeles aboard the company jet, fuming all the way west about Davis's attitude. "I thought, What am I doing in this company now? I can't function this way. This is the end for me," he later recalled.

Shortly thereafter, he telephoned Marvin Davis and suggested that Davis sell him half of Fox. Davis countered with an offer of 25 percent. Diller later succinctly summed up their conversation. "It began a discussion."

Twentieth Century-Fox got its start in 1904 when William Fox opened a nickelodeon theater in New York City. Ten years later, Fox began producing his own movies under the company name of Box Office Attractions Film Rental Company. He soon joined other early movie producers and moved to California where he changed his company's name to the Fox Film Corporation and discovered such silent-movie stars as Theda Bara and William Farnum.

Despite his aggressive pursuit of new technology and acquisition of movie theaters, Fox was hit hard twice in 1929: he was seriously injured in a car accident, then lost his studio after the stock market crash. Several rocky years followed until 1935, when Fox was merged with a small but successful production company run by Darryl F. Zanuck, and Twentieth Century-Fox was born. Zanuck was soon producing 50 movies a year, featuring such headliners as Shirley Temple, Don Ameche, Loretta Young, and Henry Fonda, who starred in the 1940 Fox classic, *The Grapes of Wrath.*

The studio fared well through the war years and into the 1950s, thanks in part to a new technology, known as Cinema-Scope, and a sexy new superstar named Marilyn Monroe. But by the end of the decade, the competition from television combined with the departure of several key production people—including, in 1956, Darryl Zanuck—marked the beginning of hard times for Fox.

Zanuck, along with his son Richard, returned some years later to save the studio and salvage the movie that almost single-handedly destroyed Fox: the crisis-laden *Cleopatra,* which cost millions more than anticipated.

The Zanucks revived the cost-cutting, efficiency methods that Darryl had instituted 27 years earlier when Fox and 20th Century had merged. But despite such hits as *The Sound of Music,* their reign lasted only until 1971, when a series of disastrous flops created losses exceeding $100 million. The two Zanucks were replaced by businessman Dennis Stanfill, an Annapolis graduate who had worked on Wall Street and knew next to nothing about making movies. Stanfill installed as head of production Alan Ladd, Jr., son of Alan Ladd, Paramount's famed tough guy of the 1940s and 1950s.

The two men were not a good fit; Stanfill was notoriously tight-fisted, and Ladd felt that he was penny-pinching all the creativity out of the studio's operation. Ladd had to fight hard to make and distribute George Lucas's 1977 megablockbuster, *Star Wars.*

Despite its success, the tension continued until 1979, when Ladd, along with a number of key production people, left Fox.

Stanfill replaced him by hiring Alan J. Hirschfield to run the movie side of the operation and C. Joseph La Bonte to handle the nonmovie operations. After the 1980 success of the *Star Wars* sequel, *The Empire Strikes Back,* Stanfill became intrigued with the idea of implementing a leveraged buyout of the studio, which now not only was cash-rich, but also boasted assets that ranged from its movie and television companies to real estate in Pebble Beach, California, to a 63-acre studio lot in Los Angeles. But over the course of the next several months, even as he plotted with Hirschfield and La Bonte to secure the financing that would allow the deal to go forward, tensions developed between himself and Hirschfield over who would actually run the day-to-day operation and affairs of the company.

By January 1981, the proposed deal had fallen apart, and both men set out to find financing from other sources, independent of each other. As far as Wall Street was concerned, the company was now in play, available to the highest bidder. Among those interested behind the scenes were Herbert Siegel of Chris-Craft, who had long wanted to buy a studio and now owned approximately 20 percent of Fox's stock, as well as corporate raider Saul Steinberg, chairman and president of the Reliance Group.

Hirschfield met with Steinberg, who kept a poker face, not letting on that he was fascinated with the possibilities of making money from a Fox sale. He subsequently began buying up Chris-Craft stock, until he had acquired 5 percent of it, whereupon he suggested to Siegel that Chris-Craft move to take over Fox. But instead of mobilizing Siegel with his proposal, Steinberg threw him into a panic. Siegal saw the move as an attack on Chris-Craft. Eager to protect his company, Siegel was motivated to bail entirely out of Fox, since Fox was Steinberg's true target.

Siegel's solution appeared in the unlikely guise of Denver-based millionaire Marvin Davis, who had made his fortune drilling oil wells. Approached by investment banker J. Ira Harris, one of Salomon Brothers' top dealmakers, Davis was instantly captivated by the scenario Harris spun of a Fox takeover, with Davis leading the charge. He quickly lined up some help to enable him to make the deal: His friend, Marc Rich, a commodities trader, was prepared to become a nonvoting silent partner, in return for a half interest in the investment. In addition, Davis got a commitment from his long-time Chicago banker, Continental Illinois Bank, to back him with an unlimited line of credit.

Next, Davis got in touch with Siegel and offered to buy all of Siegel's Fox stock. Siegel agreed not to make a deal for his stock with anybody else, provided that Davis would hand over to him Fox's three television stations, which he would add to the stations he already owned. No problem, said Davis, whose imagination was fired up by the lucrative Los Angeles real estate owned by Fox adjacent to downtown Beverly Hills.

On February 20, just one month after Stanfill had pulled back from his LBO plan, he was informed by attorney Edward Bennett Williams that Williams's client, Marvin Davis, wanted to buy Fox for sixty dollars a share, seven dollars above the stock's market price. Stanfill stood to make a profit of over seven million dollars, but he might well lose his position as head of a major movie studio with all of its attendant prestige and perks.

A week later, Davis's offer was presented to Fox's board. After both sides had evaluated each other's credentials and value, the merger agreement was signed on April 7, and the deal was approved by the stockholders on June 8. Twentieth Century-Fox was now a privately held company, controlled by the corpulent oil man, who suddenly discovered a whole new world of Hollywood glamour and high social visibility.

Davis, an ex-New Yorker whose father had made a fortune as a dress manufacturer, rented a bungalow at the fabled Beverly Hills Hotel for $365,000 a year and began to commute between Denver and Los Angeles. He and Stanfill quickly found themselves at odds over issues both large and small. By the end of June, their relationship had abruptly ended, and Alan Hirschfield was shortly installed as chairman and chief executive officer.

Sherry Lansing had been head of production since January 1980, the first woman to hold that position at a major studio. Now it fell to her and Hirschfield to show Davis and his partners a profitable return on their $724 million investment. Lansing felt greatly thwarted in her efforts by a combination of Byzantine internal politics and personality conflicts. Although one of her first Fox projects, *Taps,* a relatively low-budget movie with production costs of only $15 million, became the surprise hit of the 1981 Christmas season, it did not represent the kind of blockbuster success that Davis had looked forward to seeing.

Lansing's films for the following year, 1982, opened to mostly negative reviews and tepid box office reception. Nevertheless, Davis had been working hard at ridding Fox of its $1 billion debt by finding buyers for much of the studio's real estate assets, as well as its record company and music-publishing division. As well, Davis entered into a joint venture with CBS for producing and distributing its movies in the home video market. The studio was also profiting from the exploitation of the demand from television worldwide for programs in Fox's television library particularly *M*A*S*H,* which sold in 1982 for $10 million.

Davis's wallet was getting fatter, but the studio was still losing money—$16.9 million, by the end of 1982. Although much of that could be used as a write-off and tax deduction against their investment, Davis and Rich were still greedy for box office bonanazas, and Lansing was not delivering. Her contract was due to expire on January 1, 1983, and she had already lined herself up a production deal at Paramount in partnership with another soon-to-be Fox refugee, producer Stanley Jaffe. By all accounts, Davis was happy to see her go.

The problems at Fox were not resolved, however, by Lansing's departure. Her successor, a former agent/producer named Joe Wizan, came up with a handful of hits, including *Romancing the Stone, Bachelor Party,* and *Revenge of the Nerds,* which one reviewer labeled a "high-energy, low-humor comedy." But Wizan lasted only a year before he was replaced by Lawrence Gordon, who had produced Paramount's 1982 hit, *48 Hours,* starring Eddie Murphy in his first movie role.

It had now been four years since Fox had had a winner on a scale comparable to the productions of the other studios. *The Empire Strikes Back* had grossed $25 million in 1980, but that success paled next to Paramount's 1981 *Raiders of the Lost Ark,* which grossed $175 million; Universal's huge 1982 hit, *E.T.,* at $300 million; and Columbia's 1983 *Tootsie,* at $95 million. Fox's gross earnings were up from $554.9 million in 1982 to $776.5 million the following year, thanks to the sale of *M*A*S*H* to syndication.

But aside from a few moneymakers, studio management just couldn't seem to find the winning combination to control costs and generate high-grossing movies. Marvin Davis was looking for a new chief executive officer with a proven record for creating hits. And Barry Diller was looking for a new job.

The summer of 1984 was a long, hot one for Diller, who continued to chafe under Martin Davis's thumb. He was only 32, young by most standards, but his old friend and rival, David Geffen, had already twice started his own company and was a millionaire many times over. Diller and Geffen had remained close through the years. Along with Studio 54 owner Steve Rubell, talent manager Sandy Gallin, and clothing designer Calvin Klein, Diller and Geffen formed a nucleus of influential businessmen who were charter members of what had come to be known by the socially savvy of the New York–LA axis as the "Velvet Mafia." A very deep bond existed among these men based on their being young, wealthy, and extremely successful.

David Geffen was by far the wealthiest of the group. He had moved from William Morris to the Ashley Famous agency, where he had represented pop music artists, then had gone on to managing his first client in 1968, singer Laura Nyro. By 1970, using some of the $4.5 million worth of CBS stock he had earned from the sale to CBS of Nyro's song publishing company, Geffen had started his own record label, called Asylum. A year after that, he earned another $7 million when he sold Asylum to Warner Communication, retaining the title of president of the label.

In 1976, by then vice chairman of Warner Brothers Pictures, Geffen had a tumor removed from his bladder and was told by his doctors that he had cancer. He retired from the business for four years until a subsequent battery of medical tests showed that the cancer had been misdiagnosed, and he was in perfect health. He then founded Geffen Records and resumed producing movies, both of which were to be distributed by his former associates at Warner Communications.

The competition between Diller and Geffen was friendly but real. They had gotten their start in the business working side by side in the William Morris mail room. Diller was only a year older. Yet Geffen reported to no one but himself, while Diller still had to check in with Martin Davis. And now Geffen had invaded Diller's turf by making movies. According to journalist Rod Lurie, writing in *LA Magazine,* "Person after person interviewed said Diller's real motivation is being more powerful than Geffen—from business to their sex lives to the firmness of their handshakes."

No wonder then that Diller wanted two things that summer of 1984—a way out of Paramount and a piece of Fox's action. On September 3, Labor Day, Martin Davis showed up in Los Angeles for the first time in the year and a half that he had been head of Gulf & Western. His mission was twofold: to renew Diller's contract and to reorganize the studio's chain of command, elevating Mancuso to the same level as Eisner. Davis also brought with him an offer that Diller and Eisner would have been hard-pressed to accept, a cut in their annual bonuses.

What he didn't know as he made his case during meetings with Diller and Eisner over the next few days was that both men were already in the midst of negotiations that would soon extricate them from Paramount. Diller was close to finalizing a deal with Fox. His number-two man, Eisner, had been holding discussions with top management representatives from the Walt Disney Company since the middle of August, when he had been approached by Disney board member Stan Gold. On September 5, just one day after Davis told Eisner that he thought he was paying him too much, Disney's board chairman, Ray Watson, visited Eisner at home to offer him the position of chief operating officer. But Eisner declined, holding out for the top spot, chief executive officer.

That night, Barry Diller held a party at his Coldwater Canyon home for Martin Davis, the top Paramount executives, and several Gulf & Western board members. Throughout the evening, Davis made a point of lavishly praising Frank Mancuso, who was not present at the party. Whatever message he was trying to give them, however, Diller and Eisner were to have the last laugh. The following Monday, Diller telephoned Davis in New York to tender his resignation from Paramount. Twelve days later, Eisner was chosen as Disney's chairman and CEO. In the intervening period, Diller had asked Eisner to join him at Fox, but Eisner declined. He wanted to break free of Diller and run his own show. He also felt more than a little betrayed by Diller, who had failed to tell him until the day after the Paramount party that he was leaving to go to Fox.

The courtship between Diller and Marvin Davis had consisted of an intricate dance that was conducted under conditions of utmost secrecy. Throughout their months-long negotiations, there was much that each had kept hidden from the other.

It was Fred Silverman of NBC who had helped make the match between Diller and Marvin Davis. "I heard from a Denver oilman named Marvin Davis," said Silverman. "He had acquired control of Fox. He's a strange fellow and I didn't know him at all until he called me. . . . Marvin wanted to know about Barry Diller, whom he was considering for the chairman's seat at Fox. Of course I told him that he was an outstanding executive in every way and would be a fine choice to run Fox."

The deal that was ultimately struck between Diller and Marvin Davis was built on a shaky foundation of false assumptions and unrealistic expectations. Diller had played hard to get, never letting on that he was desperate to leave Paramount. Davis, though he kept his feelings well hidden, was just as desperate to snag a prize catch like Barry Diller to rescue his debt-ridden studio.

The five-year contract that Diller signed on October 1 added up to an extremely valuable package of financial benefits: $3 million in annual salary, 25 percent of any increase in the studio's equity value during Diller's tenure plus 17.5 percent of appreciation in the value of Fox assets for three years after he left the studio; an interest-free loan of $1.5 million to pay off an equal loan he'd received at Paramount; a liberal expense account; insurance, and various other perks. Although Diller was free to terminate their relationship at almost any point, including, for example, if Davis were to sell more than 20 percent of the studio, Fox was bound to the deal unless Diller were to die or be convicted of a felony.

The contract also spelled out in great detail the limits of Davis's future involvement with the studio. It stipulated that the two men "will be in frequent and regular contact," but that they weren't actually obligated to meet more than twice a year. Davis was also prohibited from meddling in the operation of the studio; he was not allowed to have any contact with any Fox employees "in such manner as shall derogate, limit or interfere with Diller."

It was an extraordinary agreement. But Diller—who regularly played poker with Neil Simon, Steve Martin, Johnny Carson, and Daniel Melnick, until recently a Fox-associated independent producer—had paid close attention to Melnick's tales of woe about Davis. He was determined not to let Davis get in his way of running the studio, and he had had the contract tailored specifically for that purpose.

The "Odd Couple" was what industry wits took to calling Diller and Davis. Davis was a street-smart tycoon who had spent his teenage years working alongside some pretty rough characters in Midwestern oil fields, but he had underestimated how ruthless and relentless Diller could be. Diller, for all his careful planning, was wholly unprepared for what he discovered as he settled into the executive suite at Fox.

"I felt horrible," he later said, recalling his early days at Fox. "I felt as if somehow, in my forties, I had gotten off a round earth and happened upon a flat earth. I was stepping off the end of it."

7

Setting the House in Order

"Barry's going to have a little piece of Fox and a very hard job for the next two years. But he's going to succeed," predicted David Geffen, after Diller announced that he was leaving Paramount for Fox.

Diller got his first hint of how hard his job would be—and how bad things really were—when he stopped by the office of departing CEO Alan Hirschfield, whom Davis had eased out with the face-saving title of consultant and a guarantee of two more years of his half-million dollars annual salary. Davis had led Diller to believe that the studio would break even in 1984. But Hirschfield wryly informed Diller that, to the contrary, Fox would probably lose approximately $70 million for the fiscal year.

Diller was in for more shocking news. At a meeting several weeks later with Fox's bankers, he learned that Fox was on the verge of going broke. As he said, "I found out . . . that the company was not only technically bankrupt, but that on the following

109

February 11 the company literally would run out of its last re-
source, its last penny."

He was beginning to realize just how desperately Davis needed
him to keep the studio afloat. Though Diller was nowhere near as
expert as he would come to be in the culture of high finance, he
certainly understood that the banks would not continue to underwrite Davis's movie mogul dreams without a talented professional
in place whom they could count on to make profitable movies.

Through a series of clever financial maneuvers, Davis and Marc
Rich had managed to earn back all the money they had paid for Fox,
while putting almost no money back into the studio. Although the
$1 billion debt had been reduced to $430 million, the studio was
still paying approximately $70 million a year in interest.

"Aside from its financial status," Diller recalled, "which was
some sort of electric shock to the brain, there was very little of a
real company . . . with any kind of thoughtful rationale and any
kind of integration working for it."

For the fiscal year 1984 which had just closed on August 25,
Fox was showing a loss of $89 million. That year, the worth of the
company's stocks had slid from $301 million to $67 million.

Nor did Diller feel optimistic about very many of the projects
that were already in the production pipeline. Among the loose ends
he was left to deal with from the previous team were *Moving Vio-
lations, Turk 182,* and *Mischief,* all of which were 1985 releases that
would lose money. The studio had high hopes for their big summer
comedy, *The Man with One Red Shoe,* which starred Tom Hanks,
with a plot that was taken from a successful French farce, *The Tall
Blond Man with One Black Shoe.* But that also proved to be a loser,
a $16 million egg that grossed only $4.3 million.

Fox did have one hit that summer, a gentle fantasy-comedy
about a group of senior citizens that the studio had almost turned
down. Produced by the team of Darryl Zanuck and David Brown,
Cocoon featured veteran actors Don Ameche, Gwen Verdon, Hume

Cronyn, Jessica Tandy, and Maureen Stapleton; it cost $17.5 million to shoot and grossed almost $100 million.

Diller had to act fast and decisively. Ironically, he resorted to the sort of brutal cost-cutting measures that Martin Davis had instituted at Paramount. He fired many of the in-house producers who had development deals, and he decreed that every department, without exception, reduce its staff by 15 percent. He pressured Davis to dismiss the highly paid board of directors. He also wrote off about $40 million in projects already in development.

Coupled with the financial disaster in the offing, Diller was having trouble convincing key Fox executives to remain at the studio. Everybody, including Davis, assumed that Diller would be bringing his own people over from Paramount. But Diller's authoritarian and confrontational management style proved to be his undoing. Michael Eisner was deep in talks with the Disney Company, which was in disarray because of an interfamily feud. When he moved to the "Mouse House" shortly after Diller arrived at Fox, and took with him Katzenberg and other loyalists, Diller was perceived as the big loser.

He had an especially tough time persuading production chief Larry Gordon to stay on in the position he had mentally reserved for Katzenberg, because Gordon had stopped trusting Diller after an ugly incident at Paramount during which Eisner had had Gordon evicted from his office there. Gordon and Eisner had eventually patched things up between them, but Gordon was still wary of Diller and didn't hesitate to tell him so. His condition for staying at Fox was that he be made president and chief operating officer, with responsibilities for the entire studio. Diller had no choice but to meet his demands.

With Hirschfield gone, Diller quickly dispatched Norman Levy, Fox's vice president and chief operating officer, and a close friend of Davis's. He hired Jonathon Dolgen from Columbia Pictures to replace Davis's friend Buddy Monash who had been in charge of business and administrative affairs. He prevailed on Harris Katleman to continue as head of Fox's television division, at the same time ordering him to step up production of half-hour TV series instead of movies and miniseries, which Diller knew were not big profit-makers because they earned less money in syndication.

He next faced the difficult task of securing enough cash to begin paying for the product he had been hired to create. Diller soon discovered that cost-cutting was an easy policy to implement, compared with the necessary next step of generating income, which required seed money to pay for creative talent. That money had to come either from lenders or investors, and Davis, as Fox's owner, should have been the logical prime source of funds.

It hadn't taken long, however, for Davis and Diller to become mutually disenchanted. Davis's hopes of a dream team to rescue Fox had been dashed when Eisner opted for Disney over Fox. He was further chagrined to learn just how serious Diller was about limiting Davis's involvement with the studio. Though he could still play the role of movie mogul at the Beverly Hills Hotel Polo Lounge, presiding over Booth 1 at the entrance to the room, he was no longer free to wander through Fox's movie sets, mixing with actors and directors, as he had in the past. Under Diller's regime, Davis would be treated at arm's length like any other investor.

Davis was thus not inclined to put more money into Fox, in spite of his contractual obligation to do so. He had already recouped most of his original investment, so that the worst-case scenario would be that the studio might go belly-up, securing for Davis a major tax write-off. In response to Diller's repeated demands for additional funds, Davis urged Diller to make a deal with Michael Milken, Drexel Burnham Lambert's famed "King of Junk Bonds," to borrow a quarter of a million dollars in high-interest bonds to finance more product.

Diller was willing to go the junk bond route, but given the extent of his legal and financial exposure if he were to go out and meet with interested investors, he wanted Davis to sell him actual equity in Fox. Davis coolly refused. He point-blank informed Diller that he had no choice in the matter. Diller was stuck on a sinking ship and had no alternative but to start bailing if he wanted to save himself.

The brief honeymoon period was over. Diller decided against throwing in his lot with Milken and chose instead to find a way to convince Davis of the merits of investing in his own company. He marshaled Jon Dolgen, his financial watchdog, and other top executives to put together a carefully researched presentation that made the following very simple argument: If Davis agreed to pump some money into the studio, Diller and his people could make movies that would earn profits on his investment and thereby increase the value of the studio. But despite the logic behind all their well-drawn charts and detailed analyses, Davis stood firm. Once again, his answer was no.

Diller threatened a lawsuit, and although Davis professed not to be concerned, he did come up with a counteroffer to Diller's request. Instead of declaring a $50 million dividend from the money that Fox was about to be paid for the CBS home video joint venture, he would allow the studio to retain the money as working capital. He would also try to arrange a $400 million line of credit for the studio. But he refused to invest a single cent of his own money.

Diller could have quit, but he had always been a risk taker, someone who lived for meeting the next challenge. Leaving Fox would have been tantamount to admitting that Davis had outsmarted him, and Diller was not about to concede defeat without putting up a fight. Davis was contractually required to invest more money in Fox. Diller told him, "It's very simple. You either make an agreement to sell the company, or I sue you for fraud."

Some months earlier, Davis had struck a deal with the Internal Revenue Service to purchase Marc Rich's Fox stock, which the IRS had frozen when Rich fled the country rather than face charges of tax evasion and racketeering. Davis had paid the government

$116 million, only a fraction of what his erstwhile partner's stock was actually worth. He was not prepared now to sell his entire share of the studio; he and his family loved Hollywood and all the prestige that accrued from his being the owner of a movie studio. But he needed Diller to keep the bankers at bay—and he needed to keep his bankers happy in order to get the loans for the next attractive deal that caught his fancy.

He cast around for somebody who would be willing to buy half the studio, a situation he felt comfortable with because of the arrangement he had had with Rich. The perfect candidate—or so Davis perceived—presented himself in Rupert Murdoch, the freewheeling Australian media entrepreneur who already owned the *New York Post, New York* magazine, and other American newspapers, as well as a television network in Australia and various newspapers there and in England.

Murdoch was interested in buying a company capable of producing programs for his present and future investments in television—and despite Fox's bleak economic picture, he believed in Diller's ability to resuscitate the studio. Although he would have preferred to buy 100 percent of Fox, he was willing to settle for the 50 percent that Davis was willing to offer. He paid $250 million, most of which Davis agreed to use to pay down Fox's debt. Murdoch also contributed an additional $88 million as an advance against profits so that Diller could begin to properly conduct studio business by generating product.

Diller used this opportunity to negotiate a new contract for himself, according to which he was entitled to leave Fox at any point during the next year, if he so desired. He also embarked on a campaign to further isolate Davis, by imposing a strict accounting of all his Fox-related expenses and refusing to provide him with the freebies and perks to which he had become accustomed.

Davis was furious, but he had essentially cornered himself in a trap of his own making. He was not willing to put any of his own money into the studio, nor was he willing to let go his control of it. He had virtually no choice but to hold on to Diller, which meant that now he was stuck with Murdoch, who would quickly prove to be a very different sort of partner from Marc Rich.

Murdoch had no intention of remaining a silent, nonvoting partner. Moreover, he saw Fox as the cornerstone of a worldwide entertainment colossus that could serve not only as a source of programming but also as a means of distribution. It did not take long for Diller to come to share Murdoch's image of Twentieth Century-Fox positioning itself for the twenty-first century.

In March 1985, just as the deal with Murdoch was being finalized, Diller hosted a cocktail party in his Fox conference room in honor of John Kluge, which Murdoch and Davis also attended. Kluge, the 70-year-old chairman of Metromedia, a diversified communications empire, told Diller that he was thinking about selling Metromedia's seven television stations. He was asking $2 billion for all the stations, including the one in Boston, about which the Hearst Corporation had already expressed interest. Although Diller thought the price was too high, Murdoch had no such qualms.

Kluge's stations had a special appeal, because they were located in major cities, including New York and Boston. Diller had been thinking about starting a fourth network as far back as 1977, when he had tried to create one at Paramount. He and Kluge had talked then about a possible purchase, but Charles Bluhdorn had eventually decided against the idea.

Murdoch, however, was all in favor. There were two serious problems: Murdoch was an Australian citizen and U.S. law prohibited foreign ownership; and he was not permitted by U.S. law to own television stations in the same cities in which he owned newspapers, which he did in New York and Chicago. Nevertheless, Murdoch saw the potential deal as a singular opportunity, one of the few occasions when a group of unaffiliated stations in major markets could be his for the purchase price.

After several months of intense haggling with Kluge, Murdoch agreed to buy all seven stations for $2 billion, and to then resell the Boston station to Hearst for $450 million. Murdoch asked Davis, who kept vacillating about whether he wanted a piece of the deal, for an option to purchase the stations as well as the studio, should Davis decide to invest. But Davis, meanwhile, had concluded that the price was about $600 million too high for his taste, and he was still not prepared to sell the studio.

In June 1985, when the terms were close to being finalized with Kluge, Davis definitively decided that he would not buy into the package. He had also come to realize that his situation at Fox was no longer tenable. By now, he and Diller were barely on speaking terms, and Diller had succeeded in almost completely isolating him from the day-to-day affairs of the studio. Davis was determined to make his leavetaking as financially profitable as possible. He used Diller's involvement with Murdoch's newly purchased television stations as his bargaining chip, arguing that such involvement constituted a breach of contract on Diller's part.

It cost Murdoch an additional $237 million in cash to purchase Davis's remaining 50 percent share of Fox. (He also gave up his Australian citizenship to become an American and was thus legally permitted to own American TV stations.) Davis, who retained ownership of the Pebble Beach Golf Course, a ski resort in Aspen, and other pieces of the Fox real estate holdings, walked away from Fox with a hefty profit. Best estimates were that he ended up with $500 million, including several hundred million in profit.

But the money did nothing to assuage his hostility toward Barry Diller. "My mistake was in going after the wrong Paramount executive," he told journalist-author Alex Ben Block, two years after he had left Fox. "If I had only gone after Michael Eisner and got him to run the studio . . . it would be successful and I would still own Twentieth Century-Fox."

Davis's Monday-morning quarterbacking aside, it's anyone's guess whether he would have fared much better with the protégé than he had with the mentor. Though Eisner's personal style—his warmth and exuberance—might have been a more felicitous match for Davis than Diller's reserved and often icy-cold demeanor, Fox was experiencing a bottom-line crisis. The well had almost run dry, and Davis was dead-set against dipping into his own pockets to refill it. He had made his fortune drilling for oil, but he had relied on other people to shoulder the financial risk by selling them quarter shares of the potential profits, which paid for the cost of exploration.

Fox had appealed to him because it represented a piece of Hollywood history, a chance to rub shoulders with and feel a part of the glitzy show-biz crowd. Above all, it had looked to be a good deal, so long as he approached his investment in the studio with the same attitude he brought to the oil business: Find a partner, maximize profits, minimize personal risk. When asked to fulfill his contractual obligation to replenish Fox's empty coffers, he had balked.

No matter whom he might have chosen to run the show, Davis viewed the studio as a collection of assets, not all that dissimilar from his oil wells or real estate. Murdoch, on the other hand, had a much grander vision of his investment, and he had found in Diller the perfect partner to fulfill that vision. Taking a financial risk was just another step in the process to make his dream come true.

8

Creating the
Fourth Network

Rupert Murdoch and Barry Diller were eager to move forward with establishing their new network. They were well aware that if they succeeded, they would accomplish what nobody else had been able to do in over 40 years. The industry was full of naysayers who were predicting the network's demise even before it had been given a name. But the expressions of doubt and doom impressed neither Diller nor Murdoch. The fourth network was an opportunity waiting to happen, and both men were excited by the tantalizing possibility of turning a fantasy into reality.

Murdoch had built himself an empire on three continents by making tough business decisions and thumbing his nose at accepted conventions. The son of a respected journalist who had presided over Australia's biggest newspaper chain, Murdoch got his start in the early 1950s when he took over two small, failing Adelaide newspapers after his father's death and turned them into profitable operations. Toward the end of the decade, with the advent of television in Australia, he won a controlling interest in one of the country's first stations and also launched a magazine called *TV Week,* modeled after *TV Guide.* As the breadth and scope of his business grew, he became known as Australia's king of tabloids. His influence soon spread to England with his acquisition of the *Sun* and *News of the World.*

In 1973, he crossed the Atlantic and purchased two newspapers in San Antonio, Texas. From there he moved east, living up to his reputation as a master of yellow journalism when he founded a sensationalist, fad-driven tabloid called the *Star* to compete with the supermarket checkout counter favorite, the *National Enquirer.* In 1976, he bought the *New York Post* and turned it into a politically conservative tabloid with racy headlines and strongly slanted news articles that often seemed to cross the line into editorial opinion.

By the time Murdoch joined forces with Diller, he had also acquired *New York* magazine, the *Village Voice,* and the *Times* of London, a venerable and distinguished newspaper whose editorial content he wisely left unchanged. He differed from Diller in that he ran his company with a relatively hands-off management style, allowing his surprisingly small staff an unusual amount of independence, so long as the various groups met their performance objectives. This left him free to concentrate on the bigger picture, which in the fall of 1985, suddenly included the chance to make television history.

According to Federal Communications Commission regulations, a network—defined as a group of stations that offered a minimum of 15 hours a week of programming—was not permitted to sell programs for syndication. Thanks to Harris Katleman and the various series being developed by his department, Fox was earning a great deal of much-needed income through syndication. With few new movies in the pipeline, the studio was dependent on that money.

On the other hand, advertisers paid more for network programs than for local or syndicated shows. The conundrum that Diller and Murdoch faced therefore was this: How could a group of affiliated television stations achieve an identity as a network in the eyes of Madison Avenue, yet not be identified as a network by the FCC?

The solution was relatively simple. The network that was not a network would put programming on the air one or possibly two nights a week during the prime-time slot from 8 to 11 o'clock. Diller's hope and intent was to find shows good enough to convince affiliates, advertisers, and—most importantly—viewers that the former Metromedia stations had changed in more than name only.

He had to build the network from its foundation upward, to create a structure that could support the fledgling enterprise. At the same time, there were the normal duties involved with running the studio. Although he and Murdoch had decided to maintain the studio, the stations, and the network as three distinct legal entities, Diller still had responsibility for the overall operation. He also needed the cooperation of the Hollywood community to provide him with product for the network.

That fall and winter, Diller entertained the top echelon of Hollywood's producers, writers, and studio executives at a series of intimate lunches in his private conference room. He knew that by virtue of their profession, his guests were simultaneously skeptical and optimistic. Always in search of additional markets for their services, they had been burned so many times by failed projects that they were naturally apprehensive. Diller was hoping to dispel their suspicions that the Fox network was just another blue sky promise. He wanted to persuade them that Fox was open to more creative programming than the other networks, that they would have more freedom, less bureaucracy than they usually encountered.

It was a brilliant maneuver on his part. Rather than call a big press conference to announce that the new network was in business, Diller quietly pursued the cream of the entertainment world, catering to their egos, as well as to their wallets. Rupert Murdoch also was in attendance at each of the luncheons; they were, in fact, scheduled around his frequent trips to Los Angeles.

Murdoch, for all his attempts at respectability, was still perceived in many circles, Hollywood among them, as the sleazy tabloid publisher whose *New York Post* had flaunted the infamous headline about a murder in a Queens tavern, "Headless Body Found in Topless Bar." He and Diller wanted to dispel the idea that Murdoch was only interested in making more money, no matter who was offered in the process. They also wanted to reassure their guests that Diller would be running the network, and that Murdoch was prepared to underwrite the operation with the funding it needed until it could show a profit independent of his support.

Also that fall, Diller began the process of hiring a staff for the new network. He rejected the accepted method of choosing people with years of network experience and proven track records in favor of candidates who showed potential, a willingness to learn, an appetite for advancement. Whether or not he was aware of it— and most likely he wasn't, because Diller is famously averse to self-analysis—he was looking for people much like the young Barry Diller whom Len Goldberg had hired to be his assistant at ABC 20 years earlier. He had applied the same hiring standards to Michael Eisner and Jeffrey Katzenberg, and the strategy had proved highly successful.

Jamie Kellner was the first person to be employed by Diller for the network. The 44-year-old Kellner was a native New Yorker who had gotten his start in television at CBS's management-training program. After showing promise at CBS when he engineered a lucrative deal for the special products department, he had moved on to Viacom Enterprises, a government-ordered CBS spin-off that sold shows for syndication. He later worked at Filmways, where he was in charge of production for such shows as *Cagney and Lacey* and *Hollywood Squares.*

After meeting with both Diller and Murdoch, Kellner decided he liked what Diller had to say about transforming the existing network constellation. Despite the warnings he received from colleagues and friends about the pitfalls of working for Diller, he was excited by the prospect of getting involved from ground zero in showing up the other networks as aging dinosaurs that were too entrenched in tradition to consider anything different or out of the ordinary.

Kellner signed on with Fox as president of the network in February 1986. Shortly thereafter, Diller received a letter from David Johnson, a 46-year-old television consultant who had recently lost his job at ABC-TV as a result of the purchase of ABC by Capital Cities. Johnson had seen an article in *The Wall Street Journal* about Fox's new venture; in his letter, he outlined what he considered to be the mistakes made by the three established networks and urged Diller to avoid hiring people who would commit the same errors all over again. Diller was sufficiently impressed by Johnson's approach that he offered him a job as head of advertising and affiliate relations. In effect, Johnson became the resident authority on network-related business issues, the number cruncher responsible for creating projections and forecasts on which key decisions would be made.

Scott Sassa, the next person to join the team, had worked in various executive-level television jobs, most recently at the Playboy cable TV channel. He was to become the all-around utility infielder, working in finance, promotion, advertising, and affiliate relations. Sassa was responsible for bringing in Diller's next two hires: Garth Ancier and Kevin Wendle, both recruited from NBC to develop programming. Ancier, who like Sassa was only in his mid-20s, worked in programming at NBC. A former assistant to NBC's network chief Brandon Tartikoff, he had been involved with the development of such major NBC hits as the *Cosby Show* and *The Golden Girls*. Wendle became his second-in-command, moving from director of drama development to the number two programming spot at Fox.

By the end of March, Diller had gathered his core group of executives to run the still unnamed network. After an afternoon of brainstorming at a meeting that included Diller, Murdoch, and their five brand-new employees, a decision was reached. The fourth network would be called the Fox Broadcasting Company.

The management team that would launch and drive the FBC adjourned for dinner at a Beverly Hills restaurant, the Mandarin. Not all of those around the table that night would be around for many anniversary dinners, but on this celebratory evening, they were excited by their shared sense of possibility and camaraderie. Murdoch offered the toast that summarized the spirit of the occasion: "Look around and let us wish each other success for tonight is the start of something. It is a night we shall long remember," he declared. He then disclosed a piece of highly confidential information that would dramatically affect the network's image and development.

Over the previous months, he and Diller had pondered the question of how best to generate attention and credibility for the inauguration of the network. The answer had come to them by way of a phone call that Diller received in the early part of 1986 from Peter Dekom, the lawyer for comedienne Joan Rivers. Rivers and her husband, Edgar Rosenberg, were interested in exploring alternative options to her current situation as the permanent guest host of Johnny Carson's *Tonight Show*. Although Rivers felt a deep sense of gratitude to Carson for his help in promoting her career, NBC seemed to be stalling on the negotiations for her contract renewal. At her husband's urging, she was willing to entertain the idea of moving to FBC—if the terms were sufficiently attractive. Dekom wanted to know whether Diller was interested in exploring the possibility.

Diller was more than interested. ("They *skateboarded* over, and my lawyer hadn't hung up yet," was how Rivers described it in an October 1990 interview with Jonathan Van Meter that appeared in *Vanity Fair*.) A late-night talk show starring Joan Rivers was precisely the kind of high-profile program that Fox needed to generate attention and credibility. Moreover, stealing Rivers from NBC and Carson would be a terrific coup for the new network.

By Diller's calculations, hiring Rivers was a no-lose strategy. If she were to beat Carson in the ratings, she would achieve a television miracle. If she didn't beat him, the sheer audacity of her dramatic assault on the King of the Night would generate for Fox millions of dollars of free publicity, as well as the respect of the television industry.

The cost of such a show was also a crucial consideration. Talk shows were the least expensive type of format to produce for television. All that was needed was a studio with two or three cameras, an audience that came at no charge, and guest stars who worked for scale. The biggest expense was the price of the show's host, and he or she came relatively cheap. Johnny Carson, for example, earned $5 to $10 million a year when his was NBC's most profitable single show, earning the network $30 million plus a year.

Rivers had met Diller when he and some of his Hollywood friends had come backstage during one of her comedy club standup gigs. He had impressed her with his charm, and that impression was reinforced when he visited her and her husband at their Beverly Hills home to discuss her possible move to Fox. Rivers was taken in by his warmth and sincerity; only later would she become familiar with the dark side of his anger. Diller amused them both with stories of growing up in Beverly Hills. He flattered her and Rosenberg with predictions that Johnny Carson's ratings were fading, and that he would yield late-night TV to Rivers on FBC. Rivers had heard that Diller was a tough, take-no-prisoners business tycoon, but that afternoon he showed no signs of living up to his reputation.

Nevertheless, Rivers was still reluctant to jump ship. She had every hope of replacing Carson at *The Tonight Show* when he finally decided to retire, although supposedly her name had been missing from a list of the leading candidates for Carson's job that NBC was rumored to have prepared. Her loyalty to Carson also made it emotionally difficult for her to consider Fox's offer. It took a second meeting at Diller's house and subsequent discussions during which she and Rosenberg played hardball over terms of the contract before an agreement was reached.

Fox gave her the three-year commitment that she had demanded; she would receive $5 million during each of those three years. She was given "artistic control" over *The Late Show Starring Joan Rivers,* and the wording of the contract specifically stipulated, "The show will be produced with production quality and staffing equal to or better than that of *The Tonight Show.*" Rosenberg and Rivers's manager, Bill Sammeth, were named executive producers.

Nervous and insecure by nature, Rivers couldn't resist such a sweet deal, despite the enormous burden it placed on her to become the standard-bearer of FBC's success. Diller decided to break the news of her show, which was scheduled to debut in October, at a press conference on May 6. Even before the announcement took place, there were hints of tension between Fox and Rivers, differences of opinion as to who was really in charge and how things should be run. Rivers was particularly concerned about Johnny Carson's reaction. She tried to call him just before the press conference, but failed to speak with him. Deeply upset, she nevertheless appeared at the press conference alongside Diller and Kellner, answering questions like the consummate professional that she was.

The response, both from the media and non-network television stations across the country, was everything Diller could have hoped for. Rivers's $15 million price tag seemed to be worth every penny when the announcement of her show instantly conferred on FBC big-league status. The news of her defection from NBC made front-page headlines and unaffiliated station managers rushed to sign on with FBC.

Diller had told those present at the news conference that Murdoch had committed to supporting the unborn network with "$100 million . . . regardless of whether anybody other than our owned-and-operated stations sign up." Almost overnight, a scarcity of affiliates was the least of Diller's troubles.

For all of the positive publicity generated by FBC's answer to Carson, problems with *The Late Show Starring Joan Rivers* arose almost from the first day. Fox was contractually obligated to produce a show that was of the same quality as *The Tonight Show,* yet Diller now seemed reluctant to spend the money necessary to achieve that level of quality. As Rivers saw it, "The struggle for control started the very first week. I had been guaranteed by contract control of all creative aspects of the show—essentially what happened on camera. But in those first days I discovered that in his mind, Barry Diller had torn up the contract."

Rivers began to feel as if there were absolutely nothing about which she and Diller could agree: She didn't have enough space for herself and her staff. Diller wasn't paying enough to attract good writers to the show. Her litany of complaints against Diller and Fox went on and on. She and Diller disagreed about the interpretation of the overly vague wording in the contract regarding Rivers's right to complete artistic control.

According to Rivers, that clause gave her the right to decide that the show be taped, as *The Tonight Show* was, rather than be aired live. Mistakes and dull or flat material could be edited from the tape before broadcast, so that Rivers and her guests would appear at their funniest and most interesting. Taping the shows also meant that Rivers wouldn't have to rush to catch her flight from

Los Angeles to Las Vegas on the nights she was scheduled to appear at Caesar's Palace. Diller, on the other hand, wanted the show done live to give it the feeling of spontaneity that the competition lacked. His view prevailed, and Rivers lost her first fight over artistic control.

The conflicts extended to niggling matters such as whether Fox would pay for lunches for the entire production crew or just the senior staff, as well as whether the studio would pay for refreshments. Fox had originally put a refrigerator on the set and stocked it with soft drinks and bottled water, but Diller eventually had it replaced with a coin-operated soda dispenser.

Beyond such trivial but irritating issues loomed far more important questions such as who would serve as the show's producer. No agreement was reached until the end of the summer, just a couple of months before the show was set to debut, when Bruce McKay, formerly of *The Tonight Show,* was finally hired. Another major point over which Diller and Rivers argued was which guests to book and how many should appear per show. Rivers wanted four guests a night; Diller wanted fewer guests to promote more substantive interviews that might generate news stories and free press coverage for FBC.

Rivers was faced with a distinct disadvantage that she had not anticipated. The show had a limited viewing audience, which made it a less desirable venue for celebrities who were flogging their new movie or book. An even more daunting problem stemmed from Johnny Carson's anger over what he considered Rivers's betrayal, and the fact that he'd learned about her move from the news media. Rumor had it that people who appeared on Rivers's show would be banned from *The Tonight Show.* Very few rising young comedians—or established stars, for that matter—were willing to risk Carson's wrath. Nor did Diller deliver on his promise to use his considerable influence to attract celebrities to the show, so the reservoir of guests from which she could draw was severely limited.

Rivers, who had been receiving death threats, was concerned about her personal safety. She asked Diller to hire a private security service to patrol the studio where her show was headquartered. But Diller refused, not wanting to incur the additional expense.

The battle lines had been drawn. Whatever control Rivers thought she was entitled to exert over the production and content of her show, the real power lay in Diller's hands. Ever the perfectionist, he insisted on involving himself with even minute details, down to the decor of Rivers's green room, where guests and other important visitors were seated while waiting their turn to appear on camera.

Rivers devised a fitting symbol of how badly their relationship had deteriorated even before the premiere of the show. On a wall in her dressing room, she hung a photograph of herself and Diller, holding hands at their May press conference, which she had ripped down the middle. The distance between the two halves of the picture became an indicator of how she felt at any given moment about her new boss. By the time the show aired, the gap was no laughing matter.

It was a difficult time for Diller, who was also faced with the problem of how to salvage Fox's seriously ailing movie studio. Eighteen months earlier, Larry Gordon, who had presided over the movie end of the operation since Diller's arrival at Fox, had been diagnosed with a blocked heart artery that would ultimately require surgery. At the urging of his doctors, he had decided to remove himself from the studio's high-stress environment.

In December 1985, Diller replaced him with Alan Horn, formerly of Embassy Communications. The two men discovered almost immediately that their working styles were totally incompatible. Horn, who thought he had been hired to run the studio, resented having constantly to argue with Diller over every decision and project. "We could never agree on the allocation of responsibility," Horn later summarized his situation at Fox.

When Horn quit, after having been allowed to green-light only a handful of movies, Diller assumed interim control of the studio. His agenda now included determining which movie scripts to push through Fox's production pipeline; coordinating with other staff members to draw affiliates and advertisers to FBC; as well as finding prime-time programming for the much-heralded network-to-be—a pressing task.

The previous fall, he had pledged to the select group of creative types who had attended his luncheons that FBC would encourage a new level of creative freedom to propel its new network ahead of the three already existing ones. Now he had to make good on that promise. One of the incentives he offered to lure the top producers and writers—which utterly defied industry practice—was to forgo viewing and approving a pilot show before committing to a new series.

Michael Eisner and Jeffrey Katzenberg were among the first industry executives to line up at Diller's door. The bad blood between them forgotten, they met at Eisner's home towards the end of 1986 to discuss how Disney and Fox could work together. According to industry gossip, ABC was thinking of canceling the *Disney Sunday Movie* from its end-of-the-week lineup. Diller was ready and waiting to sign up the ABC hand-me-down. But Eisner, optimistic that he could keep the movie at ABC, had something else in mind. He and Katzenberg wanted to do a half-hour sitcom spin-off based on Disney's 1986 hit, *Down and Out in Beverly Hills,* starring Bette Midler, Richard Dreyfuss, and Nick Nolte. As yet, there was no cast (the original actors weren't part of the package), no script, and there would be no pilot. Diller showed his faith in his former protégés and said yes to nine episodes.

Other projects that Diller okayed during that same period included a very liberal production deal with producer/director James Brooks, who was already at Fox, working on *Broadcast News.*

Diller was so eager for Brooks to contribute to the TV side of Fox's operation that he agreed to set up a series development fund from which Brooks could draw to create pilot shows. Brooks was guaranteed a commitment of 26 episodes of any show he developed and deemed worthy of being aired.

A deal was struck as well with producer Stephen J. Cannell, who had developed *The Rockford Files* and *The A-Team,* among many other hits, to create an action-adventure show specifically targeted at young adults. The hour-long show, *21 Jump Street,* would feature a group of cops gone undercover in a high school that suffered from such problems as drugs and gang warfare.

There was also a half-hour sitcom created and produced by writers Michael Moye and Ron Leavitt, who had worked on *The Jeffersons* and *Silver Spoons.* Their concept was based on a blue-collar family that was the antithesis of Bill Cosby's very popular Huxtable family.

Moye and Leavitt had gotten to know Garth Ancier at NBC, where they had developed several pilots in addition to *Silver Spoons.* Ancier invited the two men to come to FBC because they seemed to perfectly embody the network's stated philosophy of pushing past the edge of traditional programming. Moye and Leavitt were delighted by the possibility of trying something new. "We wanted the alternative network," Moye said in a 1995 interview. "We wanted to give the viewers something that they couldn't see on any other network."

Moye, a North Carolina native who describes himself as "not one of those New York elitists that came out on the Harvard Express," met Leavitt when they were both working on *The Jeffersons.* Ironically, the two men, who supported themselves by writing for television, were drawn to each other by their shared hatred of sitcoms, which they thought were insipid, and all too much of the same thing.

Moye and Leavitt had conceived the idea for their show long before they heard about Fox's plan to do "alternative programming." They thought it would be interesting to take the abrasive stage persona of shock comic Sam Kennison and marry it to the equally caustic stage persona of Rosanne Barr. They knew, of course, that the concept was too radical to pitch to any of the networks, but they enjoyed playing with it, in Moye's own words, "just to keep our sanity when we were working for all these other hideous sitcoms. . . . Everybody was riding the Cosby wave at the time, sweaters and clean teeth." When Ancier told them that FBC was looking for material that wouldn't play on the other networks, the two men said, "Try this on for size."

"This is a long-term investment," Diller had said of Fox's network concept. "We're not going to be jumping out of any windows if we don't show a profit in six months."

Despite his cautious tone and a projected loss of $50 million for FBC's first year, Fox's studio produced several very successful, money-making films in 1986, including *Jewel of the Nile,* which grossed $100 million; *Aliens,* and *The Fly.* Diller had also found someone he could trust to replace Horn as president and chief operating officer. His friend and former ABC boss Leonard Goldberg, who most recently had been working as an independent television producer, was now responsible for Fox's television and movie production.

The new network kid on the block had almost 100 stations signed up, and $100 million to generate imaginative programming. Diller had every reason to feel optimistic in the fall of 1986, when *The Late Show Starring Joan Rivers* aired during the second week of October. Yet within two weeks of its launch date, its ratings had fallen from an initial 3 to 4 percent of the viewing audience to 2 percent, less than half the number of people tuning in to *The Tonight Show.*

The numbers were better than the ratings the independent stations had earned for that same time slot before they had carried the Rivers show. But Diller still had cause for concern, because the ratings determined the acceptance of the show by affiliate stations, a concept known in the industry as "clearances," which refers to the number of stations that will take the program and the hour at which they will broadcast it.

If, for example, a station in each of the one hundred major markets across the country aired the show at 11:30 P.M. opposite Johnny Carson, Fox would have the competitive edge because of the number of viewers it delivered to advertisers. Conversely, if few stations were clearing the show or not clearing it until 3 A.M., the audience for advertisers would be very limited, and Fox's earned advertising revenue would be low.

The size of a show's audience—and the number of viewers that the network delivers to the advertisers—is judged by a rating points system reported by audience survey companies such as the A.C. Nielsen Company. The FBC number crunchers were hoping that the Joan Rivers show would earn a 6 share, meaning that 6 percent of all the television sets turned on during that time slot were tuning in to *The Late Show*.

The high 2's and low 3's that the show was consistently earning during the fall and early winter of 1986 were in fact sufficient for the show to make money. But the ratings weren't good enough for Diller, who had fantasized about—and perhaps unwisely made predictions based on—the show garnering a 6 share. When the program didn't meet those expectations, Diller was keenly disappointed.

He had leaped at the opportunity to bring Joan Rivers to Fox, ardently courting her and Rosenberg, staying resolute in his suitor's role even as she wavered back and forth in her resolve to leave NBC. He had sold her to Murdoch, assuring the man who paid the bills that he would not regret his $15 million investment. Although his confidence in Rivers had been shaken by their disagreements over creative control throughout the five months that the show was taking shape, he had pinned his hopes for the network's successful birth on her.

Diller lacked the patience and foresight that might have helped him ride out what he perceived to be a crisis verging on disaster. Nothing in his previous experiences had prepared him for such conspicuous failure. Certainly, he had been responsible for his fair share of dismally received television shows and movies while at ABC and Paramount. But those were minor setbacks, a rotten apple or two in otherwise bountiful harvests. He had fought with Martin Davis and walked away the victor, claiming as his prize the chairmanship of Twentieth Century-Fox and a precedent-setting contract. His clashes with Marvin Davis had taken place, for the most part, behind closed doors; both men had good reason to keep their altercations as private as possible.

The problems with *The Late Show,* however, were rapidly becoming obvious and public knowledge. The industry rumor mills were working overtime, churning out delectable tidbits of gossip about how each of the players—Rivers, Rosenberg, and Diller—was reacting to the situation. Diller, one of Hollywood's most famously private figures, could not help but feel exposed and vulnerable as Rivers tried to get comfortable in her new late-night home.

She and Rosenberg had worked very hard all through the summer to prepare for their first season, but the show still suffered from the inevitable kinks that were bound to shake out over time. Diller, whose inability to tolerate imperfection was legendary, would not permit any flaws to mar FBC's gold-plated launchpad. He wanted the weaknesses shored up immediately, before the ratings took another nosedive and the damage was too severe to be contained.

Diller predictably grabbed the offensive and came down hard on Rivers and Rosenberg. He had hired Rivers because she was outrageous and different. Now he demanded that she soften her act, file down the hard edges that were so intrinsic to her stage persona.

In keeping with the pattern he had developed since his days at ABC, he isolated himself from the problem. There were to be no more visits to each other's home, no further pretense at cordiality. Their relationship quickly deteriorated to the point that Diller refused to take calls from Rivers or deal with her in person. Whenever Diller's people met with her and Rosenberg to discuss yet more changes to "fix" the show, both sides made sure to bring along their lawyers. The tense drama unfolding backstage, behind the set of *The Late Show,* would prove to be far more compelling than anything FBC had in development. It would end in a tragedy that no one could ever have predicted.

9

Truth or Consequences

"I felt like a child who was being kissed and slapped at the same time—who had been hired because she could push the limits of TV, and was now being told, 'Don't make waves.'" Thus Joan Rivers recalled her brief and unpleasant reign as Fox's late-night queen.

Seeking to exert ever greater control over Rivers's show, Diller dispatched one after another of his subordinates to communicate with Rivers and the omnipresent Rosenberg, who functioned as her advisor, protector, and spokesperson. Their presence was very much felt on the set, and it was no secret that they were reporting back to him about everything that went on.

He even went so far as to insist that the script be submitted to him and his immediate staff before each show so that he could edit the material. Diller, who once said of himself, "That's what I do for a living. I take other people's ideas and make them better," believed he was simply taking care of network business. Rivers and Rosenberg were infuriated by what they saw as his interference, which bordered on censorship.

Fox had told them, as well as the other creative teams that had signed on to work with FBC, that—unlike the other networks—there would be no censors standing over their shoulders, judging whether or not their material was appropriate for the eyes and ears of the American public. They had even gone so far as to promise that the pilots for the sitcoms and dramas in development would not be market-tested, which was standard operating procedure for new series.

Michael Moye was particularly pleased to hear that the pilot he and Ron Leavitt were writing, which for a time was jokingly referred to by them and Fox as *Not the Cosby Show,* would not be prescreened for a sample audience reaction. Such screenings were, he felt, "the biggest waste of time." Once the pilot was ready, however, Fox changed its mind and ran a test. Moye and Leavitt were then summoned to a meeting with Diller and the rest of the Fox's executives where they were lectured by an industry expert who used a series of graphs mounted on an easel to break down the demographic appeal of each of the characters on *Married . . . With Children.*

Moye and Leavitt had understood that the only rule they had to follow at Fox was that they do a show that couldn't be seen on any other network. But now the expert had concluded that the show would have a shot at success only if they made the husband and wife, Al and Peg, more loving toward each other, and the children more respectful of their parents. For Moye, this was tantamount to being told, "Make it like every other sitcom on television." He and Leavitt got up and stalked out of the room, but not before Leavitt declared to the expert, "You, sir, are the reason television sucks."

The brouhaha was quickly smoothed over. The writers were assured that they could ignore the test results, and the show was picked up for 13 episodes. Moye and Leavitt were delighted. No one had any idea whether Fox would make it as a network, but "even if Fox died in total obscurity," Moye said later, "it would have been fine because it kept me away from the other networks for half a year. . . . We didn't think the network would be around that long, but we thought that at least we were actually doing a show we really wanted to do. We didn't have to do the very special episode about AIDS or the very special episode about functional illiteracy or gang violence or animal rights. . . . We were happy as hell."

Moye's impression was that, despite the ongoing tension over the future of *The Late Show,* the mood at Fox during that period was generally optimistic. His sense was that "in the early days of Fox, although Diller and I creatively might have had some differences, the thing that you could say about Fox was that they seemed to have a direction and philosophy. . . . I thought Fox had focus. And they were a bit ballsy."

"Ballsy" was certainly the word that Joan Rivers and Edgar Rosenberg might have used to describe Diller and the Fox executives, but with a very different connotation than the one Moye had in mind. As the conflict escalated, Rivers—who was also taking a drubbing from the TV critics—and Rosenberg felt besieged by a barrage of Diller-initiated criticism. Diller thought she was being too coarse and vulgar; Rivers thought she was doing just what Fox had hired her to do, what she had always done best.

Rivers depended on Rosenberg as her executive producer to run interference and make sure her interests were properly defended. But the tone of his relationship with Diller was set at an early meeting when Diller lost his temper in front of a room full of people and shouted "Shut up!" at Rosenberg across the conference table. Rosenberg was intent on proving that he was every bit as much of a player as Diller.

When Fox didn't come through with what Rosenberg deemed necessary for the show, he pushed harder than he otherwise might have, demanding that they stick to the letter of their agreement. It began to feel to them as if Fox were deliberately conducting a campaign to get them to behave in ways that would constitute a breach of contract. Communication was soon reduced to a volley of threatening messages between their respective attorneys.

Rosenberg, who two years before had undergone open heart surgery, was still in poor health and could ill afford the stress of the battles, large and small, that Fox was waging with him. Rivers was fearful that the constant humiliations and confrontations were taking their toll of her husband.

She worried as well that the hostile environment would adversely affect her ability to walk onto the set five nights a week and be charming and funny in front of the cameras. Both she and Rosenberg were exhausted from the tremendous effort of preparing a show that would satisfy their own demanding standards, the critics, and Diller's exacting requests. She was also maintaining her crowded concert schedule, regularly performing in Las Vegas and other locations around the country.

It was probably inevitable that they should begin to take out their tensions on each other. Rosenberg seemed to be using Rivers as leverage in his war with Diller. She, in turn, began to wonder whether the strain had become too much for him, especially after he called her one day while she was at the set and told her he thought he was having a stroke. Rivers rushed to the hospital to be at his side and almost missed the show; the stroke turned out to be a false alarm.

Perhaps the problem boiled down to a matter of chemistry. By all accounts, Diller was hard to please. But some people succeeded better than others in accepting his outspoken manner and forthright, often overly brusque declarations.

Matt Groening, who was doing two-minute animated Simpson clips for *The Tracey Ullman Show* when he first met Diller, had heard about his "legendary blowups." He never actually witnessed one, nor was he ever the target of Diller's wrath. He experienced Diller as "extremely blunt," yet he also appreciated how focused Diller always seemed to be.

Polly Platt was another member of Hollywood's creative community who knew Diller by reputation—she had heard that he was "blunt, outspoken, and sometimes brutal"—before she ever met him. Platt had been told by Louis Malle, a friend of Diller, that "Barry was not predisposed particularly to liking *Pretty Baby*," the 1978 Paramount film for which Platt wrote the script and Malle directed. Their initial encounter took place during a meeting about the movie on the Paramount lot.

"It was a very hot summer day, and this bullet-headed, incredibly, I thought, attractive man with blue eyes set close together came in. He was wearing a shirt that had a completely solid collar and cuff, but the rest of the shirt was transparent. It was so thin, probably the finest cotton, that you could see his skin and you could tell that he wasn't wearing an undershirt. He had two crescents of sweat underneath his armpits. . . . It was sexy, it made him look sexy. . . . He didn't look like anybody else I had ever seen . . . He didn't knock. He just walked right into the office. He stood there listening to us long enough to know what we were talking about. Then he marched across the room and exited on this line: 'I hate the title.' He never said hello or introduced himself. When he left, we all just shrugged."

Platt became better acquainted with Diller when he was at Fox, where she coproduced the 1987 Christmas hit, *Broadcast News*, written and directed by James Brooks. "You could see him thinking right on his feet," she said. "We didn't have a name for [the movie]. It was called *Untitled* while we were shooting. When we finished I got the crew jackets with *Untitled* written on the back. So Jim [Brooks] says, 'We're going to call it *Sound Bites*.' And Barry says right back to him, 'No. You're not calling it *Sound Bites*. You're calling it *Broadcast News*. That's it.' Other studio executives might have said, 'Oh, that's interesting. Let me think about it,' because it scared them to directly confront a powerful filmmaker like Jim. . . . But Barry said no, and Jim was fine with that."

The man whom Rivers and Rosenberg would have described, at best, as difficult to work with was the same man whom Platt called "the cleanest decision maker. He's made some very interesting decisions. I'm not saying he can read the future or knows the best movies. All I'm saying is that he seems to have an eye on a different ball."

Platt recalled attending parties at Diller's home and described the events as "put together beautifully. We came in limos but he had excellent valet parking. One wouldn't have to wait at all."

She especially noted and admired "his love of flowers. When I would go over to his office at Fox there would be very beautiful exotic flowers on the coffee table, not your average carnations or roses. He was way ahead of the florists who are just now making those exotic combinations.

"I found it interesting that such a powerful man would have such delicate flowers floating in beautiful glass containers in his office. His office was always very neat and organized and no papers on his desk. His office was almost Japanese.

"His house was more traditional. More color control, red flowers, white flowers. There was never what you would call a hodge-podge, His tables were beautiful, the food, exquisite."

Platt summed up her assessment of Diller as follows: "Barry will tell you what he thinks. The reason I like Barry Diller is because he never dissembles. He's simply direct. You don't walk away from Barry wondering whether he's telling you the truth or whether he got the correct assessment of what you're doing. It's very refreshing. He's different than the others."

The very same qualities that Matt Groening and Polly Platt perceived as Diller's strengths—his utter honesty and ability to focus—proved to be the stumbling blocks beyond which Rivers and Rosenberg could not see. Joan Rivers, by her own account, was ". . . a nervous Jewish lady . . . full of insecurity." She needed to be flattered and cajoled and showered with praise. But doling out compliments was hardly Diller's strong suit, and Rosenberg could be every bit as inflexible and obstinate as Diller. Their oversized egos butted up against each other, and Rivers was caught in the middle. She simultaneously had to try to keep her husband healthy and happy, and hope to find a way to please the implacable Diller.

It was an impossible task. Each accused the other of not listening. Neither side was willing to compromise its position and work together to improve the show. Diller, who held the upper hand, could not see past the immediate problem of low ratings, for which he blamed Rivers and Rosenberg. By the beginning of February 1987, less than four months after the show had premiered, Diller had judged it to be a failure.

Alan Sternfeld, a former NBC executive who joined the network in April 1987, had this to say about Diller's approach to the ratings game:

"Barry's focus for over twenty years had been the movie world where you're made or broken on your opening weekend. He'd jump to conclusions and try and overmassage things or over-read things based upon one set of numbers. TV viewing rarely produced climactic results in one single outing. Patterns form over a period of time. Intelligence and observations need to be formed over a period of time."

At a meeting in February attended by Fox's executive team, Rivers, Rosenberg and attorneys for both sides, Diller made clear that he had lost faith in Rivers and Rosenberg. The ratings were maintaining their downward spiral. He had no choice but to insist that Fox take control of the show, effective immediately. Changes had to be made in its style and content. Otherwise, they risked losing the already waning support of their advertisers and affiliates. It would no longer be Joan Rivers' show, with her and Rosenberg exercising creative control. Bruce McKay, their producer, was about to be fired, to be replaced by an as yet unnamed executive of Fox's choosing. Rivers was now just another employee, a hired performer who had no choice but to follow Fox's directives. Rosenberg was stripped of all his duties and authority.

"You're a tinhorn dictator!" Rosenberg lashed out at Diller. "I don't need this. I'm a rich man." Diller inelegantly and uncharacteristically shot back, "Go fuck yourself!"

Both Rivers and Rosenberg left the meeting feeling physically ill; Rivers was so demoralized by what she perceived as an assault on her and her husband's credibility and professionalism that she—the consummate trooper—was unable to host that evening's show.

A new producer, Joanne Goldberg, was hired in early March. In the meantime, the show's ratings had risen slightly while Rivers was away on vacation, a fact that did not escape Diller and his people. But with Rivers back on the set, the ratings continued to drop. The demographics were also working against her; the show was declining in popularity among younger viewers, the audience it had targeted and specifically promised to deliver to its advertisers.

The affiliate stations were achieving higher numbers with Rivers than they had previously. But Diller was aware that coming up very soon were the all-important May sweeps, the highly competitive period during which the networks showcased their best programming in order to win the high numbers that would determine the advertising rates for the next six months.

The April launch date of the new network, now renamed Fox, was also fast approaching. In addition to his ongoing monitoring of *The Late Show* situation, Diller, as usual, had immersed himself in every aspect of the process.

Dissatisfied with the actor who had been chosen to play the key male character in *21 Jump Street,* Diller had insisted that Stephen Cannell halt production until another actor could be cast.

The field eventually narrowed down to two sexy young men, Josh Brolin and Johnny Depp. According to Diller, the choice was obvious as soon as he viewed the audition tape: Johnny Depp was picked to play the character of Hanson.

Diller's participation extended far beyond his new role of casting director. He involved himself closely with publicity and advertising, fiddling with and reshaping print advertisements and television promo spots. Often, he would demand so many last-minute changes that the promotion department would have to work round-the-clock to meet its deadlines.

Chiat Day, the Los Angeles-based advertising agency, was briefly employed by Fox to help with the April launch of the network. Chief among the agency's contributions was the suggestion that during the week of the launch, Fox rent the famous "HOLLYWOOD" sign in the Hollywood Hills and superimpose on it the word "FOX." The maneuver attracted some significant local press coverage, and even received some national attention. Chiat Day's relationship with Fox was short-lived, however, mostly due to the difficulties posed by Diller's hands-on approach.

Fox went prime-time on April 11, 1986. Its initial Sunday night lineup included *21 Jump Street; The Tracey Ullman Show,* a half-hour variety show produced by James Brooks that featured Ullman, a talented English comedienne and an ensemble cast; and *Married . . . With Children.* Diller meanwhile was keeping a very close eye on the ratings for *The Late Show.*

He was especially concerned about potential defections by affiliate stations if the show's May ratings continued at the same low level. Diller finally made up his mind after being informed that Rivers was officially in breach of contract because of the many occasions on which Fox had previously warned her of what they deemed to be unacceptable behavior on her part.

In late April, Rivers was notified through her lawyer, Peter Dekom, that Fox had decided to terminate her contract. *The Late*

Show Starring Joan Rivers was being canceled, effective immediately. Rather than fight Diller and Fox by taking them to court, Rivers chose to settle for "somewhat over $2 million." Her last show was the following evening. Rivers signed off to a standing ovation from her audience. She was weeping as she left the set, and her tears continued to flow as she said goodbye and exchanged hugs and kisses with her staff and crew.

Although many of the people who had worked most closely with Rivers and Rosenberg were fired, *The Late Show* was kept on the air, presided over by a different guest host each night. Diller and his executives soon discovered, however, that Rivers was not as easily replaced as they had anticipated. Over the next few months, the show's waning popularity was eroded even further. Viewers who had made a habit of regularly tuning in had done so because they liked Rivers's style. Now they were being asked to adjust to whoever happened to be sitting behind the desk on any given evening. The absence of a permanent host soon turned out to be a ratings washout.

Joan Rivers might have had the last laugh on Fox had it not been for the devastating tragedy that struck her just two months after she was fired by Diller. At approximately midnight on August 11, Edgar Rosenberg committed suicide in a Philadelphia hotel room by ingesting two bottles of sleeping pills washed down with whiskey and cognac. Whatever Fox's view might have been of the role it played in Rosenberg's death, Rivers's feelings on the subject were unequivocal. A year afterward, interviewed by Alex Ben Block, she said, "Fox never did what they promised. They were totally dishonorable. . . . My husband is dead over it. Edgar killed himself over it."

10

The Plots Thicken

Barry Diller had set out to create the network of alternative programming. Whether he achieved his goal is a question of some debate. Certainly, Fox was perceived as an interesting challenge by enterprising television executives, as well as writers and producers seeking something a little bit different from their past network experiences. Alan Sternfeld was one of those executives who brought with him to Fox the hope of finding creative opportunities that were not available elsewhere.

Sternfeld was working at NBC when Garth Ancier called to explore the possibility of his coming over to Fox. After a meeting with Ancier during which they discussed the parameters of the job, Ancier ushered him in to Diller's office and introduced the two men. Although Sternfeld's first impression of Diller was that he was "low key, charming and gracious," he also thought "that he was probably like a coiled spring and potentially quite mercurial."

When Diller asked why he wanted to leave NBC, Sternfeld candidly admitted that he had worked there for eight years and was feeling underappreciated by Brandon Tartikoff, the head of programming. Sternfeld later recalled that Diller seemed very sympathetic to his plight. He commented that it had to be difficult for such a talented young person to feel that his professional growth was being stymied, and that the difficulty was compounded because he was working for someone who was preoccupied with taking all the credit for himself. It wasn't clear to Sternfeld whether Diller was intimating that the opposite would be true at Fox. Diller did say that there would definitely be a lot of opportunities at Fox for Sternfeld to make his mark, and he characterized the new network as "a growing enterprise . . . and an adventure."

Based on their conversation, Diller gave Ancier the go-ahead to hire Sternfeld to work on the prime-time series as well as help with scheduling. Sternfeld, who thought of himself as somewhat of a risk taker, had no qualms about signing a three-year contract to join the fourth network. Working at Fox struck him as exciting, a chance to be part of a new and unprecedented venture.

Like Michael Moye, Sternfeld remembered that the mood at Fox in the spring of 1986 was "very bright and optimistic. We were all excited by the challenge. By the time I got there, Fox was already on the air and they were already on in prime time . . . . Fox was in a defining mood."

There were regular and frequent meetings in Diller's conference room, located behind his office. Among the questions most often discussed were: "Do we want to be cutting edge? Do we want to be mainstream or alternative?" The meetings, which were attended by most of the top executives, would go on for six hours or longer. According to Sternfeld, they "had no agenda, a rambling focus, [and they] never resulted in any specific plan for action. They would often start out with one thing and lead to another. The next thing we knew," Sternfeld remembered, "we were having lunch in Barry's dining room and would continue the conversation after lunch."

It was never clear to Sternfeld whether Diller was "playing games with the group in terms of eliciting opinions, or if he truly wanted devil's advocates, or if he resented anything that smacked of criticism or lack of agreement. I can't recall too many instances where there was a problem defined, a solution discussed, a plan of action contemplated. I think there were a lot of amorphous, rambling conversations.

"It occurred to me at some point that Tartikoff, who initially had taken this little network less than seriously, now held it in somewhat higher regard simply because it had stolen some of his executives. But if he had known just what his former colleagues, Garth and myself, were doing, listening to Barry go on at this length, I think he would have been rather content to let the network implode. These were the kinds of meetings that certainly would never have taken place over at NBC, nor I dare say at CBS or even ABC, which by the late 1980s was clearly the doormat of the industry."

Sternfeld and the other executives in charge of prime-time series were working 60-hour weeks in addition to attending Diller's marathon rap sessions. They had scripts to read, tapings, run-throughs, and other meetings at which they were required to be present. It was not unusual for Sternfeld to return home at one in the morning. Very shortly, "the optimism and the bright sunny rise-to-the-challenge gave way to 'I'm exhausted' . . . to 'this is really hard and . . . there's an awful lot of time spent at this process.'"

Beyond the issue of the long hours, there was also a deep sense of disillusionment when the team spirit turned into what Sternfeld described as "backbiting, sniping, political subterfuge, and intrigues . . . things became decidedly darker and Machiavellian. A lot of cliques formed."

Sternfeld, who was working with Ancier on scheduling, felt that early on Ancier and Diller made a number of key mistakes that undermined Fox's effectiveness. Diller had sold the network to advertisers on the basis of its innovative programming and its specific appeal to urban, upper-middle-class viewers between the ages of 25 and 54. But aside from several notable exceptions, most of the early series were no better than mediocre. Such shows as *Down and Out in Beverly Hills, Mr. President,* which starred George C. Scott and Bean Baxter, hardly lived up to Diller's guarantee that Fox would offer programming that stood out from the other networks.

Sternfeld took it upon himself to point out that the network lacked an identity that viewers could easily recognize. Programs had been bought—and were being aired—simply because they had been made available to Fox. Advertisers had signed on because they had been promised a certain demographic, but the series were falling far short of delivering the targeted audiences.

As Sternfeld saw it, "The programming philosophy was not formed and not matched to what was going on with advertisers. Saturday [evening programming] was launched with shows that could have been on any of the networks—except that they were really bad. . . . [It was] programming without design."

Yet Diller had promoted the network as a home for writers and producers seeking greater creative freedom, an opportunity to expand beyond the ordinary conventions of TV sitcoms, without the typical interference from network executives. He had trumpeted the emergence of a designer showcase for television programming. "In reality," said Sternfeld, ". . . there was no coherent plan to launch."

Ancier and Sternfeld had similar philosophies about programming, developed under the tutelage of Brandon Tartikoff and Grant Tinker at NBC. "What's very important in the process of putting on very successful weekly series," explained Sternfeld, "is people who can produce and execute on a weekly basis. Series

Barry Diller with long-time companion, designer Diane Von
Furstenberg, 1992. (Globe Photos Inc./Lisa Rose)

Barry Diller and Brooke Shields at Harper's Bazaar Black-Tie Gala honoring Avedon, 1994. (Globe Photos Inc./Andrea Renault)

Barry Diller and Diane Von Furstenberg at 1995 "Kids for Kids" pediatric AIDS benefit. (Globe Photos Inc./Rose Hartman)

Barry Diller, QVC (center), Howard Stringer, President CBS Broadcast Group (left), and CBS CEO Laurence A. Tisch (right) announce pending $2 billion merger of QVC and CBS in New York City on June 30, 1994. The merger failed. (AP/Wide World Photos/CBS)

Ted Turner, CEO of Turner Broadcasting (left), with Barry Diller, CEO of FOX Studios (right), at U.S. Senate Judiciary subcommittee in Washington, DC, April 1992. (AP/Wide World Photos/John Duricka)

Above: Industry leaders Rupert Murdoch, Chairman of FOX, Inc. (right), and Barry Diller, former QVC Chairman (left), at the National Association of Broadcasters convention in Las Vegas, April 10, 1995. (AP/Wide World Photos/Lennox McLendon)

Diller arriving at a Leukemia Society benefit in New York City, October 12, 1993 during the time he was trying to take over Paramount Communications. (AP/Wide World Photos/David Karp)

Diller takes time out from his campaign to take over Paramount Communications to attend the Bill Bernbach Memorial Award Dinner to benefit leukemia research in New York City, October 12, 1993. (AP/Wide World Photos/David Karp)

Below: TCI Chairman John Malone (left) with Barry Diller (right) at U.S. Senate Judiciary antitrust subcommittee hearing about communications industry mergers in Washington, DC, December 16, 1993. Malone and Diller are involved in an attempt to take over Paramount Communications. (AP/Wide World Photos/John Duricka)

Diller talking to Senator Howard Metzenbaum (D-Ohio) at U.S. Senate Judiciary antitrust subcommittee hearing on telecommunications industry. Left to right, Metzenbaum, TCI Chairman John Malone, Diller, and Senator Bob Kerry (D–Mass.). (AP/Wide World Photos/John Duricka)

QVC Chairman Diller with Diane Von Furstenberg attending Metropolitan Museum of Art and 25th anniversary party for CBS show "60 Minutes," November 10, 1993. (AP/Wide World Photos/Mark Lennihan)

Panel on cable television consisting of actor Robert Redford (right), Turner Broadcasting's Ted Turner (left), and Barry Diller (standing) at cable television Western Show in Anaheim, California, November 29, 1995. (AP/Wide World Photos/Kevork Djansezian)

Cable television mogul Ted Turner expounding and gesturing to the amusement of actor Robert Redford (center) and Barry Diller (right) during panel presentation at cable television Western Show in Anaheim, California, November 29, 1995. (AP/Wide World Photos/Kevork Djansezian)

Above: FOX television
head, Barry Diller, with
his keynote late-night star,
Joan Rivers, in happier
times during May 1986.
(AP/Wide World Photos)

Barry Diller faces
reporters as he leaves CBS
headquarters in New York
City after his planned
merger of QVC and CBS
hits a snag that ultimately
blocks the deal, July 13,
1994. (AP/Wide World
Photos/L. M. Otero)

are nothing without execution." Diller, however, ". . . bought concepts. . . . Barry had a hair-trigger response to everything. Barry would have a meeting with Disney and wind up buying a *Down and Out in Beverly Hills* without a clue as to who was going to write and produce the show. Or whether it was even a good concept."

His mode of operation defied the television industry's conventional wisdom of choosing a writer or producer with a proven track record, people "with whom you'd like to be in business," as Sternfeld put it. "Producers come in, they pitch shows, the ideas get refined and honed down. It's like going into a tailor and saying, 'I'd like a suit. Let's pick out some materials and talk about the style.' Then it's custom-made to your body. That's in effect what the network sees as the development process. You start by picking out a tailor—Jim Brooks, for example—to create a show. Going to a studio and saying let's do *Down and Out in Beverly Hills* is the wrong way to go about it."

Sternfeld felt that Diller, who had "clearly set himself up as the Archduke of Programming," had unrealistic expectations, not only in terms of the ratings his shows could hope to achieve, but how long it would take for them to get there. "I think he tried to read too much into whether a number was an eight share or a nine share—a 2.2 rating or a 2.3 rating. Based on Nielsen numbers, in the 20s range there's a substantial error margin because their statistical reliability is only so great. When your base of rating is 2, your entire rating is, in effect, an error margin. So it's meaningless to anguish over whether it's a 2.2 or a 2.4 and whether a trend has been established because you were 2.4 last week."

Meaningless it may have been, but Diller nonetheless did dwell on the numbers, and never more so than in the summer of 1987. In July, Fox had added Saturday night programming to its schedule and had been officially designated as a network by the Nielsen Company, the major TV ratings service. Fox could now charge higher prices for advertising time. But the need to score high ratings was even greater because the new network was being reported on the same list as—and therefore being compared with—the three established veterans.

By the end of August, the network was losing approximately $2 million a week. Rupert Murdoch was feeling increasingly edgy about seeing some return on his investment. Murdoch was in the process of expanding his empire to four times its previous size. Among other recent acquisitions, including the largest newspaper chain in Australia, several months earlier he had paid $300 million for the publishing house of Harper & Row. In addition, he was taking heavy losses on his investment in Sky Channel, a direct-by-satellite (DBS), English-language, European television system.

The debt being carried by Murdoch's company, News Corporation, had risen to $400 million, an increase of over $300 million since 1985. He was growing tired of best-face-forward promises. He, like Diller, was anxious to see some solid Nielsen ratings listed next to their shows.

Diller's modus operandi in such pressure situations was to resort to a survival-of-the-fittest technique. He pitted people one against the other, not explicitly perhaps, but implicitly by permitting (some might say encouraging) confrontational and abrasive behavior among his executives. "If he was not satisfied with the results he got immediately from someone, he would give somebody else the same responsibilities and wait to see who survived the process," recalled Alan Sternfeld.

Scott Sassa, who had labored over publicity and promotion for the network's launch, had come to feel overwhelmed by his impossible workload and the lack of support from his colleagues. In February 1987, he was eased out of doing promotions and into the area of operations, to be replaced by Brenda Mutchnick Farrier, a public relations executive whom Diller had worked with at Paramount. From then on, Diller ignored him, and several months later he was gone from Fox.

The constant faultfinding and finger-pointing took its toll of Fox's top-level staff. Sternfeld said, "I think I had a cold for about two months, which was probably a function of stress and exhaustion."

Garth Ancier found himself in an ugly power struggle with his friend and close associate, Kevin Wendle. It was Wendle who had originally suggested to Jamie Kellner that he recruit Ancier to be in charge of programming. After Ancier had decided to accept the position, Wendle, too, signed on with Fox because he believed that Ancier, whom he greatly respected, would be an excellent teacher and mentor.

"Then the next thing you knew," remembered Sternfeld, "these two friends and colleagues were at each other's throats. Kevin was whispering in Barry's ear, 'He's doing it all wrong. I can do it much better.' And Garth was just a walking, suffering mess. . . . Garth took all the potshotting to heart and let it get to him."

It was fairly common knowledge around Fox that Ancier was going through a particularly rocky period. The general perception was also that Wendle had Diller's encouragement to call the producers who had been talking to Ancier about shows already on the air and those in development, and insert himself into the middle of process. As it was, Ancier had limited authority to commit to projects or expenditures without Diller's express approval. He had to consult with Diller about items that were matters of free choice for his counterparts at the other network entertainment divisions.

Alan Sternfeld's impression was, "Barry played games with Garth. I remember specific instances where Garth would say, 'I promised so and so I'd answer them by four o'clock tomorrow. What do you want to do?' Four o'clock would roll around and Barry would make himself unavailable, and Garth would tear his hair out because he had promised to come to some conclusion by that deadline.

"Then the next day Barry would say, 'What did you do with so and so?' And Garth would say, 'I couldn't do anything with them because I don't have the authority to make this decision and you wouldn't return my phone calls.' And then Barry would chastise him for his poor treatment of the person on the other end of that decision.

"I have no idea what Barry thought these games would accomplish. Somebody else might have looked at the situation and said, 'You do it to me once, you do it to me twice, third time, I'll just take it upon myself to do what I think is correct, and if you don't like it fine. Deal with it then.' That wasn't Garth's way. He would just leave people hanging."

Ancier wasn't the only executive whom Diller kept on a short leash. "Every promo, every ad, everything that Kevin Wendle did," said Sternfeld, "was likewise subject to Barry's review."

Although Ancier was "not a strong leading executive," Diller had hired him because he had come so highly recommended by knowledgeable people in the industry. Ancier was a key player in the NBC hierarchy, and NBC executives were a hot commodity in the mid-1980s, "a talent pool for the industry," according to Sternfeld, who was himself an NBC alumnus. Ancier had never worked in development, but he had a solid reputation as a series programming person, especially in the area of comedy.

Michael Moye's sense was that Ancier had a big part in helping Fox to develop its sense of direction. "Because Garth was one of the few executives who actually did follow his gut. He did love his stats, but if something just turned him on, he would fight for it rather than say, 'Well, this has never been done before so I'm just going to let it go.' Which is the way most executives are."

Diller, of course, wanted executives like Ancier, people who were willing to listen to their intuition and fight for what they believed in. The success of *Married . . . With Children,* with which Ancier was closely associated, further enhanced his reputation.

The pilot episode was aired on Fox's first Sunday night, but it was by no means an instant hit.

"When we first started out, nobody heard of us," said Moye. "The ratings were just a bluff. Garth would call us when the ratings were very low and try and make us feel better because we didn't get nearly the coverage we have now. It's hard to make people change their habit of watching ABC or NBC."

Whatever pressure Diller put on Ancier to improve the ratings, Ancier did a good job of keeping the heat off Moye and Leavitt. Moye's previous network experience had taught him that "because everyone's into immediate gratification, you've got to score big out of the box. So what you get is a bunch of pilots that try and be all things to all people in about twenty-two minutes. They're dancing, they're singing. 'Please like us. Look, we're hugging and we're funny. Look, I'm gruff, but I have a heart of gold, and my wife can work and take care of the home. Please like us!'" Fox, on the other hand, "gave us a chance to go slowly."

Moye's sense was that "we were kind of their fill until they could get something better," which may have been another reason why Diller stayed out of their way, and the show was able to develop and catch on over time. Diller left Ancier to oversee *Married . . . With Children,* while he stayed more deeply involved with *21 Jump Street* and *Tracey Ullman,* whose producers—Stephen Cannell and James Brooks, respectively—were important names in the industry.

"You have to remember that when Ron and I went to Fox we weren't well-known at all," said Moye. "As a matter of fact, I still have the article in *LA Magazine* where we're referred to as 'and others.' Fox was so proud that it had gotten the services of Weinberger, Cannell, and all of those guys. And then there's us: 'and others.' Even given the philosophy of the network, I'm not sure that *Married . . . With Children* was Fox's idea of alternative."

Married initially did poorly in the ratings. The audience didn't know what to make of Peg and Al Bundy. As Moye put it, "At first you watch the show and go, 'These people are wild. He's insulting his wife, he doesn't want to sleep with her. He doesn't care.' But then you go, 'Oh I see. They bicker a lot but when an outside force comes in, they band together.' People think, Hey, they're like my family. They really do like each other. After six or seven episodes, you understand. It's handed to you gently instead of with a sledgehammer."

The show was different from most sitcoms, which, said Moye, ". . . try and cram in everything because they've got to score. . . . But look at some of the great classics. They built up, because the better shows are usually the ones that are different. And they all started slowly."

The same was true of *Married . . . With Children.* The show didn't really begin to take off until the middle of the second season. "Rather than it being hyped in the papers and on TV, this show was being hyped by the water cooler. People would get together and say, 'Did you see what they did on *Married . . . With Children?*' And that's kind of how we grew. People talking in offices or filling stations or battleships. We do real well in prisons, colleges, and the military. Anywhere there's one TV and people have to watch it, we do very well. It became a great cult thing through colleges."

By the third season, thanks in part to the attention drawn to the show by Michigan housewife Terry Rakolta, who took public issue with what she considered overly explicit sexual content, *Married . . . With Children* had begun to beat the competition. Its strong ratings were beyond everyone's wildest dreams, including Moye and Leavitt.

But the publicity generated by Rakolta's outraged protests was certainly far from the whole story of why *Married . . . With Children* became so hugely successful. The show offered the viewing public something totally new and different, a sitcom that altered people's expectations of the genre, much as Norman Lear's *All in the Family* had done in the 1970s.

Cocreator Moye credits as well other factors that influenced the show's popularity. "I think that people can identify with these characters, as cartoonish as they get. . . . I think they like the honesty of it. Al Bundy has said things that probably no television husband has ever said. Al Bundy's kids were the first kids that didn't particularly want to learn anything from their father. Why would they? He sells shoes. People recognized a lot of the characters, and you didn't see them on television.

"I really think that our audience won't sit back and feel like they've been conned. You know how sometimes you'll watch an episode of situation comedy and it's over and suddenly you feel oily . . . you feel dirty. Someone just slipped you this message and you weren't prepared for it and it pissed you off. And that makes people mad. You don't have to worry about that with *Married . . . With Children*. People know they can totally let their guard down with us.

"Another thing I think contributed to the longevity of the show is . . . there's a blue collar audience out there that I'm proud to be a part of, and they're going, 'Might we have some entertainment, too?' There aren't as many shows for them. I thought there was an audience that didn't particularly care about the sitcom goings-on of an obstetrician who wears clean sweaters and gets witty with his kids. Even today, I think there's an audience that doesn't give . . . much of a damn about the bitching and moaning of Generation Xers. . . . People just want to come home and laugh."

Moye believes that Fox's most successful comedies were those that adhered most closely to their original philosophy of alternative programming. But he also suspects that because of the particular type of humor on *Married . . . With Children*, Diller and other Fox executives might have preferred to have some other show become their runaway biggest hit.

"I think that Fox got typecast as the toilet joke network, the bad taste network, the network that's been left home alone. And I don't think that's what they were going for. They were going for something alternative—Tracey Ullman wacky alternative—rather than what they perceived as bathroom humor. I think that when the Rakolta thing broke . . . they distanced themselves from us quite a bit. I never thought that we were defended the way we should have been defended by Fox. . . . [W]e would read in the paper that a Fox spokesman said that 'we are going to stand by our writers' . . . . All the while we were getting phone calls from Fox saying that we had to tone it down."

Not surprisingly, Moye and Leavitt ignored Fox's demands that they create safer, less provocative scripts and shows. They felt that any publicity was good publicity, and that Rakolta didn't necessarily represent the majority of public opinion. As Moye put it, "The people who like the show don't write in. . . . When you get a car that you like, you don't write, 'Dear Ford, I love this car. Absolutely nothing went wrong with this car. It stops when I want it to stop.'"

Moye wanted to appear with Rakolta on the TV talk show circuit, to personally counter her charges. But Fox told him not to, and Moye harbors bitter feelings about that. "This show bought a lot of people a lot of nice houses and porcelain things and all we wanted was a little backup."

He sees their refusal to let him go up against Rakolta as being about "the fact that they might have been a little ashamed of [the show]. This show helped a lot of careers, but publicly they tried to distance themselves from it because it's not a correct kind of show. It's not *Cosby,* it's not *Murphy Brown* or *Frasier.* It's not your Emmy-winning, let's-all-meet-at-Mortons-and-pat-ourselves-on-the-back-after-the-taping kind of show. So it was hard for them to stand shoulder-to-shoulder with us and defend us. . . . I think that when the Rakolta incident happened, it brought [the network] notoriety, but it wasn't the type of notoriety that they liked."

Did the success of *Married . . . With Children,* the first of Fox's shows to be featured on the cover of *TV Guide* influence the content of shows that Fox subsequently signed up? Moye thinks the answer is yes; that the network's philosophy changed once *Married* began to score in the ratings game. "Their own success started scaring them. After this happened very rarely did I see shows in development that were different. I think . . . an amendment was written: We want other shows that you can't see on other networks as long as they're within certain parameters. . . . We want different shows but not that different that they will get us into trouble."

He even believes that "we were lucky with our timing"; that once the network became more established, he and Leavitt would not have been able to sell Fox on the same concept that they had pitched to Ancier and Diller in 1986. "I think if someone asked me in a nutshell what Fox's problem is, I'd have to say that they got successful and they started playing it close to the vest."

A careful and seasoned observer of the television game, Moye offers several convincing examples of shows that seem to meet the definition of alternative programming, yet debuted on networks other than Fox: HBO's *Dream On,* which has been shown (sans nudity) on Fox in syndication; the *Larry Sanders Show,* another offering from HBO; and MTV's *Beavis and Butthead.*

"These are the shows that Fox should have had. And I honestly think that if this were the slate, they would have stayed on course through it all and rewritten television history."

For all of his criticisms of Fox, Moye still believes that Barry Diller was the best possible person to have headed up the emerging network. "He was, to me, about the only one who had any direction at all. I always like being part of an underdog team. When this show first started . . . we'd walk around town with our

Married . . . With Children T-shirts and people would come up to us and say, 'How refreshing to see someone that is so proud of his family that he would wear a shirt.' But it was exciting back there. And we kicked a pretty good amount of tail."

Michael Moye may have been correct that *The Tracey Ullman Show* was the kind of "good" alternative programming that Fox was looking for, but it never achieved anywhere near the level of ratings that *Married . . . With Children* did. Alan Sternfeld, who appreciated Ullman's enormous talent and the work of her very able cast, felt the show was "niche programming," and therefore not necessarily the show he wanted to see scheduled on Fox's Saturday night roster.

Ullman had been discovered and was being produced by James Brooks, "a big fish in the Fox pond," according to Sternfeld. Doug Wick, a producer of *Working Girl*—a 1988 Fox hit directed by Mike Nichols that starred Sigourney Weaver, Harrison Ford, and Melanie Griffith—met Diller at a lunch arranged by Brooks. Wick described Brooks's relationship with Diller as "very interesting . . . . Diller surrounded himself with talent, and Jim Brooks is one of the biggest talents I've ever seen."

Brooks's movies, *Big* and *Broadcast News,* were earning lots of money for the studio, and he was looked upon as one of the network's major creative stars. *The Tracey Ullman Show,* in spite of its consistently low Nielsen numbers, "had an aura about it and a virtually untouchable cast," according to Sternfeld.

It also earned a stack of favorable reviews and an Emmy nomination that brought prestige to the network at a point when it was desperately in need of some positive attention—when its only major hit, besides *Married . . . With Children,* was an animated half-hour cartoon series that satirized and celebrated a typical dysfunctional nuclear family of the postmodern era.

11

"Don't Have a Cow, Man"

Matt Groening's first meeting with Barry Diller took place on the set of *The Tracey Ullman Show*. Groening had no real reason to be there, but he made a habit of showing up on Friday nights, when the show was filmed in front of a live audience.

As Groening recalled, "Diller and other Fox executives were standing over on the side watching the proceedings, and in between sketches the audience was shown clips of *The Simpsons* shorts. I think that Barry and the other executives were laughing quite a bit." Groening remembered Diller as "immaculately dressed in an expensive suit . . . the Alpha Man." He, on the other hand, had "been there plenty of times, but I dressed shabbily. I think TV writers are one level below teamsters in our fashion sense. So I can't imagine that Barry was very impressed. After that I ran into him from time and time, and he was friendly."

Groening came to Fox after Polly Platt saw his comic strip and showed it to James Brooks. Platt telephoned Groening and said that she loved his work and wanted to use it somehow. The "somehow" became *The Simpsons* shorts that were interspersed between sketches on *The Tracey Ullman Show.*

The animated clips were originally meant to be two minutes long, but as time went on, they were cut back to one minute, and then to four 15-second segments. Groening used the experience as a way to learn about animation, about "how much information you can get across in 15 seconds." He discovered that it was very hard to develop characters, but "amazingly enough, the characters were vivid enough to stay in people's minds. And so they caught on."

Soon Groening was approached by Fox to do either a "Simpsons" special or a series of specials. But, says Groening, "I designed *The Simpsons* to be a TV series. That was always my secret plan. The idea of putting animated characters on at prime time was considered very controversial. *The Flintstones* and *The Jetsons* are the only [prime-time cartoon series] that people remember. There have been a couple of others that failed along the way, but it really hadn't been done since the 1960s." Groening told Jim Brooks that he was "adamant that we hold out for a TV series. I was worried that just having one shot at getting people's attention would not do it. And I always felt comfortable about doing a series of shows in which people could catch on to what the humor was."

Groening's concern was that viewers might not have a chance to grasp the concept of *The Simpsons* if it were shown as a one-shot special. He felt certain that children would appreciate the show, "just because I saw the horrible cartoons on TV. I thought *The Simpsons* was better than most of the other stuff." His worry was that adults might not immediately understand the humor. "And I thought that if you get enough shows on the air, adults would find out about it and then they might start to watch it."

Groening had the opportunity to make his case for a 13-episode commitment at a pitch meeting attended by Diller, Ancier, Brooks, and other Fox executives. As he explained his idea for *The*

Simpsons, he was "quite nervous because I had what I considered fairly oddball ideas about what was funny in television: a family that lived in a mythical Midwestern city called Springfield—the most popular name in the United States—a family that drove each other crazy." He neatly summed up the series with the kind of high-concept tag line that Diller loved: 'a celebration of the American family at its wildest."

He offered thumbnail sketches of the characters, beginning with the father. "Homer Simpson was a really dumb guy who loved his family but wanted to kill them because they drove him crazy. The part that I thought they'd have trouble with was . . . I said, look, this guy's a dumb guy and guess where he works—a nuclear power plant. And I thought, if I get past that, then they'll go for it. . . . They all laughed."

Groening recalls that Diller asked him, 'Where did you say they lived?" Groening reiterated that the family lived in the Midwest, whereupon Diller commented, "For some reason I thought they lived in the San Fernando Valley." Groening said, "Well, they could. But I see it more as this fake Midwestern city." And Diller said, "I tend to agree with you, but I don't know why."

Says Groening, "I've thought about that for years, and I don't know what it means. And I think it's a brilliant thing to say."

His responses apparently satisfied Diller. "We got an announcement for the go-ahead." Fox agreed to take 13 half-hour episodes of *The Simpsons.* At that same pitch meeting, Diller queried Groening about whether there was such a thing as "family entertainment that appealed to every member of the family," whether "you could tell jokes that five-year-olds wouldn't necessarily understand but that fifteen-year-olds might."

He seemed "a little dubious," said Groening, although "that's always been my idea of how to make the best use of television. Don't try and aim for stuff that doesn't confuse Junior and not offend Grandma. Do stuff for everybody. With animation in general, people can really take advantage of that because you can cram so much information in every second of the show."

Groening was eager for Fox to buy the series; he was, he said, "nervous, but I wasn't thinking, 'If I don't do this, it's the end of my life.' If they didn't want to do it the way I thought it should be done, then I didn't want to do a half-assed version. . . . [I]t wasn't a desperate pitch. I really thought the show was funny . . . that the characters were funny. I knew that if we could get it on the air, it would be a smash hit. I have never met anyone in the entire process, from the beginning to after it became a hit, who didn't think it wasn't funny."

To this day, Groening does not know whether the show was audience-tested, as *Married . . . With Children* had been. Nor was he given any notes on character development or plot situations. But the show did pass a test of sorts that could not have gone unnoticed by Fox. Before the series premiered, several of the shorts that had been produced for *The Tracey Ullman Show* were used as teasers that appeared before Fox movies, including *Weekend at Bernie's* and *War of the Roses*.

Groening had the enviable experience of being present at a Marina Del Rey movie theater where *Weekend at Bernie's* was being shown, preceded by a Simpsons short. As soon as *The Simpsons* title came onto the screen, the audience burst into applause. It was the first time that Groening had ever seen such a large group of people react to his work, and he thought, "This is going to be a smash." It's likely that the people at Fox had a similar reaction.

In Groening's view, what set *The Simpsons* apart from other animated shows was "the emphasis on writing. People who can write generally don't pay any attention to the intricacies of animation. And people who animate don't care about character or story as much. If you grow up wanting to be an animator, your aspirations are fairly low because there's so much junk out there. I always wanted to do whatever the alternative was—funny, sophisticated animation."

Groening had tremendous confidence in his idea. He had grown up watching TV, and he was sure that "if kids could see this stuff, they'd go nuts for it. And I thought perhaps adults might get it too." Like Moye and Leavitt, he had no qualms about hooking up with the fourth network, even though he knew it was being ridiculed, because he knew that none of the other networks would even have considered the possibility of what he was suggesting. But he was not especially persuaded by Fox's espousal of alternative programming.

His take on their programming choices was that they were often "desperate, crass. . . . I think they were smart to do alternative stuff but . . . it's really hard not to have amnesia when it comes to television." As he puts it, "There were a lot of really bad Fox shows."

He would hear Fox executives discussing their upcoming season, touting shows like *Baxter* or *Mr. President,* which turned out to be major flops for the network. But as with *Down and Out in Beverly Hills,* the charm of these shows was not so much that they exemplified alternative programming at its best—or alternative programming at all—but rather that they were *available,* and Fox was hungry for product.

Groening recalled another Fox offering called *Babes,* a show about overweight women. Groening thought the idea was not a bad one, but that the writers should include no fat jokes, an insight he shared with one of the executives in charge of the show. "And then I watched it, and that's all it was—fat jokes."

The point was, as he saw it, that "they didn't do fat jokes on *Rosanne.*" But Fox's development executives, for all their claims to seeking a higher television ground, nevertheless chose the low (and much traveled) road when it came to putting new sitcoms on the air.

The Simpsons, on the other hand, was little short of a grand experiment in how to develop an animated series. Groening had never done animation before, and Fox had given him the green light to put the first 13 scripts into development all at the same time. What this meant, therefore, was that he and his associates would have put together 13 episodes before they actually got to see a single show.

The creation of *The Simpsons* was anything but smooth sailing. The animators were fairly new to the business, with no prior TV series experience. The director, who did have TV-animation experience, unilaterally decided that the script for the first episode lacked humor, so he added his own visual jokes.

Says Groening, "There are a series of rules that every cartoon makes up and follows for movement—facial expressions and mouth charts and all these things that we were just learning on *The Simpsons.* He threw out what ideas I had and did his own bizarre interpretations. For example, in the background he put a picture of a horse, a horse's ass, the tail lifting, and stink lines. He framed it in such a way that two characters would be having a conversation, and this picture would be between them."

Neither Groening nor anyone else involved with the show was consulted before the changes were made, nor did the director give them any warning of what he had done. Groening's first inkling of the additions came the day before Diller and other top Fox people were scheduled to see the first episode. A screening was held at Gracie Films, the home of James Brooks's production company on the Fox lot, attended by Groening, Brooks, and all the people who had worked on the show, including the writers and animators.

"Everybody was very quiet through the whole thing," said Groening. "He [the director] sucked out whatever charm there was in the show and out of the characters. It's really easy to wreck animation. It was a horrible, horrible experience. Then the tape ended, and we all sat there in silence for about a minute. Nobody said anything. . . . And Jim Brooks said, 'This is shit.'"

Groening blamed himself for the director's miscalculations and was convinced that his career as a creator of TV sitcoms was over before it had even begun. The screening for Diller was post-poned. Groening then paced the floor and waited to see the re-sults of the second show, which had been directed by David Silverman, who had worked on the Tracey Ullman animated shorts.

After spending what he described as "the most agonizing week of my life, as far as worrying," Groening was extremely re-lieved and gratified to see that Silverman had created "a completely different world." The first director was fired, and the four shows he had worked on had to be completely reshaped.

Diller and his team seemed "mildly amused" at the rescheduled screening. Citing "technical problems" with the first episode, Groening showed them the second one, which Silverman had directed. Afterward, Diller remarked that perhaps *The Simpsons* should air at 9:30 on Sunday nights. Groening, who felt that 8:00 would be a more appropriate time slot, was concerned about the possibility. But Diller soon changed his mind. Groening thought "he was just musing out loud," as he frequently did. The final upshot of the incident was that the show's production was badly enough disrupted that *The Simpsons* debut had to be rescheduled from the fall of 1989 to mid-December.

Ironically, given the network's assurances to writers that they would have more leeway on Fox's shows, the Standards and Prac-tices people made their presence felt very early on at *The Simp-sons.* According to Groening, the censors were very nervous about sex on the show, because, they said, cartoons were the medium as-sociated with Mickey Mouse, and that medium could not be cor-rupted with jokes about sex.

Groening considered the sexual humor on the *The Simp-sons* to be fairly mild and very much in a spirit of fun. The first showdown occurred over the pilot episode, in which Homer and Marge go off to a motel for an evening. The censors were upset because Groening had Homer say to Marge, "Wear your pink thing with the things," and they were afraid to see what the "pink thing with the things" might be.

Groening held firm and won the fight, as he did almost every other disagreement that came up with Standards and Practices. He lost one major battle—Fox's decision to move *The Simpsons* from Sunday night at 8:00 where it consistently ranked among the top 10 shows, to Thursday night at 8:00, which put it up against *Cosby,* NBC's number one show. Groening got a phone call from Diller who informed him of the time change; "This is what we're going to do," Diller said. Groening argued with him. "He was very polite but was absolutely unmoved. And that was that."

Groening denies the rumor that the character of Mr. Burns, the owner of the nuclear plant where Homer Simpson works, was based on Barry Diller. He likes Diller, he says, and adds that Diller was one of the few Fox executives who understood the show and how it should be marketed.

Indeed, because of the huge success of *The Simpsons,* marketing soon became an important part of the picture. "You had to wipe off the saliva from the conference table at meetings with these Fox executives who were so happy to cash in on this stuff," said Groening. "People wanted to cash in, in every possible way, as quickly as possible. But Diller seemed to have some sense of the longevity of the show, and he thought about keeping the show alive. And there were lots of things that he thought the show shouldn't do, and I think he was right."

It didn't take long for the Simpson family, despite (or perhaps because of) its dysfunctionality, to become a pop culture phenomenon. The marketplace was soon flooded with millions of cheap, mass-produced Simpsons T-shirts and other merchandise.

By the time Fox had geared up to do quality merchandising, most people had had their fill and the market had dried up.

Groening's impression was that although Fox was very pleased with and proud of the success of *The Simpsons,* many people there saw the show as "a flash in the pan that would be over any second," and wanted to cash in on its popularity as quickly as possible. When the issue came up at a meeting, Groening said, "You guys can be as greedy as you want, but if you are as greedy as possible, you won't make as much money as you would if you take the second or third greediest position."

There were those at Fox who felt the next best thing would be to package a behind-the-scenes special about how the show was put together. Diller, however, disagreed, and Groening thought that his decision was "a savvy choice": "I think that showing the man behind the curtain isn't always that interesting," he explained. "And also, there were many dark personalities in the making of the show whom people didn't really need to find out about."

He did not count Diller among those "dark personalities." To the contrary, his sense of Fox's chairman was that he was "an extremely vivid personality who was really, really decisive." Groening felt that Diller was "particularly aware of the subject at hand. He's not distracted. He was very focused on the show."

Speaking in 1995, three years after Diller had left Fox and moved on to other ventures, the cartoonist said he feels Diller's absence from the studio. "Since he's left, there have been plenty of nice people, but I don't sense any overriding plan or vision. No strong personality has made himself or herself apparent. You were aware of Diller in the commissary. I can't say that about anybody else, including Rupert Murdoch."

12

In Development Hell

It took a solid three years of prodigious effort on the part of both Barry Diller and Rupert Murdoch before Fox established itself as a force to be reckoned with among viewers and advertisers. During this period, Murdoch was expanding his empire to four times its previous size. He was also embroiled in a far-reaching controversy with Massachusetts' powerful Senator Edward Kennedy, because the politically conservative Murdoch had used the *Boston Herald*, which he owned, as a bully pulpit to blast Kennedy. In the final weeks of 1987, Senator Kennedy had tried to sneak a law through Congress that would have made it illegal for Murdoch to own both the *Herald* and his Boston TV affiliate. Murdoch subsequently won the battle in federal court, but ultimately lost the war and had to sell his Boston television station.

Some months later in 1988, Murdoch stunned the trade media when he purchased Walter Annenberg's Triangle Publications for an astonishing $3 billion. Murdoch was now publisher of the *Daily*

Racing Form as well as *TV Guide,* which not only had enormous influence over the television industry but was also the largest selling weekly magazine in the United States. In 1989, Murdoch launched Sky Television in England with four channels of programming, one of which was the Disney Channel. When the project began to flounder, however, Michael Eisner ignored the pleas of his former mentor and withdrew Disney's presence. A lawsuit resulted that was settled out of court in the spring of 1989.

Diller, in addition to his involvement with every detail of the network's evolution, was also continuing to oversee Fox's movie studio. As Diller characterized his own management style, he was good at beginnings and endings, but not very interested in the in-betweens. He was very hands-on at the beginning of a project and would then stay out of the way until the project was nearing completion, at which point he would once again involve himself in the details.

His obsession with details extended even to choosing the graphics for program credits and the color schemes on the sets. Polly Platt remembered the day he made a surprise visit to her office on the Fox lot, the first time he had come to see her there. Diller sat down and started talking to Platt about the Fox news broadcasts. "I want you to come look at the new set where we shoot the news," he told her. "I want you to revamp it completely. I want you do redo the set. I'll pay you."

Although it was beyond the usual scope of her producing responsibilities, Platt was delighted to have the assignment, "because I love the news." Diller invited her to come to the set that evening. "He was more cordial, much more animated, than I had ever seen him be. He was talking about something of his own. And that's when I began to understand his pride of ownership. The pride of creativity. I saw a different person. I didn't see a man who listens to creative people, coming to him for money, or to make movies, or this or that. I saw a person who was really excited about what he was doing."

She was so impressed by his excitement that "I went over there. He put his arm around me and introduced me to all the people in the news, the head of the news department, the president of KFOX. And he kept going on about how brilliant I was . . . I loved it."

Platt toured the set and then offered Diller her critique. She began "with these phones. Just painted red and green and yellow. They didn't even look real. They were just stupid phones on the wall like those car rental places. They didn't even have dials. So I told him that they were stupid looking and he said, 'Oh really, you think so? That was my idea.' I said 'Cheesy,' and he took it very well."

She assumed that he brought the assignment to her because she had produced *Broadcast News*, and had an outstanding reputation as a production designer. "But it was the first I ever knew he had any respect for me. His choice was very flattering. I ended up not doing it because I asked for a lot of money. And he said, "The reason I can't pay you that is because I'm trying to exhibit fiscal responsibility as president of the network. . . . I can't be pulling the purse strings on one hand and then spend that much on revamping the news set. Of course, he took all of my ideas anyway."

"This hands-on approach," says Alex Ben Block, "to even the most minor detail was both Diller's greatest strength and greatest weakness. It drew Diller away from the bigger issues and sometimes threw a monkey wrench into the decision-making process. Anyone who worked for Diller soon came to realize that the real power was concentrated at the top."

The fact that Diller made no attempt to disguise his need to control every aspect of his operation did nothing to lessen the impact of his critical comments and incessant demands. One of his colleagues said that working for Diller was like trying to put out a fire on the Alaska oil pipeline: If you got too close, you were bound to get burned, and if you got too far away, you froze.

The word "abusive" comes up often in discussions about Barry Diller. Brenda Farrier, who inherited Scott Sassa's job to become head of Fox's corporate public relations, said of Diller, whom she had followed from Paramount, "You see his name and your heart stops."

One of Diller's close associates at Fox said that Diller's desk phone had 10 "hot lines" that connected him directly to his top 10 executives. Another, quoted in *New York* magazine, November 1, 1993, claims that he received so many calls from an angry, ranting Diller that after awhile he could no longer bring himself to answer his hot line.

Diller used the argument of honesty and candor to defend himself against the charge that he abused employees. "What people don't understand about me and I think about Mr. Murdoch is that what we do is on the table," he said. "It's sometimes noisy, but it's without artifice and it's very direct. It's very clear. There's no back channel, second agenda or much subtlety."

Fox-TV's strategy, which would be sorely tested by Diller's management style, was to introduce the new network gradually and avoid having it classified as a network by the FCC until it had sufficient revenue rolling in to ensure its ultimate success. As mentioned earlier, this meant keeping prime-time programming under 15 hours a week, and focusing on programs in the time slots that would best attract the audience it needed to pull in advertisers.

Launching the network with a late-night show meant that, because the show aired outside the 8–11 P.M. prime-time period, it wasn't counted as network programming. This allowed Fox a Monday-to-Friday presence that gave them visibility and had the additional advantage of being inexpensive to produce. The second part of Fox's strategy was to air programs on Sunday night, traditionally considered the best night for TV watching, which could therefore attract the biggest potential audience.

Fox executives then decided that Saturday night should be the second night to be added to the schedule, which would provide the network with an entire weekend block of programming. The error in this logic was that Fox had pledged to make its network different from the other three, and to focus on the demographic segment of the population that advertisers loved: young people between the ages of 18 and 35. The problem that Diller and his executives did not foresee was that those young people whom Fox was courting with their youth-oriented programs didn't spend their Saturday nights at home, watching television. In a sense, Fox was programming the right programs to the wrong audience.

The third piece of Fox's strategy was to create programming for the 7:30–8:00 P.M. time slot, which was still considered prime time, but according to FCC regulations may not be filled by the networks. The FCC hoped that by taking the half-hour away from the networks, they would be providing independent producers with the opportunity to create PBS-style programming. Unfortunately, the discussions of Shakespeare, poetry, and ancient Greek culture that the FCC commissioners had envisioned never materialized. The time slot became instead the sinkhole for game shows. But it also offered a chance for Fox, as long as it maintained its non-network status, to fill that time period with situation comedies and dramas that might help them capture the prime-time audience.

In the summer of 1986, with Joan Rivers gone from the late-night slot, Fox-TV executives decided to fill her shoes with a different host each night—a sort of rotating, live audition for a permanent host until they found the right chemistry. This solution quickly proved to be a terrible idea. It ignored two realities about broadcasting that Diller and his associates failed to recognize, a failure that probably could be attributed to Diller's stated preference for hiring new, young blood whom he could develop in his own image rather than previously established stars. Too many decisions thus had to be made through the process of trial and error, instead of being based on information gleaned from past successes and mistakes. The question of what to do with *The Late Show* became a perfect example of how the collective inexperience of Fox's staff hindered and delayed the network's success.

One of the cornerstones of broadcasting—of all the other media, for that matter—is dependability. Newspaper readers expect and demand that they find the crossword puzzle, the financial section, the sports pages, and the comics in the same place every day. A radio or television station that is building an audience for a certain program or type of programming must likewise be dependable. A particular program has to run every Tuesday night at 9:00. Otherwise, audiences get confused, irritated, and ultimately desert the medium.

A loyal audience cannot be built without dependability, but Fox violated this principle when it chose a nightly parade of different faces with different styles for *The Late Show*. People tuning in to Fox would find an actress who featured musical guests one night, followed the next night by a male host with a collection of talking heads who would have been comfortable on the *The McNeil-Lehrer News Hour*. The problem was exacerbated because *The Late Show* staff had taken over the show and begun to run it their way, so that it had no chance of reflecting a particular personality or style.

A second principle of communication is the medium must know its audience. The formula that Jack Paar and Johnny Carson pioneered and honed to a fine rating point was based on the knowledge that most people watching late-night television were either actually in bed or about to go to sleep when they watched the show. They didn't want any heavy messages or complicated formats to deal with at that hour. They wanted a few minutes of mild and soothing fun before they drifted off to dreamland.

In August 1987, Diller hired David Letterman's producer, Barry Sand, to create a new late show under a million dollar contract and the promise of complete freedom; whatever idea or format he came up with was guaranteed to go on the air. The parade of daily hosts continued all through the summer and fall, including a talented young black comedian who seemed to connect well with his audience because he was hip and funny. But Arsenio Hall, who went on to host the hugely successful syndicated late-night talk show for Paramount, was allowed to slip through Fox's fingers because Sand was developing Fox's new late-night offering.

The show was called *The North Wilton Report*, after the street on which the show was produced at KTTV studio in a tacky section of Hollywood. It was meant to be a mix of humorous sendups of daily news stories plus offbeat comedy and skits overseen by Phil Cowans and Paul Robins, two radio disc jockeys from Sacramento. *The North Wilton Report* was set to air on November 30, but when Diller previewed the show, he saw a hodgepodge of sketches that lacked sophistication and humor. Diller ordered that the show be subjected to a complete makeover, but the real problems—the writers, producer, and hosts—went unmended.

The North Wilton Report debuted on December 11, 1987. It became an instant television classic—a disaster of classic proportions that would become a legend in television history. It achieved the one thing that Fox executives had hoped for—a lot of attention—but the press coverage it received was hardly the kind that Diller, Sand, and the rest of the Fox team had anticipated. The critics savaged the show, and viewers kept their sets tuned to the competition.

Fox was trying to connect with the audience that in most markets watched programs on independent TV stations. Obviously, Fox-TV was not about to get picked up by the affiliate stations of any of the other three networks. Thus, by definition, Fox's affiliates were independent stations whose audience profiles were different from those of the network stations. One of them, KLJB-TV, Channel 18, in Davenport, Iowa, was a Fox affiliate until its owner, Gary Brandt, realized that reruns of old movies were pulling in bigger audiences than he was getting for Fox's programs. Brandt decided to show the movies during the weekend evening time slots and push back Fox's shows to run after midnight.

This was precisely the sort of time shift that could badly hurt Fox-TV, especially if other affiliates decided to do likewise, since it would not be able to deliver the number of viewers it had promised to the national advertisers. But Brandt, a no-nonsense veteran of the business side of television, refused to allow a group of inexperienced Hollywood types to mess with his television station. "They came out with all these grandiose plans, but they had analyzed the marketplace incorrectly. They all came from a network background. Nobody had independent-station experience. They made decisions based on the network pattern that I felt was incorrect for an independent."

The question arises as to how well Diller's management style—particularly his system of passionate advocacy—worked in the first two years of Fox-TV's existence. As noted earlier, he tended not to hire seasoned executives who perhaps could have avoided some of the network's more costly and obvious mistakes. By all accounts, he tacitly encouraged his staff members to engage in underhanded office politics and back-stabbing to determine who would emerge the victor.

These power struggles often exacted a terrible price on the lives of those involved. As reported in Alex Ben Block's *Outfoxed,* in remarks made while he was still at Fox, Diller himself said that the politics at Fox were too tough on Garth Ancier. "The process was damaging him personally. It was brutalizing to him. It is an enormously demanding and harsh environment."

Yet Diller seemed driven to create an atmosphere of conflict and confrontation. It was as if he required such an ambience to function and achieve the best results. Matt Groening associated Diller's extraordinary drive with creativity, a great compliment coming from such a creative talent. He felt that Diller's creativity expressed itself through the form of business manipulation, that he had a "sense of vision" that set him apart from other studio executives. His impression was that Diller's decisiveness "made people feel comfortable. They might not agree with him, but at least he did seem to have a vision."

Comfortable, of course, is a highly subjective condition. Many people—including some of Diller's closest associates, past and present—might take issue with the image of Barry Diller providing a comfort zone for his employees by dint of his resolute and unyielding choices.

Alan Sternfeld, for one, came to a rather different conclusion about Diller. Sternfeld, who had to interact with Diller on a frequent basis, found him difficult to work with and extremely demanding. "Barry's very willful, very success-oriented," said Sternfeld. "I think that in pursuit of his goals he was very wasteful on a human scale. He cared not for the body count that he created in his wake."

Sternfeld felt that fear, competitiveness, and jealousy were the forces that ruled in the Kingdom of "Killer Diller." "Barry played favorites. It seemed clear that once he made up his mind about people there was very little dissuading him." But his favoritism seemed to be based not on any personal rancor or a desire for revenge, but rather on his need to achieve his agenda. As Sternfeld put it, Diller had "very lofty ambitions." He didn't set out to make people fear him, but in pursuit of those lofty ambitions, "he chewed people up and left them by the roadside with very little regard."

Diller's embrace of rule by intimidation defied all conventional definitions of good leadership. He did little to support or encourage his associates, and he made no attempt to create an atmosphere in which employees felt they were working together as a team to accomplish a goal. He failed to inspire a sense of loyalty or devotion among his staff; to the contrary, said Sternfeld, he not only "did a very poor job at delineating goals and strategies," but he also "depended on some level of fear and a bullying posture."

Sternfeld, who perceived Diller as a "micromanager given over to minutiae as well as the big picture who trusted no one," brought an unusual perspective to his job at Fox. Before he began his career in television, Sternfeld had operated greenhouses in Boston. His approach to TV programming was similar to his attitude about gardening: "It's a lot like running a greenhouse. You want to maximize your efficiency so that you have plants growing in every square inch of growing space. And if you want to bring something to market next Mother's Day, you'd better seed last week."

In other words, you plan, you plant, you wait and see what grows instead of giving up after one season. Diller, however, had what Sternfeld called a "feature film mentality," which led him to believe that the fate of a show was made or broken on its opening weekend, and that such assessments were basically irreversible. Sternfeld agreed that weekend box office was a fairly good indicator of future performance for feature films, and movies usually did not recover from an initially poor showing. But he was convinced that TV was an altogether different situation.

"TV takes time," he said. "Of course, there's no greater challenge in TV than to make the audience aware of a new series. A full-scale network is on the air seven nights a week—morning, noon, and night—and there's time to promote the network during other network time slots."

But with Fox on the air just two nights a week, the question arose as to when to run the promos for the series that aired on Saturday nights. The network had no control over—and no way of knowing—whether any of the affiliates were running promotions for the network shows on Friday, Thursday, or Monday. The only time that they could control on-air promotion was on Saturday nights, when the spots that ran during the network shows were mostly for the shows that aired on Sundays.

Sternfeld's opinion was that the promos that ran on Sunday were virtually valueless, because they advertised shows that wouldn't be seen until the following weekend. He said, "Basically, you've got a seventy-two-hour shelf life for the effectiveness of on-air promotion in TV. Beyond that, people are bombarded with so many messages that they tend to forget what they've seen. In effect, Fox couldn't control its own destiny because it was on the air only two nights a week."

When the network began looking at adding Friday nights to the programming schedule, Sternfeld went to Diller and told him that Friday night was a poor choice. He cited two reasons for his thinking: (1) Fridays were the affiliates' strongest night of the week, both in terms of ratings and revenues; and (2) the promos for the Friday night series would have to run during network time on the previous Sunday, a full five days earlier.

Sternfeld felt that it made much more sense to add either Monday or Tuesday to the network schedule, so that the promos that aired during the Sunday shows would encourage viewers to return to the network a mere 24 to 48 hours later. "It's a simple thing," he told Diller. "Work your additional nights in a forward direction rather than backwards."

As was so often the case, Diller chose not to take Sternfeld's advice. A similar situation had arisen when Sternfeld first came to work at Fox. "When I got there, I said, 'Barry, you're buying twenty-two episodes here. There's fifty-two weeks in a year. Well, twenty-two times two—which is an original and a repeat telecast—is forty-four. What do you think you're going to be doing for the other eight weeks in that time period?' And he said, 'I don't know. Come up with a plan.' So I came up with a plan, and he said, 'This is going to cost too much money. Just rerun all the same shows.'"

Sternfeld's experience was that Diller would "seemingly seek out counsel," and he would find himself in the position of having to say to Diller, "Here's the downside. Here's why I wouldn't do thus and such." He recalled one instance when "we were standing in a parking lot talking about something, and I found myself saying, 'Once again I find myself in the minority here. Here's why I wouldn't do that.' I gave him all my reasons, and he said, 'Don't apologize for being the minority. I depend upon you having an independent point of view. Don't ever tell me what it is you think I want to hear. That's not what I'm paying you for.'

"About four weeks after that I realized that I hadn't been invited to any meetings in Barry's office and I wondered what that meant. It may have been me just coming to the wrong conclusion—that what he was saying was quite different than what he truly believed, namely, 'I don't need another critic standing over my shoulder. If I really needed your opinion about anything I wouldn't be Barry Diller.'"

Sternfeld tried to find out from Garth Ancier whether there was any truth to his suspicions. But by that time Ancier was too preoccupied with his power struggle with Kevin Wendle to shed any light on Sternfeld's situation. Although Sternfeld never directly discussed the matter with Diller, his impression was that, like everyone else in turn, he had found himself in Barry's doghouse for some unknown reason.

Sternfeld claimed that he wasn't overly troubled by the apparent rift with Diller. "I still had plenty of work to do, so I figured it was less time wasted sitting around in his office. I pretty much saw very little of him other than chance encounters and the weekly Tuesday meetings which everyone attended, where there was a review of the weekend ratings and press-related issues, a general catchup. Sales would be on the speaker box from New York. You could generally spend two hours in that meeting, and only about four or five people would actually get to speak."

Sternfeld, who now works at ABC and says he wouldn't "trade ABC for any other network," left Fox in 1988. "I was glad to leave," he said. "I had a three-year deal at Fox and it had become quite an unpleasant experience. By the spring when the writers' strike took effect, production shut down because there were no scripts. There was no scheduling to do because there were no shows to move around. There was little to do and there was bad will. Mercifully, Kevin Wendle came into my office and said, 'I'm in charge now. You and I have had disagreements in the past, and I don't like disagreements, so it would be fine with me if you leave.'

"I said to myself, 'In my contract, I only report to the president of my division and Kevin's not the president. Even though it's not in writing, it's a significant enough of a breach that I'm probably free.' Shortly thereafter, I made a list of people I thought it would be really pleasant to work for. I put Grant Tinker's name at the top of the list, so I called him up and asked if I could come over and meet him for lunch. By the time lunch was over he had offered me a job.

"I went to see Barry and said, 'This hasn't worked out, and I've gotten a new job offer.' He was very gracious and said, 'Fine, if you're not going to start with Grant until Labor Day and it's July 30, why don't you not come to the office for the next five weeks and tell us where to send the checks.' So I found myself with that rarity as a grown-up—a paycheck and a vacation."

Diller's oppressive and domineering ways cost the network the contributions of Alan Sternfeld, Scott Sassa, and other talented young executives. Confusion reigned at Fox as it searched, often at cross-purposes, to find those programs that would capture the attention of America during late night and on weekends.

Many programs were ordered into development or production. Some, including *Werewolf, The Tracey Ullman Show, Duet,* and *In Living Color,* made it onto the air; others, such as *The Dirty Dozen: The Series,* and *Down and Out in Beverly Hills,* never got past the development stage; still others, including *The North Wilton Report,* would have been better off if they'd never made it past the pilot episode. The programs that did do well did not necessarily succeed because of the abilities of those guiding them from the start: *21 Jump Street, A Current Affair, Married . . . With Children,* all eventually took hold; *Married . . . With Children* became a big hit.

But it wasn't necessarily thanks to any grand master plan, as Diller himself admitted. "Fox found its path not in the way people think. People think Fox decided to be this young, edgy network. It wasn't true. We started Fox in the same birdbrained way that everybody does it. Which is we said, 'Okay, let's go out and get the best people and we'll do their programs.' And, so we got some very good people, Gary David Goldberg, really great television people to start Fox's programming. And the early shows on Fox looked just like the competition. Slowly—and actually *Married . . . With Children* helped us a great deal because it was a real alternative program. And when we found it, we said, 'Ahh, traction. You can be something with that. People get attention that way. This is gonna be true tomorrow. You gotta find it as you find it.'"

Diller learned over time that Americans were interested in watching something different on Fox from what the other networks ran, but not *too* different. They wanted the fourth network to be slightly edgier, but they rejected anything that they deemed too rough or obscure. Thus, *The Tracey Ullman Show,* aside from being very expensive to produce at $400,000 an episode, was too far out, too edgy, and was soon retired to a second life of syndication reruns.

Married . . . With Children cost the same per episode as *Tracey Ullman,* but it pulled in the ratings. *Married* took the traditional situation comedy format with which audiences were familiar and gave it a piquant flavor that made it a winning moneymaker for Fox. However, the real push that would salvage the network came from a truly unexpected sector. Of this big break in programming, Diller admitted, "After a year I learned that we go at our peril by copying the three television networks. We began by trying to copy their best. It was a mistake. It was the wrong way to go."

It could be argued that the Fox network was saved from extinction by 24 people who recognized a Staten Island, New York, hospital employee. The man's face was flashed around the country on a low-budget Fox network show called *America's Most Wanted,* which premiered a new genre of TV show, that of true crime. The man was quickly recognized as Bob Lord, a well-known advocate for the homeless, who was unmasked on *America's Most Wanted* as David James Roberts. Roberts had escaped from prison where he was serving time for rape, murder, arson, and robbery. Twenty-four people telephoned the FBI, and four days after the show aired on February 11, 1988, Roberts was arrested. His recapture was picked up by the media everywhere, giving Fox the benefit of millions of dollars in free publicity.

America's Most Wanted quickly became an American TV phenomenon. As Alex Ben Block observed in *Outfoxed,* his book about Fox's television network, "Actually, it became a phenomenon in more ways than one. It was the show that marked the turnaround of the fledgling Fox Broadcasting Company and its rise toward credibility and profitability. It was the show that changed the economics of television programming, proving that it wasn't how much you spent on a show, but rather the appeal of that show for the audience that mattered."

Diller immediately ordered that the show be moved into the 8 P.M. Sunday night slot, where it drew big ratings and advertising dollars for Fox. *America's Most Wanted* cost Fox $125,000 per half-hour show, about a third as much as Fox's sitcoms, partly because it was produced in Washington, DC. Because Fox owned the show, it could rerun it as many times as it wanted for almost no additional cost, as opposed to shows that cost them $400,000 and belonged to somebody else. It was a no-lose situation for the network.

It had taken two years and the costs—financial and human—were far higher than anyone would have predicted. But by July 1989, Diller had proven yet again that he was an extraordinary executive and visionary with the ability to transform ideas into reality—more importantly, into profitable reality. The Fox Broadcasting Company had carved out a firm place for itself in the television market, with programs that attracted strong, faithful audiences.

Twentieth Century-Fox Films paid the price during this period for the extent to which Diller had concentrated on carving out the future of Fox-TV. Whereas by the end of the 1990 fiscal year, the network that had suffered $90 million in losses would finally show a profit, Fox Films's profits would plummet almost 40 percent from the previous year to $55 million. A major Hollywood talent agent summed up the problem thusly: "Barry's been distracted."

Statistics underlined the sorry state of Fox's theatrical film production division. In 1988, Fox had released *Big, Die Hard,* and *Working Girl,* whose combined success had earned Fox third place in the ranking of the eight major studios. But by mid-December of 1989, Fox had fallen to seventh place; the only one of Fox's 1989 releases to gross over $50 million was *The Abyss,* which earned tepid reviews and cost more than $60 million to produce and distribute.

According to some sources, Diller allowed his former boss, Leonard Goldberg, to run the film division as he saw fit. Doug Wick was among those who thought that Diller "made a conscious effort to let Leonard have his own ground. It's a complicated relationship, they started out at ABC. But Barry was very respectful of Leonard Goldberg."

Wick had "very minor contact with Diller on *Working Girl.* Barry would occasionally show up on set. But Barry's so smart, he would never waste energy where it wasn't needed. He would basically show up on set to be supportive. . . . I mean, there's a lot of people who pretend that they have control by making stupid contributions. Barry isn't like that.'

On the other hand, "it's not like Nichols said, 'I have this project I want to do,' and Diller said, 'Okay, here's fifteen million. No questions asked.' Barry had very constructive thoughts after seeing the first cut of the movie. He would come down and see the producer's cut, and the director's cut."

Wick thought that the reason Diller and Mike Nichols got along was that "Nichols always delivered what he promised. Even if it looked like it was going to be impossible Nichols would stay up all night and figure out a way for it to work. Not unlike Diller himself."

Although Diller "was not involved with the day-to-day discussions about the script," he did get engaged with "the pivotal things, like the poster for the movie, the premiere party, anything that would publicly represent Fox.

Wick and Diller had met over lunch. "I knew James [Brooks] from a previous project, and he thought that we should meet for future business. . . . He knew that at some time Diller and I would be interested in each other. I was basically a pisser . . . down the totem pole. . . . I was curious about Diller from the stories, good and bad. And it was a great lunch.

"Diller, when he's focused on you, he's totally there, totally listening, totally present. Not like a lot of executives who are half there. I was surprised how intimate he was. How conversational. He made me feel at home. We basically talked about life, getting to know each other."

Wick's sister, who at one time was head of marketing at Fox, was also a friend of Diller's. They shared a mutual interest in motorcycles and often rode their bikes together.

Unlike most of his other colleagues, "Diller never tested my confrontational skills," said Wick, who later made a great deal of

THE BARRY DILLER STORY

money by investing in QVC when Diller went over there. "It's sort of a chemical thing, either you get along or you don't."

Others, however, took a far less generous view of Diller's relationship with Goldberg, asserting that Diller chose to second-guess the man who had taught him his earliest lessons in television. Former employees of Fox Films say that Goldberg had to fight hard to convince Diller that Bruce Willis was worth $5 million for his starring role in *Die Hard,* a 1988 action-adventure movie that earned Fox more than $80 million.

Goldberg also had to battle to get Diller's permission to use the steel-and-glass Fox Plaza skyscraper for the set of the movie. One of Goldberg's former associates at Fox said, "Barry tortured Len over using Fox Plaza for *Die Hard.* The whole county of Los Angeles was more cooperative than the chairman of the company that was financing the movie."

Whatever the truth of his relationship with Diller, there's no question it had to be complicated, Goldberg left Fox in 1989 after only two years there and resumed his career as an independent producer. Diller replaced him with 41-year-old producer-director Joe Roth, who had formerly been head of Morgan Creek, where he gained a reputation for producing low-budget hits, including *Young Guns* and *Major League.*

Roth was Diller's fifth hire for the position in as many years, and this time around Diller decided to give his studio head more responsibility and leeway, including the right to sign up and produce a movie without first having to get Diller's permission. "Up until Joe," said Diller, "no one in any company I was associated with could make the final decision to make a film without my approval. I always felt that was a decision you could not unilaterally delegate."

Roth's mandate was a three-year goal to triple the number of films produced by Fox, for a maximum total of 30 movies. He seemed undaunted by the task, which would also include asking

Rupert Murdoch and the News Corporation for a handout in the first year of $70 to $100 million to pay for the additional films. Roth said, "I was brought in because I ran a company that made eleven movies in eighteen months. Fox simply hasn't been productive enough. We can triple production and not have to add any more people to the overhead to release the pictures."

Roth spoke of producing high-concept movies, Diller's favorites, and a series of sequels to previous Fox hits, including *Young Guns 2* and *Die Hard 2*.

It could not have been easy for Diller to relinquish control of this area. Perhaps he was motivated by the studio's dire situation, or the realization that simultaneously running a brand-new network and a movie studio was simply too much for even Barry Diller to handle. "I owe it to the business not to stick to some selfish way of operating that's no longer appropriate," he said in a 1990 interview that appeared in *Forbes*. "I'm shakily proud of my ability to change."

The facts and figures could not be ignored. The company was not functioning properly as it was presently structured, and Diller was too hard-nosed an executive to sacrifice the bottom line for the sake of his ego.

13

Saying Goodbye

When Barry Diller invoked his "ability to change" in 1990, few, if anyone, would have guessed at the extent of the changes that were shortly to occur in his life, and at the far-reaching effects of those changes. Diller may be a visionary or a control freak, a prince or a fire-breathing dragon—or he may simultaneously encompass those qualities. But one thing his fans and detractors agree on: Diller thrives on competition. He loves and draws energy from being challenged, both personally and in his career. He also has an astonishing capacity to embrace the unexpected.

On February 24, 1992, Diller shocked the movie and television industries, and the business world at large, when he announced that he was leaving Twentieth Century-Fox. What was probably just as startling was that he wasn't resigning to take over another major studio or to buy up either NBC or CBS, both of which were rumored to be for sale. He wasn't starting his own

THE BARRY DILLER STORY

independent production company, nor going into business with one of his wealthy Hollywood friends.

He was leaving Fox with no immediate plans for his future. "Killer Diller," who had been working since the age of 19, was giving up his fancy title, a raft of executive perks, and his elegant office and conference room with the grid on the wall of all the networks' prime-time shows to do *nothing*.

The question on the lips of everyone in Hollywood and Wall Street was why. Rumor had it that Diller's departure was the result of tension between himself and Murdoch, caused by Murdoch's increased involvement in Fox's affairs. Others whispered that Diller had long hoped Murdoch would set Fox up as a separate company from the News Corporation and allow Diller a piece of the action.

The truth was more complex. Diller had made television history and conquered the movie industry. In 1990, *Daily Variety* headlined a front-page story, "Barry Diller-baiting Hot Hollywood Sport," in which the reporter observed, "The two most over-used words in the Hollywood vernacular these days are 'Barry Diller.' Old-timers are hard put to remember a time when the machinations of one individual so riveted industry attention."

But Diller had another challenge to face down that he would rarely admit to aloud—which was the challenge of keeping up with David Geffen. He had tried once before, in 1984, when he had moved from Paramount to Fox. But by the end of the 1980s, Geffen had become one of the most powerful men in the music industry, if not in all of Hollywood.

Geffen would never earn the title of "Mr. Congeniality," nor would he care to win any popularity contests. He was—and continues to be—every bit as smart, mercurial, generous, vengeful, thoughtful, and vicious as Diller. The late superagent Swifty Lazar said of Barry Diller's close friend and rival, "Geffen went nuclear about five years ago. Nobody knows where he's going to land next and you're lucky if you're not in his sights."

Geffen's approach to the entertainment business is similar to that of the early Hollywood movie moguls: He has an instinctive sense of the public taste, and he relies on personal relationships to capitalize on that instinct. He makes a point of working with people whom he trusts and with whom he has a close relationship— almost a family kinship. But such close connections require loyalty, and when conflict severs the connection, Geffen reacts as if he has been betrayed by a member of his family.

By 1989, his empire included Geffen Films, which produced such films as *Risky Business* and *Beetlejuice;* financial and producing involvement in the Broadway shows *Cats* and *Dreamgirls;* and Geffen Records. As he developed Geffen Records into a major force in the music industry, he worked closely with Steve Ross— some characterized their friendship as a father-and-son connection—until the relationship turned sour because Ross entered into the Time-Warner merger without first informing Geffen about it. The rift turned bitter; Geffen felt double-crossed and put his Geffen Records up for sale.

He rejected offers from several companies because he felt a lack of rapport with the top executives, but found what he was looking for at MCA. In 1990, Geffen sold his record company to MCA for $545 million in stock, making him one of MCA's largest single stockholders and bringing his personal fortune close to a billion dollars. Soon after that, Geffen scored a huge profit when the Matsushita company of Japan purchased MCA in 1992, making Geffen the first billionaire-mogul in Hollywood.

Diller was admired, feared, respected, sought after, and wealthy. Yet he had fallen behind in the race with Geffen. As much power as he commanded, he still had to answer to someone who was wealthier than he and more powerful. He had asked Murdoch to make him a principal in the company. Murdoch's response was, "There is only one principal in this company." As to what his future plans might be, Diller was typically cryptic.

"There will not be substance until there is. When I left Paramount it was a surprise. When I left ABC, it was an even bigger surprise. Now it's a surprise that I'm leaving Fox. That's the way I like it and I'm proud of that."

As the *Los Angeles Times* reported, "Barry Diller, the volatile, but innovative Fox, Inc. chairman who built a fourth TV network . . . unexpectedly resigned Monday. Diller—whose razor-sharp tongue and impatient management style earned him the nickname 'Killer Diller'—said he plans to work for himself. Sources speculated that he will make a play for an existing network or start his own company. Members of Diller's senior management team said they were shocked by the announcement."

"I think I've completed one phase of my life," Diller declared to the press. "Now I want to go on to the next. I want to put myself a bit at risk." He also apologized publicly for the suddenness of his announcement. "I'm sorry to be so dramatic. I've had three bombshell announcements—when I became chairman of Paramount, when I left Paramount for Fox and—but it ain't over."

He had discussed his plans with no one but Geffen, his close friend, Sandy Gallin, and Diane Von Furstenberg. When asked to comment on Diller's departure, Geffen said, "He made billions for Charlie Bluhdorn and Rupert Murdoch; now he's got to do it for himself. He's the premier entertainment executive in the entertainment business today, he's 50 years old, he made the decision. He doesn't want to work for anyone else anymore."

Because of the dramatic circumstances of his leave-taking, and the high regard in which Diller is held in the entertainment industry, the press rushed to air its assessments of Diller, his management style and his business accomplishments.

The *New York Times* summed up the impact of Diller on his industry and his company as follows: "Perhaps no other Hollywood executive has left so strong a mark on his company in the last decade as Barry Diller. No only did Mr. Diller create the Fox network, but he helped make Fox Inc. into a cornerstone of its overall corporate parent, the News Corporation, owned by Rupert Murdoch. Fox is crucial to the News Corporation's profits."

The *Times* went on to note the unusual circumstances of Diller's leave-taking. "Such a departure is almost unprecedented in Hollywood, where lavishly paid executives are treated two ways: They are either dismissed leaving with a golden handshake worth millions, or, if they are burnt out, are given a set of offices, a staff and a studio development deal to keep them happy.

"Instead, Mr. Diller has taken a career step that in the highly visible, gossipy, back-biting world of Hollywood is extremely risky, especially for a man who has been treated like show business royalty."

Financial analysts noted that Diller was gifted not only on the creative side of entertainment, but also on the financial side. Paul Marsh of Kemper Securities said, "Rarely do you find a Hollywood executive with both a creative reputation and a good eye for watching the bottom line." Jessica Reif of Oppenheimer & Company opined, "Some may say he's been too hands-on, but he has to be credited with achieving what many people thought was impossible."

Not everyone, however, felt as positive about Diller's management skills. Kevin Maney, the "Money" section reporter for *USA Today,* assessed Diller's management abilities in less complimentary terms.

"Diller is an executive out of the old Hollywood school, where it was not uncommon for arrogant, self-centered bosses to micromanage creative products, berate employees in public, throw tantrums and fight with their peers and superiors. Diller is famous for all of that; one tale has Diller hurling a videotape at a staffer. The staffer ducked and the tape knocked a hole in an office wall. That's not the kind of executive who will build bridges to megamedia, which is becoming a cross-industry collaborative business.

Diller's style may work in Hollywood, but it won't work around companies like AT&T or Compaq."

Maney seemed to be in the minority. It did not go unnoticed that even as he was launching Fox-TV, Diller also personally revamped the Fox commissary food service, insisting on healthier menus that included careful notations of fat content and calories. For many Fox employees, these benefits were far more important in their lives than the success of any of Diller's blockbuster movies. As one employee put it, "It was that Barry did it personally. The most powerful man in our studio worried about the food we were eating!"

Polly Platt recalled that after *Broadcast News* had finished shooting, she waited to hear whether Fox was renewing its option with Gracie Films, James Brooks's production company. "Barry was not renewing it, which surprised me. I couldn't believe that Barry would let Jim go off to Sony or any other studio—Jim Brooks who created *The Simpsons* with Matt Groening, and *Broadcast News, Big,* and *War of the Roses.*

"I'd have lunch with people at Fox and ask, 'Why?' I didn't think he was ungrateful; I just couldn't figure it out. And of course now we know why. He was leaving Fox. He might have told Jim, but I doubt it because Jim is famous for not being able to keep a secret."

Brooks emphasized the career risks that Diller was taking when he decided to leave Fox. "What he's doing now is tough, extraordinarily tough. I don't believe anybody has left a job like his in Hollywood and, at least for a period of time, put themselves at risk the way he has."

Another producer, however, believed that Diller was able to make the move because he had absolute faith in his own judgment and confidence in the rightness of his decisions. "He's a difficult guy, but brilliant, a brilliant strategist. It was Diller who made *Die Hard* a hit, by sitting with us and strategizing and working out the marketing and the pattern of release. Some of the younger executives wanted to cut the film. They said it was too long. We had a preview. Diller came out and said, 'Don't you touch a frame of that movie.' He was absolutely right."

Peter Bart of *Daily Variety* had a more personal assessment of Diller, which touched on traits that many other journalists could not know, not having been as close to Diller as Bart had been over the years.

"To understand Diller, it is necessary to confront the fact that he sees himself as the ultimate outsider. He feels a compulsion to be a consummate risk-taker, to test himself against new dangers. Far from being reclusive, he is surrounded by, indeed protected by, a circle of friends who understand and nurture him.

"Diller's technique as an executive has been to prod, to argue, to search for a better, more original way to achieve a goal. If there was an 'accepted' way, Diller felt impelled to improve upon it. He often did."

Diller had just celebrated his fiftieth birthday. He had no family commitments, no pressing financial need. For all of his many accomplishments, he was not yet his own boss, and he was still chasing the elusive goal of independence. Now he had set himself free, with a $150 million settlement from Murdoch and the purchase of a $5 million Gulfstream jet, to pursue his dreams in his own, idiosyncratic way.

14

The Odyssey

$\int$everal months before Diller announced that he was leaving Fox, he bought himself a present—a top-of-the-line, $3,900 Apple PowerBook.® He hired a tutor to teach him the multiple functions of the laptop computer and began toting it with him everywhere he went.

"He had an unbelievable love affair with his computer," said his closest confidant and former lover, Diane Von Furstenberg. "I learned it to leave Fox," said Diller

The present and future possibilities of the PowerBook caught his imagination. Apart from its obvious and already existing uses, he was fascinated with the potential it seemed to offer, if only he could master the technology. "It has expanded his horizon," said Von Furstenberg in a 1993 interview. The PowerBook gave Diller a new way to think about television programming, about the power of cable, about interactivity and consumer choice, about interactivity and information services.

In May 1992, three months after he had tendered his resignation, Diller embarked on a journey of discovery across America. He later referred to that period in his life as an "odyssey," and it took him from one end of the continent to the other in search of the future—not only his own, but also the future of media and communications technology.

Homer's *Odyssey* tells the story of the Greek hero Odysseus, a brave and able warrior known for his daring achievements. After Odysseus triumphs in the battle of Troy and embarks on his journey for home, his ship is blown off course. He visits many unknown regions, and is shipwrecked and marooned for a time before finally reaching Greece where he is greeted with great joy and acclaim. Diller did something similar.

His PowerBook in tow, Diller visited with the outstanding names in computer technology, including Bill Gates, the genius behind Microsoft®; Steven Jobs, the cofounder of Apple Computer®, who had moved on to establish NeXT Computer®; and the Media Lab at Boston's Massachusetts Institute of Technology.

Rob Glaser, Microsoft's vice president for multimedia and consumer systems, accompanied Diller on a tour of the company's corporate headquarters in Redmond, Washington. Glaser later remarked, "Of all the folks that have come by"—and those folks have included Rupert Murdoch, Martin Davis, and John Malone, the CEO of Tele-Communications, the country's largest cable company—"Diller was the most engaged in the stuff we are doing."

Diller's reaction to his visit to Microsoft was simply stated and to the point. "Everything blew my mind."

That same summer, Diller and Diane Von Furstenberg traveled to an unlikely destination, the sleepy town of West Chester, Pennsylvania, home of the QVC Shopping Network (the initials stand for "Quality, Value, and Convenience"). Von Furstenberg had spent time at QVC in late February, talking to people there about creating a line of clothing to be sold exclusively through QVC. She had returned home amazed by the efficiency of QVC's direct-to-consumers marketing system, and by the volume of their sales.

Now, Diller had come to West Chester to see for himself QVC's remarkable merchandise money machine, as well as to negotiate Von Furstenberg's pending contract with the home shopping network to design a fashion line called Silk Assets. The backwater, slightly flaky operation, located next to a horse barn and a cornfield, was being embraced by major manufacturers around the country. Brand-name companies, including Saks Fifth Avenue, Bill Blass, Kodak, Pentax, and Panasonic, were all finding their way to West Chester. Kodak had given QVC the exclusive retail rights to its newest camera, the Cameo Zoom Plus, for three months. Nine thousand four hundred of the cameras were sold at $150 apiece in just a shade over an hour on the first day. John Tesh sold 45,000 of his CDs in one night.

Diller, like Von Furstenberg, was bowled over by the operation: a 24-hour-a-day synergy of television, telephone, and computer with one of the most fully automated and effective sales operations Diller had ever encountered. He subsequently heard more about QVC from Brian Roberts, the president of Comcast®, America's fourth-largest cable company, founded by his father, Ralph Roberts. Comcast was a major stockholder of QVC, along with TCI's John Malone, one of the television industry's most powerful figures; Roberts and Malone, whom Diller had known for some years, had been among the most ardent of the 33 executives who had called and courted Diller after he had announced his resignation from Fox.

TCI and Comcast were already technologically plugged into what they believed to be the future of television. But the almost endless number of channels that their cable lines could offer to viewers had little value if there was nothing for audiences to see when they turned on their sets. They lacked programming expertise—and they saw Diller as a programming genius who could bring stature to their operation.

Comcast had been founded in 1963 by Ralph Roberts, who had been in the business of distributing men's clothing accessories. Working out of Tupelo, Mississippi, Roberts senior had seen an alarming trend that had threatened to ruin a big part of his trade—belts. The invention and popularity of beltless slacks forced Roberts to conclude he had to move on to another line of work.

People in Tupelo were willing to pay for cable TV to get clearer transmission from the Memphis stations, and Roberts arranged to provide it to them. After his initial success, he began investing in other cable companies. Roberts often brought along his teenage son, Brian, when he negotiated cable buyout deals, bank loans, and franchises with local politicians. Diller liked Brian, characterizing him as someone who "has got a snap, crackle mind and he's not afraid to exercise it." Young Roberts quickly learned the business and became enamored of the excitement and the money it offered. Later, he would work as a pole climber, installing cable lines, and would graduate from the Wharton School of Business at the University of Pennsylvania, before he joined his father in Comcast's executive suite.

In hindsight, Brian Roberts believed that one of the strongest impressions made on him about the viability of the cable TV business occurred when his father put him in charge of Comcast's Flint, Michigan, cable system. Michael Moore's movie, *Roger and Me*, graphically but humorously depicted the difficult economic situation of many of Flint's citizens when the local unemployment rate rocketed to 22 percent after General Motors closed their factory there. Yet most people held onto their $20-a-month cable TV, and surprisingly, more signed up for it. Roberts concluded that when times were bad people wanted their cable even more to provide a much-needed distraction from their financial troubles.

In August, Diller went to see Malone, a reclusive figure who lives on an 83-acre ranch outside Denver. His QVC partner, Brian Roberts, called him ". . . the smartest businessman I've ever met." Defending Malone from the charges leveled by his many enemies,

Roberts added, "But, like everyone, he does have some flaws. Unfortunately, one is not caring what people say about him. . . . It's a shame. It's a tragedy. He's truly a great visionary."

Others used less flattering terms when they talked about him. Competitors thought of him as a "cold, trash-talking automaton, intent on cramming every cable system, studio, and telephone company in the U.S. into the maw of TCI." A Washington insider referred to Malone as "the Darth Vader of cable," the chief executive of a cable-programming company called him "an evil genius," and Vice President Al Gore pointed a finger at him as the head of "the cable Cosa Nostra." His Liberty Media, a TCI spinoff designed to create programming for cable systems that Malone also chaired, owned pieces of QVC, the Family Channel, Court TV, American Movie Classics, and other cable networks.

Malone had grown up in Milford, Connecticut, the son of a conservative-thinking engineer who worked for General Electric. After graduating from Yale with a electrical engineering B.S. Malone married his sweetheart, Leslie Ann Evans and followed in his father's path by going to work for a major corporation, AT&T. He subsequently earned two more degrees, including a doctorate from Johns Hopkins in 1967.

After a stint as a consultant with McKinsey and Company that required too much traveling to suit himself and his wife, Malone joined General Instrument, where he worked on building cable TV equipment. This led to his friendship with a western rancher, Bob Magness, who had become involved in the cable TV business because he couldn't get a decent TV image through regular transmission. By 1972, Malone had been appointed president of Magness's Tele-Communications, Inc., a small cable company based in a suburb of Denver.

His wife approved of the move because it meant more family time together; Malone frequently joined her at home for lunch, and they spent several months a year at their vacation place in

Boothbay, Maine. Although the first years at TCI were lean and demanding, Malone persevered to make the outfit financially solvent and to purchase more cable systems.

One of his key moves—rarely talked about—was to convince a group of insurance companies in 1977 that because cable TV held the future of home entertainment, they should financially back TCI. Satellite programming was just then exploding, cable company stocks were skyrocketing, and TCI, Malone, and Magness were the beneficiaries. Armed with cash put up by the insurance companies, Malone gobbled up every cable system he could find that made sense in the TCI mix. By the end of the 1980s, TCI was the King Kong of cable. Malone held so much power that if an owner of a channel fell out of favor with him, he could freeze that person out of cable systems all across America, to the point that the channel would not be financially viable because it couldn't deliver the requisite audience numbers to advertisers.

Politicians, whether local or federal, were automatically suspect in Malone's universe, because he believed they dealt in emotional matters, vague political concepts, and people-related issues, all of which were alien to him. He preferred the nonhuman universe—the realms of physics and mathematics, where all is quantifiable, certain, and predictable.

The garrulous Malone managed to provoke just about everyone he came in contact with, from civic leaders to members of Congress. He lashed out against those politicians brave or foolish enough to cross him, employing blatant hardball tactics that bespoke a ruthless use of power. If local politicos thwarted one of his regional cable systems, he would strike back by blacking out that community's cable TV system and broadcasting the politicians' home phone numbers so the public could call and demand that they agree to Malone's demands.

He also preferred not to deal with the human side of management at his own company, leaving those duties to his chief aide,

Brendan Clouston, while he occupied himself with the strategic thinking, deal massaging, numbers crunching and technical analysis that were his forte. The sole exception to his dislike of people was his wife, Leslie. Malone aggressively demanded a separation of his business and personal lives, so much so that even most of Malone's closest business associates have never met her.

Meeting at Malone's offices in suburban Denver, he and Diller talked about the future of the "media landscape." TCI was already the single largest industrial consumer of fiber-optic cable in the world, and Malone foresaw a scenario in which the communications industries—phone and cable companies, network broadcasters, computer companies, and so on—would all be dependent on one another to create a brave new world of 500-plus television channels operated by means of a digital-compression system whose signals would be delivered via fiber-optic cable.

Two things struck Diller about Malone: (1) He prided himself on being an outsider, which was how Diller also saw himself; (2) Malone, unlike so many other people in the business world with whom Diller dealt, was giving such serious consideration to exactly the areas of technology that Diller had recently begun to consider. Malone, with his PhD in industrial engineering, possessed an understanding of technology that deeply impressed Diller, who had come to believe that computer and cable technology would be key factors in the future of communications.

As his discussions with Malone and the Robertses progressed, Diller simultaneously continued to explore his options, the most attractive one being the purchase of NBC. Its parent company, General Electric, was asking four billion dollars for the network, far more than Diller thought he could raise.

There were other serious drawbacks to pursuing a deal with NBC. Increasingly, he had come to believe that the proliferation of cable channels meant a diminishing audience for the networks, which were still dependent for revenue solely on advertising, whereas cable was also supported by subscription fees. Diller had also been lately persuaded that the need for networks to serve as programmers would be eliminated before too long, because viewers would soon be able to make their own programming choices through the use of computer mouse-type remote control devices.

Despite his reservations, he also suspected that owning NBC "would be fun," because of the challenge he would face to revive the financially ailing network and the range of creative opportunities that would be available to him. But almost in the same breath, he admitted that "even as I say it, I bore myself. In the end, I thought, it only involves ego."

In fact, John Lippman reported in the *Los Angeles Times* that Diller had made a swing at acquiring NBC in the summer of 1992. People from General Electric said they were surprised at the weakness and poor organization of his proposal, but Diller told colleagues at the time that there was still a chance for a successful revised proposal that he was preparing.

Executives in the entertainment and communications industries had relished the idea of Diller at the head of one of the major TV networks because they felt he would restore the kind of savvy that the networks were sorely missing since the influx of cost-conscious accountants and business school graduates.

J. Max Robins, writing in *Daily Variety* shortly after Diller resigned from Fox, said, "High on the list of what Diller may do is lead a consortium that will go after one of the Big Three webs. 'If Barry Diller were to buy a CBS or NBC, you'd have a true showman running a major network for the first time in a long time,' says a senior Fox executive, 'These places have been run by bottom-line guys for too long. Don't get me wrong—Barry knows how to run a tight fiscal ship. But he's somebody who cares about the product first, and that's what you need at the top. Barry would look at an NBC the same way he looked at Fox when he came in. Remember, it was basically bankrupt back then. He'd start with

zero-based budgeting, put together a tight group of talented executives, pare the staff down to several hundred and start looking
for much more visionary ways of programming."

Washington communications attorney Michael Gardiner also
saw Diller as a network savior who could "turn it around in 12–14
months. . . . With his brilliance and disdain for mediocrity he could
really energize a network."

Diller's vision of programming was to make it more appealing
by creating series that were more realistic and geared for adults. It
was on Diller's watch that Fox aired shows like *Cops, America's
Most Wanted, Hard Copy,* and *Married . . . With Children.* Peter
Brennan, executive producer of A Current Affair, said of Diller,
"He understands what people want to watch. He's not afraid to do
TV that cuts through all the saccharine extemporaneous bullshit.
He doesn't mind when people on TV speak plain English."

The prospect of having "a true showman" running NBC or CBS
was widely anticipated throughout the industry. Everybody agreed
that with Diller in charge, the network would get involved in cable
programming. They assumed that he would opt for what the industry calls "cume running," short for cumulative running, meaning
that the same program and commercials are shown at different
times of the same day on different channels. The rating for the program is the cumulative number of viewers who have watched it at
some time during a 24-hour period. This means higher ratings, legitimately so because advertisers pay for numbers of viewers, and
therefore higher advertising revenues. It would have the additional
effect of providing extra quality programming for material-starved
cable channels.

Pundits in the television industry also expected that Diller
would cut back NBC's prime time programming to fewer than 15
hours in the 8–11 P.M. time period. As had been the case at Fox,
this would exempt the company from the technical definition of
a network, subject to the financial interest/syndication rule that

prohibited networks from earning income through syndication. Diller was vehemently opposed to the "Fin-Syn" rule, and even after leaving Fox, he went to Washington to lobby FCC commissioners to rescind it.

David Gerber, the president of MGM/UA television, who worked with Diller when they were both at ABC-TV, weighed in with his prediction about Diller as network head. "I think if Barry were running a network, the news division would be a major obsession with him. He'd be like Roone Arledge, obsessing on the packaging, the talent, the content. Everything."

Other rumors that circulated after Diller left Fox included one that had him becoming baseball commissioner, and another that had him taking over Time Warner from Steve Ross, then dying of prostate cancer. There were those who predicted he would create a new entertainment TV network in conjunction with Malone and TCI. This scenario saw Diller melding his programming talents with Malone's financial clout and cable TV's reach (twenty percent of the cable TV subscribers in the country are served by Malone's TCI systems).

There was also talk that Diller would go together with John Kluge to revive the sinking Orion Pictures in which Kluge had a major stake. Yet another rumor had Diller teaming up with millionaire businessman Ronald Perelman, which Diller dismissed out of hand as "stupid." Other predictions going the rounds had Diller buying the Fox-TV network from Murdoch or taking a shot at acquiring Paramount Communications, thereby giving him the pleasure of ousting his former nemesis, Martin Davis.

Whatever his future plans included, Diller had let people know he no longer wanted to be anybody's employee. Wherever he landed, his presence would affect the television industry because many still considered him its most powerful and influential figure. In the meantime, he would only say that he intended to finish a documentary about the history of Hollywood in which he had a personal interest. Reporting on the documentary, Brian Lowry of *Daily Variety* wrote, "Right now, however, what Barry Diller knows about Hollywood history is of far less interest than what he can tell us about its future

David Geffen promised that Diller would soon put an end to the suspense and the guessing games. "He won't rest for long. He loves a challenge. He's not afraid. He's got elephant balls."

Diller meanwhile derived enormous pleasure from the various stories and rumors. The buzz kept everybody guessing, while he enjoyed his freedom, quietly figuring out his next move and learning more about computers.

"Part of the euphoria in this is that I don't have a timetable. It's enormously freeing," he told *Newsweek* reporter Emily Yoffe. Even so, he gave some clues about what he was seeking. "The only things that have interested me are the things I've started. Like building that fourth network from a blank piece of paper. Things that haven't been done before don't scare me. So today I feel euphoric and lucky. I can put all my energy into this new project. Whatever it will be."

The "whatever" finally came down to throwing in his fortunes with the cable interests. "They're livelier than most of the competition in their thinking. Talk to the cable people, as opposed to senior people in the news-gathering business, or at the TV networks, or in the studios. Just line them up, and you find that people in the leadership of cable are students of technology and spend vast amounts of time and capital thinking issues through."

The approach of Malone and the Robertses to the confluence of the new technology and the consumer differed from that of computer industry leaders. Steve Jobs, for example, took the view that it didn't make any difference how complicated his computers were; it was up to the consumer to learn how to use them. Diller argued with him that such a viewpoint was stupid and limited. Jobs needed to make his computers sufficiently easy and user-friendly for the average person to understand.

Diller also saw a weakness in the telephone companies that for years owned the only communication wire into American homes. But its copper wire was limited to carrying just a few signals, while cable had the capacity to carry hundreds of different signals through its coaxial cable and its fiber-optic wires. This gave the cable companies an enormous advantage over the phone companies in terms of handling communication and entertainment software.

What cable lacked was the expertise in bridging the gap between the technocrats and consumers. Diller had built his entire career on doing just that with spectacular results. Of all the companies Diller had seen, QVC was the closest to merging technology possibilities and consumer marketplace realities.

The marriage arrangements between QVC and Barry Diller began on September 28, 1993, in a suite of the Four Seasons Hotel in Philadelphia, where Comcast was headquartered; the meeting was attended by Diller and the two Robertses. (Ironically, this was the same hotel where Edgar Rosenberg had committed suicide almost six years earlier.)

Brian Roberts shared with Diller some compelling statistics about QVC's operation and revenues: Best estimates put its audience of regular customers, most of them middle-income women between the ages of 45 and 55, at the 5 million mark, with a monthly increase of 100,000 new customers. In the five years it had been in business, over 200,000 people had been repeat purchasers, buying items 50 times or more. It had grossed $992 million in 1991 with a profit of $19.6 million, which was expected to double within a year, and it was almost completely free of debt. So impressive were its numbers that *Inc.* magazine had named it the "fastest-growing small public company" in the United States.

Joseph Segel, the chairman of QVC who had started the company with Comcast's help, was considering selling his stake in the business. "There's an opportunity if it is something of interest," the older Roberts told Diller.

If Diller became a partner in QVC, he would also have a foot in the door of cable programming. "After that meeting, I thought I was really on to something," he said. "Once I left that day, I thought it would be QVC."

No deal was reached, but after hours of talk, most of the major points were at least covered. Diller's imagination had been ignited by fantasies of what he could do in the future with the still-primitive combination of telephone, television, and computer. Although he was strongly inclined to finalize a deal, he needed more time to think it over, and discuss the matter with Malone. He met again with the Robertses at the Atlantic City Cable Show in October.

Then, at the beginning of November, Diller accompanied Diane Von Furstenburg to West Chester for the introduction of her Silk Assets line. Diller watched as Von Furstenberg pitched her line to QVC's eager at-home audience. Within two hours, Von Furstenberg had sold 29,000 Silk Assets items for a gross of $1.2 million.

That was the clincher for Diller. He said, "It was the closest link I've ever seen between action and reaction." Said one of his former employees, ". . . Barry was hooked. He loves visual representation of success." Soon thereafter, he and Brian Roberts flew to Colorado. After a daylong session with Malone, an agreement was arrived at, pending Segel's cooperation and the approval of the board.

In an interview that appeared the following January in *Multichannel News,* Diller described his decision-making process thusly:

"What I really did is spend some time looking at where I thought the real world—meaning not the world I was just engaged in with my feet nailed to the floor, but looking at it on the basis that these feet could ostensibly take you anywhere—was going in all forms of media, communications, and entertainment. And where were there opportunities today and tomorrow. . . . I decided that I thought the world was going to be dominated by the interests of cable, and I believe that it's going to come through a TV set and there's going to be a microprocessor next to it of some kind. I think the interests represented by cable have a better chance to be the delivery system."

Malone and Brian Roberts met with Segel on December 1 and presented him with their request for a change in management. Given that between them Liberty Media and Comcast owned 53 percent of the company, Segel bowed to the inevitable and agreed to leave his position in January. Other QVC senior executives, including the chief operation officer Michael Boyd, would stay on for the time being. Segel, who got the usual golden handshake with a 10-year consulting contract, called the arrangement "an entirely friendly transaction."

At a board meeting eight days later, the financial terms for Diller's involvement were spelled out. Diller, through his company Arrow Investments, would pay Segel and his wife $12.6 million for their 420,000 shares of QVC, the same amount he had paid two days before to Liberty Media for an equal number of shares. Beyond that, Diller was to get a signing bonus of 160,000 more shares. In total, he would put up $25 million to get a total of one million shares of QVC.

Since at the time of the deal, QVC stock was hovering around $30.70 a share, Diller's one million shares added up to a hefty worth of approximately $30,700,000. The $25 million would not be a strain on his wallet, thanks in part to the $34 million severance bonus he had received upon leaving Fox. Although his stake in QVC added up to a mere 3 percent, compared with Liberty's 22.3 percent, his partners ceded him one-third voting control of the company. Brian Roberts said, "This is a genuine partnership. It's not Barry working for Malone."

His salary would be $500,000 a year, only one-sixth of what he had been paid at Fox. The discrepancy was balanced out by an option on another six million shares of QVC at about the price they were selling for when Diller bought into the company. Diller had to exercise 80 percent of his option in the first year, the objective being to put his stockholding position on a par with that of Liberty Media and Comcast.

On December 10, Diller shocked his friends, colleagues, and the business world at large for the second time in 10 months when the announcement was made that Diller was joining QVC in partnership with Malone and the Robertses. "We are at the very beginning curve in the home shopping industry, and I am wildly enthusiastic about playing a role in that future," he said in a written statement.

Brian Roberts was equally passionate in his assessment of QVC's future with Diller at the helm. "You've got a guy starting the Fox Network doing it for cable. Here's somebody who wants to take all his programming skills and create cable networks," he said. "Comcast hasn't participated in programming before. This is the dawning of a new era.

15

"What's the Idea?"

For many people, Diller's jump from Fox to the home-shopping network was comparable to leaving the 21 Club to run a hot-dog stand. Diller, obviously, had a vision that others did not share. The cynics saw QVC as an electronic flea market selling jewelry and beanbag chairs. Diller saw a money machine generating the cash flow that would enable him to finance other, far more ambitious projects. As one of his colleagues expressed it, "When Barry went to QVC, he saw this mainly as the platform to do a big, transforming acquisition."

"I want to buy my own store," Diller had said when Rupert Murdoch had turned down his request for an equity stake in Fox. No matter how much power he wielded, how lavishly he was compensated, he had always worked for somebody else. He had reached a landmark birthday. Now he yearned to control his own destiny. But why QVC?

One investment banker, who had been predicting just such a move for Diller, nevertheless said he was 'stunned" that Diller would park himself so far beyond the Hollywood orbit.

"All they care about is status," Diller said of those who wondered loudly about his motives and his sanity. "That's why they can't understand why I'm doing this. They say, 'It's not very glamorous.'"

Diane Von Furstenberg understood, and she brought to the operation enough glamour to satisfy Diller. Aside from her poise and innate sense of style, Von Furstenberg was attractive to Diller because she was an excellent businesswoman who achieved great success in the cutthroat world of fashion. Indeed, she made her name on New York's Seventh Avenue, the heart of the American fashion industry, as the woman who made fashion affordable for the average woman.

Von Furstenberg was born in Belgium to financially secure Jewish parents who had survived World War II in Europe; her mother was imprisoned for 14 months in a Nazi concentration camp. After attending schools in Spain, England, and Switzerland, Von Furstenberg became engaged to a fellow student at the University of Geneva, Prince Eduard Egon Von Furstenberg, the scion of the ancient Italian family that owns the Fiat business empire. They married in 1969 against his father's wishes and moved to New York.

After an informal tutoring course from Angelo Ferretti, a renowned textile manufacturer, she designed three simple shirtwaist dresses that she tried to peddle to New York garment manufacturers. Most turned her away, but designer Bill Blass encouraged her to the point that she was able to stage the first New York showing of her collection in April 1970, only nine months after her wedding.

Rather than creating an expensive designer line, Von Furstenberg priced everything in her collection between $25 and $100. The public loved it even if the established designers and manufacturers did not. With $30,000 that she borrowed from her father, she established Diane Von Furstenberg, Ltd., in April 1972, and grossed $1.2 million during her first year. By 1976, she was selling

20,000 dresses a week and grossing $64 million. That jumped to $142 million a year later.

One of her most famous creations was the wraparound dress, which became a centerpiece of her collection for many years. Like other designers, she also branched into jewelry, furs, handbags, cosmetics, perfumes, shoes, scarves, and sunglasses, which added another $60 million a year to her grosses.

In 1975, after six years of marriage and two children, the Von Furstenbergs separated and, ultimately, divorced. Diane Von Furstenberg moved into a 10-room apartment on Park Avenue and also bought an eighteenth-century farmhouse in Connecticut. "It's an unpretentious place," she said of the country house. "But I love it. It's a real luxury because it's all for myself and the children. I never entertain there or use it in a social way. If I invite somebody up, they are either a lover or very close friends."

Von Furstenberg's dramatic sales results at QVC gave Diller his first glimpse of what would soon come to be known as "convergence" in the entertainment and communication industry. This, coupled with his excitement over the computer in all its permutations, made him believe that he had seen the future in West Chester, Pennsylvania.

The involvement of such a legendary media mogul as Barry Diller was equally exciting to the key QVC players. Malone and the Robertses felt that with Diller in the picture, QVC gained instant credibility with the other big players who had previously regarded QVC as an overhyped, electronic swap meet for people who lived in trailer parks.

Media reaction to Diller's latest move was predictably heated. John Lippman, writing in the *Los Angeles Times,* characterized Diller as the man who accomplished the impossible at Fox and saved it when it didn't look as if anybody could save it. He assessed Diller thusly: "The conventional wisdom dictated a deal in network television where Diller made his mark as the force behind the Fox network. But the volatile executive sees stronger opportunities in the new technologies that are already driving QVC's success.

"For nearly a year he's been boning up on the brave new world of signal compression and video on demand. Diller plans to use QVC as the springboard into the multichannel, interactive program environment that experts are trumpeting as the next wave in television."

Wall Street felt the impact of Diller's deal with QVC, as the company's stock rose 18 percent within a few days of the announcement that Diller had joined up. This meant a boost in value of $5 million for Diller on the stock he owned, a potential profit of $30 million if he exercised his stock options, and more money in the pockets of Malone and the Robertses who, of course, also benefited from the jump in QVC's stock price.

In the long run, however, Diller's partners foresaw that joining forces with Diller could bring benefits that extended beyond the imponderables such as credibility and stature. Malone and the Robertses were faced with the prospect of treading on unfamiliar and possibly unfriendly territory. If their cable operations were to progress as they hoped, they would have to go to Hollywood and Washington for assistance.

But Malone disliked finding himself in the public spotlight, preferring to sail the Atlantic in his boat mixing with stars and power brokers. Tact was not one of his virtues, and his outspoken views of legislators and regulators had won him few friends in Washington, DC. The Robertses, father and son, had always felt they were not fully appreciated by their colleagues in the communications and entertainment field, despite the importance of their cable channel. Both they and Malone were uncomfortable dealing with Hollywood executives as they moved forward to expand their cable operations.

But cable and Hollywood were coming to realize that they had a mutual interest in getting to know each other. Hollywood needed an outlet through which to distribute its films, and cable needed Hollywood to provide it with viable entertainment that could fill the yawning chasm of 8,760 annual programming hours, multiplied by 50 or 100 or 500 channels. The Robertses and John Malone were looking to Diller to bridge the cultural and communications gap between their technology and the entertainment industry.

Hollywood seemed to agree that Diller was a brilliant choice to achieve that end. "The goal is to expand the home shopping concept into broader forms of entertainment," said an entertainment executive in an article that appeared in *Daily Variety*. "That's where Diller's expertise comes into play."

For those who didn't quite grasp the vast opportunities available to a merchandising colossus such as QVC, Wall Street analyst James Meyer of Janney Montgomery Scott, Inc., explained, "They don't need Barry Diller to sell pots and pans. Liberty and QVC Network are trying to posture themselves to be a leading vendor of product for an era when you have digital-compression technology being employed. Right now you're at the beginning and Diller has the opportunity to be entrepreneurial." (Digital-compression technology refers to the system whereby cable TV companies can compress their programs so they can transmit 10 programs on a channel where they previously could transmit only one. Thus, with a 50-channel cable system, they could up their transmission range from 50 to the 500 channels.)

Jessica Reif of Oppenheimer & Company, taking note of the rumors that QVC's biggest competitor, the Home Shopping Network, was on the verge of being absorbed by QVC, weighed in with this opinion: "Having a vehicle like QVC combined with HSN will be used for more than selling knickknacks. They will be selling airline tickets, records, books and pay-per-view movies using the system that's already in place for home shopping." Reif envisioned Diller expanding QVC "into a full cable network. It's sort of like the network of the future."

The talk of a QVC merger with Home Shopping Network grew louder and more credible when Malone's Liberty Media made a quick deal with Home Shopping to buy $150 million of its stock, an 80 percent voting stake that would give Liberty control of HSN. Roy Speer, the chairman and co-founder of HSN, sold Liberty 20 million shares of his class B stock for $60 million and an additional $85 million of Liberty's stock. Speer minimized speculation that the channels would merge, but red flags were triggered in Washington as Wall Street and cable executives predicted an impending merger between the two companies. The antitrade implications of such a deal were that it would allow QVC to dominate the cable TV-home shopping world and reach into a combined 67 million homes.

Other analysts were equally excited about the QVC-Diller connection. "There are many ways to combine programming and selling. Another interesting possibility is a TV shopping network during the day and four hours of Diller programming per night," said Peter Siris of UBS Securities.

John Field of Hanifen, Imhoff, Inc. saw Diller applying the telephone banks and specialists QVC already had in place for order placement and fulfillment for other mass merchandising situations. QVC's existing fulfillment system could handle 20,000 telephone calls per minute. "It could be in pay-per-view, fulfillment of pay-per-view, a back office if you will. It is obviously more than just a shopping channel," said Field.

The advertising industry also registered its approval of the Diller-QVC connection. "In the long term, if people like Barry Diller are getting into this, it gives us optimism. It's really a vote for interactive TV," said Gaye Sussman, senior vice president and media director at Kobs & Draft Advertising.

Diller, with his Hollywood connections, would be the perfect ambassador to open the doors, talk the game, and make the deals. An added bonus for QVC was Diller's close relationship to newly elected President Bill Clinton, whom Diller had supported. *Daily Variety* underscored Diller's importance by citing the view of one cable industry executive: "Malone has some very big potential problems on the near horizon. TCI (Television Cable Inc.—largest multiple cable TV system operator in the world, serving one out of every five cable TV subscribers in America, and Malone's main operation) was raising its rates at a time when there's a lot of anti-cable sentiment in Congress. He also has Hollywood terrified about his increasing clout as a gatekeeper. Diller can help him out in both these areas."

Diller started showing up for work at QVC in January 1993. He took his new job responsibilities very seriously, attentively scanning the nine television sets lined up next to his desk, keeping as watchful an eye on the products being proffered for sale by QVC as he had to the movies and television shows that only recently had been the focus of his attention.

Seated in his corner office on the second floor of QVC's red-brick building in West Chester, he expounded on his vision of QVC's future, and the role he would play in making that future a reality. He foresaw QVC changing and growing over the next three to seven years, as it developed into a multimedia company with interests in electronic retailing as well as what he referred to as "interactivity."

His primary focus would be, not unexpectedly, in programming, because, he said, "my background is in programming, whether it is in television programming, or motion-picture programming, or figuring out what a network could be programming. It's all relative to what is on the screen."

At ABC, Paramount, and Fox, his concern had been with traditional broadcast programming. Now, his awareness had expanded way beyond the traditional Hollywood definition of the word, to encompass programming for computers, for electronic retailing, for information processing, and for what he called "interfacing programming." But when pressed to articulate more precisely the nature of his role at QVC, he would not—or could not—set forth anything more concrete. "Not only is it premature, it's inappropriate," he declared rather defensively, sounding as if he had been pushed into a corner not to his liking.

He batted away questions posed by John Higgins for *Multichannel News* about the possibility of QVC using its $185 million cash flow to create other forms of entertainment networks, labeling such queries "too speculative." Nor was he willing to get involved in any discussions about areas of the company that needed improving. Displaying uncharacteristic diplomacy, he begged the question and instead touted QVC for offering "an enormous number of individual products for sale. I think as is appropriate it will grow and develop."

He predicted that some changes would be necessary as QVC grew, but he hastened to praise the existing operation, citing management for having ". . . done a fine job until now." And the same chief executive who had not hesitated to install new regimes and make sweeping changes when he took control of Paramount and Fox, was now inquiring rhetorically of an interviewer, "Do you just throw the cart over and start restocking?" He gave an definitive and unequivocal response. "Of course not."

It was almost as if Barry Diller had undergone a transformation of sorts during his odyssey across America. He no longer had all the answers, even going so far as to admit, "I'm just entering this business and I have a lot to learn about it."

But the Diller of old was still there, lurking beneath the new, more modest version of his former self, so that he couldn't resist admitting, "People say, 'Gee, that didn't work. How come you think it might?' I've heard that since the beginning of my time. I don't mean this arrogantly at all, but the question, I think, does not inform the issue."

Because he was determined that he would make it work—whatever *it* was. He seemed—again, uncharacteristically—

uncertain as to what lay ahead for cable TV, this bold new venture, with all its uncharted byways, in which he had enlisted. When he talked about interactive television, and QVC in particular, he couldn't quite differentiate between "what's the idea" and "what's the programming." Pressed to describe a few of what he had cited as "the many good ideas in the area of interactivity," he declined. Programming was his strong suit, what he'd been hired to do, but he said, "The problem right now is you've got so many voices and noises and people and speculations talking that to a very large degree what's conceptualized by all of that is an awful lot of noise and skepticism.'

He reiterated this point in a subsequent conversation with Mike Freeman of *Broadcasting,* as his first month at QVC drew to a close. "The speculation in this area is just providing more confusion," he said. "The things that are clear are that there are real changes taking place. They have been germinating now for several years. In the next three, five, seven years they will, many of them, be deployed and it will be a world that will be more understood than it is now."

In the meantime, he admitted that he was attracted to electronic retailing because it was a new and as yet unrealized area, "in the very infancy of its business opportunity." He anticipated that the whole concept of programming was on the brink of undergoing major changes and redefinitions, and that companies like QVC would take the lead in effecting those changes.

His interest in broadcasting hadn't changed. But the lesson he had taken from his experiences at Fox was that the four networks, which he called "mass program engines," would have to more clearly distinguish themselves, to develop a "distinct program philosophy that underscores all their activities." He wasn't talking about "weird or obscure demographic profiles," but rather alternative in the sense that he had defined the concept while at Fox—"as a network alternative to the three, not simply an alternative network."

For all of his talk about interactivity and the new technology, Diller's heart still seemed to beat for Hollywood. He had recently implied that the broadcast networks were destined to suffer the same fate as American car manufacturers. But he sounded like a man who hadn't yet recovered from a failed relationship, so intent was he on enumerating his lost love's strengths and weaknesses.

As he saw it, the networks were at severe risk of losing their dominance of the airways. For the first time in television history, broadcasters needed to take a long, hard look at not only who their audience was, but who they themselves were. "It doesn't take a mathematical genius to see that with more fractionalization, pro-pelled by more diverse program alternatives, you can only divide 100 percent so many ways. And more program diversity is going to present a continuing challenge to the 'old club' who used to con-trol the vast majority of it."

He held up Fox as a role model for the other networks to emu-late. Six years into its network existence, Fox had won 13 percent of the television-viewing audience, and Diller attributed its success to what he referred to as "niche definition," which was ". . . broad, but not all-inclusively broad." He couldn't resist giving himself some credit for focusing in on an audience that was younger, not chrono-logically, but "younger in sensibility. . . . I was interested in every single program that Fox put on as an idea myself, which is the only way I think you can program much of anything."

Now, the ideas that preoccupied Diller had taken on a very different shape and texture—direct-broadcast satellites, 500-channel cable systems, digital compression, and back-end equip-ment—the future of a technology he referred to as "enablers" that would convey programming to consumers's television sets. But ul-timately, he said, it all came down to his "age-old discipline," which he had first studied at William Morris and ABC, and which posed the following questions: "What's the idea? Is the idea any good?"

For Diller, the way to quantify those ideas was by [...]
tionalizing as best you can a process that involves a progr[...]
as its defining reality," which was what he expected to do a[...]
Because "if the idea is any good, then proceed on its develo[...]
until it's proved not so good, and then understand that and [...]
on to the next idea."

Although he had broadened his conception of what t[...]
ideas might encompass, one element remained a constant: "I[...]
television screen: It is going to be watched because people eit[...]
are entertained by it, and make that choice, or it gives them an [...]
ditional benefit in their lives in terms of either making a transa[...]
tion to purchase something, or making a transaction to receiv[...]
information the way they want it, or a whole series of goods and[...]
services. Those are essentially program ideas. Are the goods being[...]
offered any good? Is the program in which those goods lie any [...]
good? Is it better than its competition? Are the transactions in [...]
terms of news and information and other goods and services good[...]
program ideas, i.e., have they been well-founded and well-thought-
through and well-marketed? These are the issues. There are no
other issues."

Diller sounded like a man who had grown bored with television's ceaseless demand for more and better product, a man who
desperately wanted to broaden his horizons. The question was,
could the medium of QVC really satisfy his need to push past the
boundaries of traditional television entertainment? Because try as
he might to defend QVC against its critics' charge that it was just
so much "commercial clutter" on the television screen, the network still offered nothing more than "the attractive showcasing of
products," to use Diller's own words.

All that could change, however, and Diller's imagination ran
riot with visions of the directions in which he could lead the shopping network. *New Yorker* writer Ken Auletta, with whom he
shared his thoughts, said:

to persuade QVC to think of itself as more than
C can also be a shopping catalogue, and a brand
ean—a catalogue that Diller can program pic-
ks that QVC's full shopping potential won't be
ecomes truly interactive. As Diller envisions it,
ll say, 'I want a raincoat. Instantly! I want an um-
ll figure out the cheapest ones, and deliver them

s, 'Three years from now, you'll say, 'I want shoes.'
button and see yourself in various shoes on the
their homes, he says, consumers will be able to roam
Bloomingdale's; avoid the last-minute Christmas rush
up a special selection of gifts for the 'special person,'
one, and having it delivered the next day; find a hotel in
obean, inspect its rooms and amenities on the TV screen,
en press a button to make a reservation."

At least one viewer of CNN's *Larry King Live* took issue with
er's futuristic scenarios when Diller appeared on the show
the early spring of 1993. King's guests also included John
endricks, chairman and CEO of Discovery Communications, and
Diller's former employee, Scott Sassa, who had since moved on to
become president of the Turner Entertainment group. They and
Diller, whom King introduced as a "visionary," had been invited to
the show to discuss TCI's just-issued announcement that by the following year, the company expected to have laid out billions of dollars on fiber-optic cable and equipment to bring the 500-channel
system into American homes.

Diller was happily expounding on his new favorite theme of
home shopping as the wave of the future because "people don't
have the time to shop anymore," when a caller from Virginia posed
this question to him: "Listen, Barry, I want to know what happens
to the millions of employees that you're fixing to put out of work.
To name a few, the department stores, the pet shops, the video

sales clerks, the record shops, travel agents. . . . What about the lost jobs? And don't say they're not going to be there."

Diller, momentarily at a loss for words, managed to summon up a less than satisfying response. "I don't think there will be this grand displacement," he said. "It just seems unlikely to me."

Ed Martin, reporting on the exchange in *Inside Media,* underscored the weakness of Diller's answer when he commented, "It's perfectly legal for a handful of outspoken, powerful individuals to utilize media platforms to get very, very wealthy, pumping their product into people's homes, through cable or over the air, and using a vast array of technologies, whether people like it or not. . . . The moguls will continue to get richer, regardless of the consequences. And we are all, like it or not, pawns in this game."

Diller had suddenly become the target *du jour* of the media pundits. Another entertainment industry watcher, Michael Schrage of *Adweek,* issued an even harsher assessment of Diller's plans for QVC, as outlined in Ken Auletta's article.

Trying to reconcile the man who created Fox-TV with the man who had bought into QVC, Shrage characterized the Diller of Auletta's piece as "a man with less a golden gut than a silicon spleen. He is a genuine techno-twit whose grasp of new media betrays a mindset that wildly misunderstands what made him successful in the first place."

Shrage took Diller to task for putting his faith in technology, rather than content. He disparaged Diller's description of a hassle-free, pre-Christmas interactive shopping expedition to Bloomingdale's, saying, "All this from the fellow who gave us *The Simpsons?* Say it ain't so! This is precisely the sort of vision a Barry Diller parodies, not one he propagandizes and entrepreneurs."

The problem, as Shrage saw it, was that Diller seemed to have forgotten that the American public had so warmly embraced the Simpson family because they were "dysfunctionally compelling characters." And character, said Shrage, not digital compression or interactivity, was still the key to success for the new media technology.

"That's why Nintendo still makes more money than Microsoft and QVC put together. The video-games giant doesn't just sell interactivity. It sells the characters of Mario and Street Fighters. It uses technology to create new contexts for both interaction and character."

The founders of QVC had actually grasped this idea, Shrage noted. "That's why they have such perky hostesses and encourage viewer call ins. The feeling is as much talk radio as it is televised flea market. The goal isn't just to structure human/television interaction, it's to project an environment that people can dip into for narrowcasting."

In case his readers—and perhaps Diller was among them—had missed his thesis, Shrage hammered home his point. "Trust me—technology is not the key to understanding. The issue is no longer programming for television or computer. It's creating characters and experiences. The challenge is crafting the next generation of media formats and genres—not figuring out how to replicate the pseudo-intimacy of a Bloomingdale's aisle on your high-definition television set."

Without mincing words, he summarized his conclusion. "Lord knows what 'The Simpsons' of QVC will look like. Or what the Home Shopping counterpart to Studs should be. Or if this genre can generate its own proprietary Howard Sterns or Rush Limbaughs. I only know that these are the issues that will determine the future success of Diller's QVC—not pea-brained projections about the coming uberconvergence of cable, telephone, and computer companies."

16

Of Paramount
Importance

Barry Diller had an unlikely date on July 21, 1993. He had been invited to lunch at the top of Manhattan's 15 Columbus Circle, headquarters of Paramount Communications, formerly known as Gulf & Western. It was the first time Diller had returned to his old stomping grounds since he had stepped down as head of Paramount Pictures nine years earlier. His host in the private dining room was his ex-boss and nemesis, Martin Davis; the agenda, as set by Davis, was very simple and straightforward.

Davis had heard that Diller was on the verge of organizing a hostile bid to buy Paramount. "Look, Barry, I'm hearing all these stories and I have to keep telling you, we're not for sale," said Davis unequivocally. "We have no interest in doing anything with you."

After a year and a half of speculation churned out by the Hollywood–New York gossip mills about Barry Diller's next move, rumors had begun to spread about his interest in Paramount. In spite of his protestations that he had found his niche at QVC, no one believed he would be content to sit still much longer in suburban Pennsylvania. He hadn't lost money on the deal: His original investment of $25 million—which had bought him approximately 12 percent of the QVC and sent the company's stock soaring from $30 to $70 a share by the summer of 1993—had increased his personal fortune by $70 million.

Now, industry onlookers anticipated such a move by QVC with greedy excitement. Paramount was ripe for the plucking, and a victory for Diller would be poetic justice, the stuff of which Hollywood dramas were made.

Four years earlier, Davis had sold the last of Paramount's non-entertainment-related operations, to create a tightly run company that consisted of Simon & Schuster, then the largest publishing company in the United States; the Paramount Studios, including its film library and production facilities; Madison Square Garden; and two New York sports teams, the basketball Knicks and the hockey Rangers. Since then, as Paramount's stock prices had sagged, Davis had been sitting on $1.8 billion in cash, precisely the sort of situation that was destined to attract hungry corporate raiders.

Seeking to expand his empire, Davis had been exploring various acquisition and merger opportunities in the entertainment, media, and communications field. In 1989, he had almost destroyed the Time Warner merger with an eleventh-hour tender offer for *Time.* He had subsequently pursued potential deals with Elsevier, a Dutch publishing company; Polygram, Bertelsmann, Thorn EMI, and Geffen Records; Sony; McGraw-Hill Publishing; Gannett Newspapers; AT&T; and all three of the major networks.

The main drawback, aside from government regulatory issues, was Davis himself. No one had rushed forward to woo Paramount's chairman to join forces. Apparently, few CEOs were eager to throw in their lot with the man about whom one of his closest colleagues said, "Martin does not generate feelings of great warmth on behalf of prospective merger partners. Whether it's accurate or not, he is seen as a difficult person to work with. [People] weren't too eager to jump into bed with a man like Martin." Davis is not unaware of his difficult reputation; indeed, he seems to revel in it. Referring to Reed Publishing, a British publishing company with whom Davis met only once to discuss a possible merger, he said, "I was told they were petrified of me."

In the film industry, Davis was considered "the ultimate suit" and "the most hated man in Hollywood." Not the least of his sins was that he had all but forced the resignations of Diller, Michael Eisner, and Jeffrey Katzenberg.

"He is a man who got rid of the three most talented people in the world he inhabits," said David Geffen. "That right there was one of the most monumental screwups in the history of show business. These three gentlemen have created billions of dollars in value for their companies that could have gone to Paramount. He threw them out. That right there is the seed that led to what is happening right now."

"Some people get passed over," said Davis, defending himself against the charge that he had engineered Diller's move to Fox. "It is part of the discipline of the business that you do that. You don't pout. . . . Some people misinterpret me. If I have something to say, I'm direct."

But one of his own Paramount executives disagreed. "You just don't treat people the way [Davis] does." A former associate described him as "a man with a tiny, cruel heart." A business rival put it more succinctly. "Marty Davis would enjoy pulling the wings off flies."

A close friend offered this insight on Davis. "Martin can be the most charming man I know. Why he insists on creating this macho image, I'll never know. He has a very fragile view of himself. He's not a man with a lot of innate self-confidence."

The macho side of his personality ruled at Paramount, where he was viewed as an "icy dictator who terrorizes LA's creative community from his wind-swept Central Park aerie," the man who was known to call his aides to his office so that he could scrutinize the shine on their shoes. Davis himself was a well-turned out autocrat. He sported starched white, monogrammed, and cuff-linked shirts beneath a pinstriped suit, and his crisply parted silver-gray hair was never out of place.

Diller, however, knew how to play Davis. Over a lunch of red snapper, he tried to calm Davis's concerns with the carefully phrased and well-rehearsed lines that he had worked out with his attorneys. "When and if I have something to say to you," he told Davis, "I will call you and say it to you. Until then, I suggest you believe nothing."

In fact, Davis had good reason to be worried about a QVC strike on Paramount, and he took little comfort from Diller's response. "I got a vacant answer," he later said.

Davis had been half-expecting just such a move ever since Diller had gone to QVC. ". . . we knew something was up. Common sense told you that. Home shopping? I mean, come on." For his part, Diller "had thought of Paramount [before] leaving Fox, but I didn't think the time was right. I was pretty sure something would happen within two years. I was sure Paramount would get sold, one way or another." When that moment came, he was determined to be in on the action.

In the spring of 1993, at John Malone's behest, Davis talked to Ted Turner about possibly merging Paramount with Turner Broadcasting; Malone owned 25 percent of the latter company and served on its board of directors. But after many hours of conversation with Malone, Davis concluded that a deal with Turner, who owned CNN and TNT, could put Paramount at risk of falling under Malone's thumb, which was where he perceived Turner to be.

Meanwhile, with the full blessings of both the Robertses *and* Malone, Diller had been keeping a sharp eye on Paramount. That same spring, Herbert Allen, a leading New York investment banker with the consulting firm of Booz Allen & Company, had approached him with the possibility of moving on Paramount. Diller gave him the nod to proceed, just as Robert Greenhill, chairman of Smith Barney Shearson, began talking to Davis about doing some kind of deal with Viacom, Inc., Sumner Redstone's $1.9 billion cable company that owned MTV, The Movie Channel, Showtime, and Nickelodeon, among other entertainment operations. On April 20, Davis met for dinner with Redstone, whom he'd known for over 40 years, with Greenhill present to smooth things along.

The 70-year-old Redstone had grown up in Boston's West End, graduated from Harvard Law School two years after the end of World War II, and worked as a young lawyer for Harry Truman. By 1954, Redstone's father had expanded from night club ownership to opening one of America's first drive-in movies. Redstone joined the family business and turned it into a multistate theater chain, National Amusements, with 843 screens.

A driven, determined, and shrewd dealmaker, by 1987 Redstone had positioned himself for his first megadeal when he acquired Viacom, a diversified cable and programming company. By 1993, Redstone was ready for his next big leap, a merger with Paramount.

But Davis had also gone back to the drawing board regarding a merger with TCI. He had even worked out terms with Malone, which stipulated that TCI would acquire a 17 percent stake in Paramount, in return for which Paramount would get Liberty Media and its 22 percent stake in QVC, which Davis dismissed as "just a programming channel."

Malone was, in effect, playing both sides against each other, courting Davis at the same time that the QVC board had given Diller permission to make a move on Paramount. Word of Diller's go-ahead was leaked by Malone's lawyer, Jerry Kern, to Don Oresman, Davis's number two man and closest associate.

Davis had spent years cultivating his relationship with Malone. "The guy is a genius but then, so was Al Capone," he said. "He's the smartest guy you'll ever meet. He's brilliant. But he stands for nothing, believes in nothing, and has contempt for everyone that walks and talks. . . . He talks too much. And when he talks, no one is spared. . . . He has nothing good to say about anyone, whether it's Barry Diller or Ted Turner. . . . There's nothing John Malone would ever do that would shock me. Except perhaps send me a warm, affectionate note."

Furious with Malone for what he considered a form of blackmail, Davis called him on June 18 and curtly demanded, "Quit trying to use Diller to put a gun to our head!"

But Malone, while confirming that Diller was ready to make a raid on Paramount, blamed the impetus on Brian Roberts. Malone, still playing the middle, tried to assure Davis that he didn't support Diller's bid, but that there wasn't much he could do to prevent it. There was good reason for Davis to be concerned about Malone. If Diller did launch a successful hostile takeover of Paramount, Malone stood to gain control of a major supply of programming for his cable channels and network—and he would be able to control the access as well.

In fact, Malone excused himself from ongoing discussions within QVC about a possible takeover; soon thereafter, Peter Barton, president of Liberty Media, informed Diller that the company would not be involved in a hostile takeover of Paramount. The implicit message was that Diller had lost Malone's support—and without it the bid was good as dead.

On July 12, Diller announced that QVC would acquire the Home Shopping Network in a stock swap worth $1.1 billion. In a cover story for its July 26 issue, *BusinessWeek* referred to Diller as "a guru of the new media age." It called the proposed transaction "long-awaited" and commented, "Together, QVC and Home Shopping will virtually corner this market. Without so much as redecorating a TV studio, Diller has put himself at the helm of a $2 billion media company."

But lest readers were naive enough to believe the obvious, the article went on to note that ". . . nobody thinks Diller will stop there. . . . It's Diller's grander ambitions that have people buzzing."

"I see unlimited horizons," Brian Roberts gushed. It was anyone's guess whether he had in mind the QVC-HSN merger or some far grander scheme. Also mentioned in the piece were the rumors of a Paramount-TCI deal. "Linking up with Paramount would be an ironic move, even by Diller's standards," remarked the writers.

Nobody was more cognizant of his former employee's "grander ambitions" than Martin Davis. Although he was quick to boast, "I don't consider Diller then, or now, a threat. Rightly or wrongly, I never considered Diller as anything other than a puppet of Malone," he was eager to cement the deal with Redstone. With Felix Rohatyn of Lazard Frere, the prestigious investment firm, representing Paramount's interests, serious negotiations had begun in early July. "This has nothing to do with money, this has nothing to do with glory," said Redstone.

A tentative agreement was reached: Davis would serve as the chief executive officer of Paramount/Viacom, while Redstone would be the chairman and controlling stockholder of the new company, with nearly 40 percent of the common stock and 70 percent of the voting stock. Viacom's offer was a combined package of cash stock, most of which would be Class B nonvoting stock, at an approximate market value of $51 a share. But Davis was looking for $70 a share. "Until we get to seven, we don't have a discussion," he told Rohatyn.

The talks broke off, and Davis invited Diller to lunch to warn him away. Meanwhile, the price of Viacom's Class B stock was rapidly rising; it jumped from $46.875 on July 6 to $57.25 on August 20. People wondered: Was Redstone and/or people acting on his behalf buying up the stock to increase its value and thus sweeten the deal for Paramount?

Davis and Malone met for a final meeting on August 10. Ten days later, Robert Greenhill persuaded Davis and Redstone to sit down for more talks. But once again, Redstone failed to come up to Davis's coveted "seven," though he did raise Viacom's bid to $65. Negotiations continued, however, and on September 7, the two men reached a compromise. "Hiya, boss," Redstone greeted Davis by phone that day, after Redstone had brought Viacom's offer up to $69.14, and Davis decided to forgo his "seven."

The deal was too tempting to resist. Several months later, he was still smacking his lips. "I could just taste the asset mix. I could taste the opportunities. I could taste the future."

The proposed merger, which was valued at $9.2 billion, $2.2 billion over Paramount's $7 billion market value, was presented to Paramount's Board of Directors on September 9, along with a financial analysis of the terms, prepared by Lazard Freres. The board convened again on September 12, and unanimously approved the merger agreement, which stipulated the following:

❖ Each share of Paramount common stock would be converted into .10 shares of Viacom Class A voting stock, .90 shares of Viacom Class B nonvoting stock, and $9.10 in cash.

❖ Under a No-Shop Provision, Paramount pledged not to "solicit, encourage, discuss, negotiate, or endorse any competing transaction," unless either a third party submitted an unsolicited written proposal "which is not subject to any material contingencies relating to financing"; or Paramount's board deemed necessary third party discussions in order "to comply with its fiduciary duties."

❖ A Termination Fee Provision entitled Viacom to a $100 million termination fee for one of three conditions: (a) "Paramount

terminated the Original Merger Agreement because of a competing transaction"; (b) "Paramount's stockholders did not
approve the merger"; or (c) 'the Paramount Board recommended a competing transaction."

♣ A Stock Option Agreement guaranteed Viacom an option to
buy approximately 19.9 percent of "Paramount's outstanding
common stock at $69.14 per share if any of the triggering
events for the Termination Fee occurred."

Davis and Redstone, accompanied by Greenhill, held a press
conference on the same day that the merger received the approval
of Paramount's board. "This is an act of destiny," Redstone exulted.
"This marriage will never be torn asunder." "I never thought it
would happen," he said. "Several times last summer, [Davis] broke
off negotiations."

Asked about the QVC threat, he added that he had known
Diller a long time and didn't believe he would try to squelch the
deal, but that he and Davis felt "inhibited" from saying any more by
their desire not to attack Diller personally. Now, only a "nuclear
attack" could destroy the $8.2 billion "synergistic" merger, he
boasted.

Seeking to forestall just such an attack, Redstone took the pre-
caution of calling Diller, who had been caught by surprise by the
announcement. "Despite the rumblings of war, I thought there was
going to be no dawn raid. You believe what you want to believe,"
he said. "I didn't want something to happen in the fall. I wanted
them to wait until spring. When the [Home Shopping] merger
was done."

Recovering quickly from the sneak attack, Diller waited only
eight days to launch his assault. On September 20, he sent a letter to
Davis in which he proposed a $9.5 billion counteroffer that would
result in the fifth-biggest entertainment-oriented conglomerate in

the world. He also declared his eagerness to sit down with Paramount to discuss the details. According to QVC's terms, the company—with the backing of TCI and Liberty Media—would pay approximately $80 a share, well above Davis's dream number of $70, consisting of 0.893 in QVC common stock and $30 in cash.

The first salvo had been fired, and war had been declared. Kurt Andersen, writing in *Time,* set the tone for the battle that was about to ensue when he wrote, "The decision to spend billions to take over a company is seldom either strictly logical or strictly emotional." Andersen went on to point out that what everybody had initially assumed would be a friendly joining of two corporate giants, Viacom and Paramount Communications, was about to turn into a ride as wild and murky as Disneyland's Space Mountain attraction.

The situation had an ironic element as well. CEO Martin Davis and Paramount Communications were about to have done to them what they had earlier tried to do (i.e., play the spoiler) to Steve Ross and Warner Communications during Warner's friendly takeover of Time, Inc. An outsider, Barry Diller, had stepped onto the playing field and announced that he wanted in on the game.

"The collective id of the players was already breathtaking," said Andersen. "Now comes Barry Diller."

Then, of course, there was Viacom with its many holdings in the entertainment field, including the Showtime programming channel, which depended on Malone's cable television systems for transmission.

"Most deals are 50 percent emotion and 50 percent economics," said Felix Rohatyn, and emotions were running as high as the economics on both sides. Some Wall Street insiders were calling the Paramount-Viacom union a "shotgun marriage," specifically designed by Davis to stave off any moves on his kingdom by Diller. "With these egos involved, things could really get out of hand," said one media industry executive.

Davis sounded matter-of-fact and blasé in his response to Diller's bid. "You can't compete with this future [the Viacom/Paramount deal]." Diller's offer would have "to be so extraordinary that Sumner and I would look at each other and say, 'It has to be.'" Redstone accused Malone of seeking a cable monopoly with Diller as the front man. Of Malone, Redstone said, "I respect him, but I don't fear him."

Diller took pains to deny that his attempted raid was a vendetta. "Our proposal had no emotional aspect other than the fondness I have for the ten years I spent at Paramount," he said. But in subsequent statements, he was all over the map in terms of his feelings for Davis. In October, *People* magazine quoted him on the subject: "We've had cordial relations for years," he said.

A Viacom executive remembered otherwise. "I was at a party once, and Diller and Mike Eisner, a couple of barracudas, were telling me what a mean son-of-a-bitch Davis was," he said. "Diller may be very talented, but Martin is not going to take it lying down."

In an interview that fall with Bryan Burrough (which later appeared in *Vanity Fair*) Diller waffled, "I didn't leave [Paramount Studios] because of Marty Davis. On the other hand, if Charlie [Bluhdorn] had lived, I'd probably still be there. . . . I don't think he's a bad guy or a sadist, he is just uncomfortable with people."

Diller's friends and colleagues had their own thoughts about the deal. David Geffen said, "Barry's always been interested in Paramount." Diane Von Furstenberg agreed with Geffen. "Barry's been dreaming of this for a long time; [Paramount was] the first mountain he climbed." Later, she added, "He's tough, but he's not a pig."

One friend, who preferred to remain anonymous, saw Diller's bid as his way to make a Hollywood comeback. "He misses it terribly. It's so difficult for him to be out of that loop." Another said, "He has the personality of a Ted Turner or a Rupert Murdoch. He's a visionary who wants power, influence, and the ability to change things. He wants to go down in history as having made a difference."

Joan Rivers, wary perhaps of badmouthing the CEO of QVC, where she was now peddling her own line of costume jewelry, seemed to have decided to forgive and forget. "I've mended fences. He is absolutely brilliant," she said. Another unnamed associate put it differently. "He's compulsive in his need to test himself against new challenges."

Herbert Allen quickly organized a round of meetings on Wall Street so that Diller could talk to stock analysts about the advantages of a QVC versus Viacom bid. Diller went on the offensive, harshly criticizing Paramount's executive officers for their lack of corporate strategy.

Larry Haverty, a Boston-based investment analyst of media stocks who worked at State Street Research and Management Company, attended one of Diller's presentations. He described to Christopher Byron of *New York* magazine the convincing case Diller made when he detailed Paramount's current management's inadequacies: disturbingly high staff turnover at Paramount's studio; underutilization of Madison Square Garden; too much money spent on television without adequate control over its distribution; a failure to establish Paramount as an important programming presence; a lax approach to investing the company's cash stockpile.

The real issue, however, was which was the better deal? QVC promised three times the cash at $30 a share, but the higher payout meant at least $3 billion in additional debt for Viacom/Paramount. On the positive side of the ledger were the strengths Diller himself brought to the equation.

Christopher Byron posed this question to *New York* readers: "But was he really worth more than the combined talents of the entire management team of Viacom? In fact," opined Byron, "the real appeal of Diller's offer was not so much his creative talents and managerial abilities as the distribution muscle of

Tele-Communications, Inc. (TCI) and its head, John Malone." He cited the *Wall Street Journal,* which called Malone the man "behind the scenes . . . pulling many of the strings."

Paramount's board met again on September 27 to weigh the two offers. Davis reminded board members that according to the original merger agreement, Paramount was not allowed to hold discussions with QVC unless QVC could prove that its proposal was financially sound. At the same time, Lazard Freres, Davis's hand-picked financial adviser, submitted its analysis of QVC's proposal.

On October 5, Diller provided the Paramount board with the evidence it needed to assess the financial viability of QVC's offer. That same first week in October, he attended a dinner in New York, accompanied by Von Furstenberg. What if he didn't win the battle for Paramount, he was asked. "I'll be sad," he conceded.

Von Furstenberg would also have good reason to grieve if Diller were to lose Paramount. A filing submitted in July to the Securities and Exchange Commission declared, "Arrow [Diller's personal holding company] has entered into a consulting agreement with Diane Von Furstenberg in which it agreed to pay Ms. Von Furstenberg 10 percent of any profits realized by Arrow upon the sale of common stock owned by Arrow."

Von Furstenberg preferred to let the filing stand at face value. "It's all very simple and there's nothing to discover. I was helpful in introducing him to QVC. We've been very helpful to each other." Still, there was no denying that a victory for Diller would mean big money in the bank for his favorite dress designer.

However Diller colored it, the general consensus was that winning Paramount would not only enable him to reclaim his crown as king of the mountain, but also to dethrone the man who had robbed him of that crown.

He had left his job as chairman of Twentieth Century-Fox because he wanted to head up a company that would have enough clout to launch a merger or LBO with a media giant when the opportunity presented itself. One of the reasons Diller landed at QVC instead of a more glamorous media company was because there he could be his own boss, instead of having to report to a Martin Davis or Rupert Murdoch. He was looking at the Holy Grail, the chance to run Paramount *and* be the boss.

Compelling business interests also spurred him to make a run for Paramount. Through his partnership with Malone and the Robertses, Diller owned cable interest on the electronic superhighway. If QVC merged with Paramount, Diller would instantly acquire the programming he needed to fill his cable channels. Through QVC, he owned the cable wire into one-quarter of all cabled homes in America, and Paramount owned the software that could provide programming for those channels.

Diller's key word for the deal was *interactivity.* "For us, investing in interactivity is part of our lifeblood," he declared. But by the time Diller had positioned himself for a takeover, Paramount was the only major studio left that could provide the sort of interactivity he was speaking of. Time Warner, Bertelsman, Sony, and News Corporation had snapped up all the other major studios. According to Frank Biondi, president and CEO of Viacom, the film studios "are the quintessential American dream machines, Everybody wants one."

In contrast to Diller, Redstone proclaimed that his goal was to create the "synergies" of a world-class media company by combining Paramount's film and publishing empire with Viacom's programming and distribution. Diller's reaction to that was, "Look, I'm not a great believer in the mostly meaningless usage of synergy." Synergy, he snapped, was just "another word for baloney."

Steven Rosen of the *Denver Post* seemed to agree with him. "In the entertainment industry," he wrote, "[synergy] is the ability to cross-promote product. . . . And the quest for the ultimate synergistic scenarios is fueling all the mergers and acquisitions. . . . But what synergy really is is hype."

Within a week of QVC's hostile bid, Viacom filed a delaying antitrust suit against TCI and QVC in federal court, claiming that the QVC bid represented an attempt by Malone to monopolize the cable-television market. That same week, Wayne Huizenga, chairman of Blockbuster Entertainment Corporation, the video rental giant, made a deal with Redstone to invest $300 million in Viacom's bid.

Redstone swore, "Short of a bullet going through me, this merger's going to take place." Inside another week, Redstone had an additional $1.2 billion investment from NYNEX®, the New York regional Baby Bell telephone company, (even though NYNEX was about to announce a year-end loss of $1.24 billion and was making plans to lay off 20 percent of its workforce.

Ted Turner had removed himself from the race on September 22 at a cable TV industry banquet. Standing side by side with Diller, he announced, "I'm calling it off temporarily." The other dealmakers speculated that Turner had been unable to line up the necessary financing. The media was hedging its bets on the two fighters already in the ring.

Writing in the *Los Angeles Times*, James Flanagan compared the combatants. "Diller is a brilliant employee, but Redstone, 70, thinks like an owner. . . . Redstone also has credibility in creating value [but] Diller is the only proven movie picker among the bidders for Paramount. . . . [Malone and Roberts'] plan is that Diller will be able to pick hit films, increasing the cash flow of Paramount."

On the same day, in the same paper, reporter Kathryn Harris credited Redstone with the greater momentum. "Redstone . . . has always vowed that he would remain the controlling shareholder of any merged company. Viacom's merger deal with Paramount would grant Redstone nearly 70 percent of the voting stock."

But Paramount's board, meeting on October 11, authorized Davis to meet with QVC. Diller had every reason to believe that with enough money in his war chest, he would soon be the man presiding over Paramount from the familiar surroundings of its executive suite. One thing troubled him, though. Diller had strategized for five months to achieve a takeover of Paramount, armed—or so he thought—with a powerful weapon, the guarantee of John Malone's financial backing. But recently, Malone had inexplicably stopped returning Diller's calls. It was as if he had slammed the door shut in Diller's face.

On October 12, just one day after Davis had been instructed to explore QVC's offer, TCI issued a stunning statement that would alter the course of Diller's hostile bid. Unbeknown to Diller, Malone had been secretly negotiating his own merger, which would completely overshadow the proposed Paramount-QVC combination. Malone was proposing to bring together TCI and Bell Atlantic in a $33 billion merger that would create the first mega-colossus of the new electronic age. At the press conference jointly called by TCI and Bell Atlantic, which hoped to acquire both TCI and Liberty Media, Malone declared that the QVC bid was "peripheral" to whatever he might do in the future.

Media observer Ken Auletta detected what he saw as nervousness in Malone. His hardball tactics were not always the wisest course for a man whose business was regulated by politicians sensitive to widespread anger and frustration over the public-be-damned attitude of the cable TV industry.

For a long time, telephone wires had not been allowed to carry television signals in competition with the cable wire and vice versa. Now, all that was about to change. Congress was considering letting the politically savvy telephone companies use the wire they owned to send TV signals; the cable companies would not be permitted to send voice messages through their wire. Aside from being vastly better at lobbying and public relations, the phone companies were far richer than the cable companies, who would have to make a huge investment to get in on the new information age technology.

Malone decided that instead of fighting the phone companies, he should join forces with them. "Eighteen months ago, I started telling Bob Magness and the board that I felt we had to do a strategic deal with a phone company or we were going to have serious problems long-term." Having secured their pro forma agreement, Malone got in touch with Ray Smith, the president of Bell Atlantic. It was an inspired move by Malone because Smith held some winning cards that Malone and his companies desperately needed, beyond the obvious issue of money.

To begin the negotiations, Smith suggested a couple of talking points for Malone to mull over and asked him to sign an agreement guaranteeing that they would both keep their discussions secret. Malone was either impressed, intimidated, undaunted, worried, or clever—depending on whom you talked to—but he was unreservedly enthusiastic about Smith and Atlantic Bell.

"The chemistry with Ray was terrific," according to Malone's version of their opening conversations. "The other guys are old school. There is no way companies like U.S. West would walk away from dividends. Ray was clearly a cat of a different color. Very entrepreneurial. He's a delightful guy. He's not the stiff three-piece suit."

A deal with Smith's Bell Atlantic would solve several problems for Malone: his adversarial relationship with Washington; TCI's need for a cash infusion; and his wife's demands for more time spent at home. Malone, who saw Smith as just the right person to run their merged companies, flat-out said as much to Smith.

Caught up in his own drama with Paramount, Diller was oblivious to all of Malone's machinations. One wonders whether he would have moved forward had he known what Malone was planning with Smith. As personally wealthy as he was, Diller still didn't have the kind of money necessary to make his own, independent deal with Paramount. He needed Malone to bottom-line the deal, and he had every reason to believe that Malone would continue to give him his support.

Diller had been very clear about his interest in using QVC to mount a hostile takeover of Paramount. Now, however, none of this seemed to matter to Malone. He had changed his mind about allying himself with Paramount in whatever configuration, and his allies and partners would have to fend for themselves.

Brian Roberts was deeply hurt by Malone's treatment of him and his father. He now faced a situation where a partner had betrayed him and his company to link up with what was bound to become a very rich and powerful competitor.

"I was disappointed on several levels," the younger Roberts told Auletta. "John was not upfront that he was talking to a phone company and might sell his company. Yet we were in the middle of ten-billion-dollar deal for Paramount that relied heavily on him. You can argue that Bell Atlantic was a thirty-three billion-dollar deal and he didn't want to risk it by telling us. But he could have indicated that something was up without revealing any details. Deep in my heart, I say he didn't trust us—or perhaps anyone—enough to take a chance."

Even while negotiating with Ray Smith, Malone continued to dicker and tinker with the deal to the point that Smith almost walked away from the bargaining table. Once they worked out a deal with each other—assuming such a thing were possible—they would have yet another hurdle to face. Because both companies were regulated by federal agencies, they would have to obtain government approval of their merger, which could take another year or so.

Marvin Davis had predicted to *Vanity Fair*'s Bryan Burrough that Malone would pull just such a maneuver. "You watch," he told the writer. "Malone will try and sell Barry down the river just like

I saw him doing to Turner." Diller was dumbfounded by Malone's perfidy. One of his friends said, "Barry was completely blown away. He felt betrayed. And he was devastated by Malone's statements."

Although he claimed that Malone had told him about the deal at least a week before the official announcement, Diller now found himself in the humiliating position of having to scramble to find other financial backing should Malone decide to withdraw from QVC's bid. TCI's merger with Bell Atlantic affected another aspect of the deal, as well.

Prior to Malone's bombshell, Diller had been holding discussions with another regional telephone company, BellSouth, about their potential participation in his QVC bid. The Atlanta-based telephone company had explored various ways to participate in the deal, alone or in conjunction with either Viacom or QVC. Eager to get a piece of Paramount's programming assets, BellSouth had warmed to a partnership with Diller and QVC. But with a major competitor, Bell Atlantic, thrown into the mix, their interest suddenly cooled.

Malone promised Diller that he would not withdraw his backing. He also offered to call and reassure BellSouth executives that his latest venture would have no impact on their participation, but the company started to drag its feet. "BellSouth may have taken unkindly to the idea of teaming up with QVC when that company's part-owner will be a Bell Atlantic-owned TCI," the *Wall Street Journal* commented.

Diller, no longer convinced that he could trust Malone, continued his search for new partners. Six days later, he hit paydirt when he secured an additional $1 billion in financing from Cox Enterprises, which also owned some cable franchises, and from Advance Publications. The battle progressed. On October 20, QVC delivered two thick binders of financial documents for Paramount's perusal.

Diller's bid still faced another hurdle. In 1988, Paramount's board had adopted a "poison pill" clause that would allow them to sabotage a hostile takeover by flooding the market with new Paramount securities, thus quickly devaluing the company. The poison pill could be invoked whenever anyone accumulated 15 percent or more of Paramount's outstanding common stock, or announced or commenced a tender offer. It was intended to protect Paramount against unsolicited two-tiered offers like QVC's. Diller argued that Paramount had relinquished the poison pill for Viacom, so QVC should be granted the same exemption.

Paramount's other protection against Diller's bid was the Termination Fee provision in the Viacom merger agreement. Also known as the "lock-up" provision, this required Paramount to pay Viacom $100 million and gave Redstone the option to acquire 20 percent of Paramount's stock if the deal fell through. The provision could cost Paramount up to $400 million if the merger was scrapped, thereby making Paramount less appealing to other takeover bids.

Viacom's offer cleared the standard antitrust review on October 21. That same day, QVC filed suit in the Chancery Court of Delaware, where Paramount, Viacom, and QVC were all incorporated, requesting a preliminary injunction to block Viacom's takeover. QVC argued that the provisions—the "lock-up guarantees"—included in Paramount's merger agreement with Viacom afforded Viacom an unfair advantage over any competing bids in the takeover battle. Just three days later, Viacom made a two-part, $9.6 billion tender offer for Paramount that was quickly approved by Paramount's board of directors.

Rumors were flying about the possibility of other suitors waiting in the wings. "While Diller and Redstone fight it out, a third party might swoop in," said Guy Wyser-Pratte, a New York stock trader. The leading candidates were said to be BellSouth and Southwestern Bell.

Viacom's tender offer became official on October 25, and QVC's was formally commenced two days later. Paramount insiders were beginning to grumble about Viacom's lower terms. To win, Redstone would have to up the ante. His bid ". . . has to be pretty damn close to Diller's," said a knowledgeable Paramount player.

But one unnamed Paramount adviser took a different view. He called Diller's offer "grandstanding," and pooh-poohed the value of QVC's offer. Diller, for his part, was pointing a finger at Paramount; the board was "demeaning" the company by not taking his offer seriously. "Our patience is at an end," he fumed. A Viacom director predicted, "This game will go on for months." Wyser-Pratte disagreed. "Diller has put Paramount under the gun."

On October 28, Diller sent a letter to Paramount in which he demanded "that negotiations begin immediately," and stated that QVC could "provide Paramount stockholders with the best deal." He also registered his objection that Paramount had failed to fulfill its fiduciary responsibility to shareholders because it hadn't met with QVC before signing an amended merger agreement with Viacom on October 24. Finally, he reiterated QVC's complaint from its Delaware court filing (i.e., that Paramount had favored Viacom by exclusively granting it special fees and concessions).

Donald Oresman responded by letter a day later, in which he stated that the proposed merger between Paramount and Viacom was "in the best interests of the companies and its shareholders, taking into account all factors, including your current proposal." Oresman nevertheless agreed to meet with QVC, "as we were before you precipitously started a tender offer."

The meeting was held on November 1, with Diller and Davis noticeably absent. No progress was made, but according to legal experts in the mergers and acquisitions field, the mere fact of attending such a meeting could eventually serve as a useful tactic for Paramount in the pending court case.

With Paramount stonewalling, Diller kept busy problem-solving on other fronts. Of major concern were the antitrust issues raised by the proposed Bell Atlantic-TCI merger, and the very real possibility of a prolonged Federal Trade Commission investigation that could adversely affect QVC's bid for Paramount. Diller resolved that point when he seemed to have persuaded BellSouth to buy out Liberty Media's $500 million interest in QVC, to cover an equal amount promised by Liberty, and to put up an additional $1 billion for the takeover battle. (BellSouth would be making the $2 billion investment just as it was about to announce a year-end quarterly loss of $276 million and plans to lay off 10,200 workers.) The arrangement would also help to resolve BellSouth's fears about investing in QVC if the Bell Atlantic-TCI merger received government approval and went forward, although Liberty would still retain 22 percent of QVC.

Geraldine Fabrikant of the *New York Times* commented that BellSouth's involvement would further benefit Diller because it would "help him break free from Mr. Malone's growing influence over the home-shopping channel. Mr. Diller very much wants to be his own boss; he was reportedly concerned that Mr. Malone's wishes for QVC were becoming increasingly impossible to ignore."

She also speculated that "if BellSouth enters the war for Paramount by acquiring Liberty's stake in QVC. . . . such a move would probably force Viacom to raise its bid. . . ." Her prediction was borne out when Viacom raised its offer on November 6 to $85 a share in cash for 51 percent of Paramount's stock, with a similar increase in the value of the securities. Meeting by telephone, Paramount's board decided to recommend the higher offer to its shareholders.

Despite the ongoing and tense negotiations with BellSouth, Diller took time off to attend the Bar Mitzvah of the son of his friend, Michael Ovitz, another William Morris mailroom alumnus who had moved on to become Hollywood's single most powerful agent and the chairman of Creative Artists Agency. Certainly, Diller was showing a zest for gamesmanship. Assessing his first attempt at a takeover, he declared, "I've matured as a businessman and no longer am creating bottlenecks by micro-management."

Industry analysts voiced questions as to how much higher the bids could soar. They were answered in part six days after Viacom's latest bid, when Diller raised QVC's offer to $90 a share, bringing the total value of his bid to $10.8 billion, compared with Viacom's $10.1 billion offer. A meeting was scheduled for November 15 for Paramount's board to consider QVC's offer, previous to which Donald Oresman sent board members a memo in which he detailed the "conditions and uncertainties" of the offer.

Davis and Oresman carried the day at the November 15 meeting. The board decided that QVC's new offer was, in fact, not in Paramount's best interests, that it was "excessively conditional" and not as strategically attractive as Viacom's.

Furthermore, as the decision rendered by the Delaware Supreme Court would later reveal, "the Paramount Board did not communicate with QVC regarding the status of the conditions because it believed that the No-Shop Provision prevented such communication in the absence of firm financing. Several Paramount directors also testified that they believed the Viacom transaction would be more advantageous to Paramount's future business prospects than a QVC transaction."

Diller's day in court was set for November 16. QVC, Viacom, and Paramount had each retained some of the most impressive names among New York's legal community to represent them before the Delaware Court of Chancery. QVC had hired the firm of Wachtell, Lipton, Rosen & Katz, and its case was argued by Herbert Wachtell, possibly the preeminent attorney in the area of mergers and acquisitions. Viacom had put its fate in the hands of Shearman & Sterling, with Stuart Baskin arguing its side of the case, and Paramount was represented by the equally prestigious "white shoe" firm of Simpson Thacher & Bartlett, with Barry Ostrager presenting on its behalf.

In his opening volley, QVC's lawyer, Herbert Wachtell, disclosed that in early July Paramount had rejected a Viacom bid that was somewhat better than the one it accepted in September. Wachtell's point was that Paramount had put itself up for sale only *after* hearing from John Malone that Barry Diller might pursue a hostile takeover of the company. He defined the merger as a sale because, he said, Viacom would end up with 70 percent of the two companies' votes, which would therefore constitute a transfer of control away from Paramount's shareholders.

Barry Ostrager responded for Paramount by making the argument that a merger with Viacom would constitute a "strategic alliance" rather than an outright sale. He said that Paramount had long been looking for such an alliance and had discussed a strategic partnership with approximately 30 companies. He also contended that the Paramount board had carefully considered the QVC offer and had made the right decision by turning Diller down.

Not so, declared Wachtell, saying that Paramount had refused to hold any concrete meetings with QVC, nor was there much paperwork that documented what had been discussed at its board meetings.

Commenting on the various arguments in the November 17 *New York Times,* Larry Cunningham, a professor at Yeshiva University's Cardozo Law School in New York, said that "QVC faced an uphill battle to prove that Paramount had been a sale." However, he noted, "that QVC might have better luck in showing that the board had not been fully informed and had not carried out its fiduciary responsibilities."

Whatever the outcome of the chancery court proceedings, it was generally acknowledged that the loser would take its case the next step up to the Delaware Supreme Court. "This is only a dress rehearsal," said one lawyer.

Davis, meanwhile, was biding his time. During an interview, he showed a reporter a draft for an "attack ad" he had considered using against Malone and his support of the QVC bid. The sketch, meant to conjure up *The Godfather,* one of Paramount's most famous films, showed a shadowy Malone manipulating puppet strings. Dangling at the bottom of one of the set of strings was Diller. "Great, isn't it?" Davis asked the reporter.

Diller sent Paramount a letter on November 19, informing the board that QVC had definitively secured the financing commitments it needed for its offer. The letter also assured them that his offer had passed the antitrust hurdle, and QVC was ready to proceed.

The same day, a QVC executive announced that the company "was a signature away from the bank agreement" with a group of banks led by Chemical Bank. "It is simply a matter of paying the commitment fees to the banks. It is not a question of whether the bank is willing to lend us the money and it is not indicative of someone having difficulty financing," he said.

The consensus on Wall Street was that QVC would have a better shot if it raised its bid again. Many in the financial community seemed to believe that the court would rule against QVC. Thus, said one trader who had been watching the case closely, "a new QVC offer has to be much stronger to force the board to deal with it."

As he awaited the court's decision, Diller acknowledged that if the court ruled against QVC, he would almost certainly forced to terminate his bid. The ruling was scheduled to be handed down on November 24, the day before Thanksgiving. That morning, in Los Angeles, Diller was feeling the tension. Needing a release for his anxiety, he jumped on his bicycle and went to work out at his gym. "I got bored silly," he said later, then corrected himself. "Not bored, crazy."

He checked his answering machine from a pay phone and picked up a message from Martin Lipton, Herbert Wachtell's partner. His heart racing, he returned Lipton's call. "We won," Lipton told him.

The preliminary injunction had been granted.

"Wow!" said Diller. At this moment of his greatest triumph, he was alone at his health club, except for the usual assortment of gym rats and trainers. "There was no one to tell!" he recalled.

Across the country in New York, a deeply shocked and disappointed Davis had to make a series of phone calls to inform Redstone and the other concerned parties. "I would not have figured it this way," he told one of his board members.

The Court of Chancery not only had decided in favor of QVC, it also had been very critical of how Paramount's board had conducted itself. As well, it chided Lazard Freres and Booz Allen for not having "provided the board with any information that would support quantitatively the conclusion reached by the board that a Paramount-Viacom merger would create higher long-term value than the QVC alternative."

Legal experts were surprised by the sweep of the decision expressed by Vice Chancellor Jack Jacobs, which nullified almost all the antitakeover provisions that Paramount had instituted on September 12. Paramount had put itself up for sale, declared Jacobs, and its board members had failed to perform its fiduciary responsibility. He particularly criticized the board's quick and poorly analyzed rejection of QVC's November 12 bid. He concurred with Herbert Wachtell's argument that the Paramount-Viacom merger constituted a sale, because control of Paramount would be transferred from the shareholders to Viacom.

Thus, Paramount was prohibited from using its "poison pill" and from taking any further action, including a modification of its stockholders' rights plan, that would advance the execution of Viacom's offer. Paramount was also forbidden from exercising any part of the September 12 Stock Option Agreement, and it was obliged to consider QVC's bid.

In his 61-page written opinion, the judge harshly scolded both management and board, stating, "Meeting with QVC was the last thing management wanted to do and by skillful advocacy, management persuaded the board that no exploration was required. Those are not the actions of a board motivated to inform itself of all available material information."

He was equally blunt-spoken when he declared, "The Paramount board is not permitting shareholders to choose between these two alternatives. [Viacom and QVC] Rather, by its selective deployment of the poison pill and other antitakeover devices to favor Viacom and disfavor QVC, the Paramount board would effectively force shareholders to tender into the lower-priced Viacom transaction. . . .

"What is at risk here is the adequacy of the protection of the property interest of shareholders who are involuntarily being made dependent upon the directors to protect that interest. . . .

"At stake here is a $1.3 billion difference between two competing proposals—value that would otherwise flow to Paramount shareholders. The directors claim that they are entitled to prevent the shareholders from receiving that value because the future incremental value of the Viacom combination will exceed that $1.3 billion. But the directors have not come forward with any quantitative valuation data to support that judgment."

Attorneys for Paramount and Viacom immediately filed an appeal on behalf of their clients in the Delaware Supreme Court. While they waited to hear whether their appeal would be accepted, Delaware Supreme Courts Chief Justice E. Norman Veasey addressed the three legal teams in conference, informing them that the court wanted "binding assurances" that neither Viacom nor QVC would alter or withdraw its bid. Both companies agreed to abide by his request.

"The shareholders have won at Paramount Communications, and judicial deference to the business judgment of directors has been knocked down another notch," declared Floyd Norris in his *New York Times* column "Market Watch," on November 28. "Cut through the verbiage of the Thanksgiving-eve opinion of Vice Chancellor Jack B. Jacobs, and it boils down to this: The Paramount directors sincerely believed that the best long-term interest of the shareholders was to merge with Viacom rather than QVC. That is a decision they are allowed to make, but only if it is reasonable.

"Unfortunately, Mr. Jacobs said, management and its investment bankers seemed to be more interested in completing the favored deal than in evaluating the alternatives, and so did not give the board the information it needed.

"'It is undisputed,' Mr. Jacobs wrote, that the board was not given 'any information that would support quantitatively the conclusion reached by the board that a Paramount-Viacom merger would create higher long-term value than the QVC alternative.'"

There was plenty of blame to pass around the next day at Paramount, as executives traded angry opinions as to whether the November 15 board meeting should have been delayed. One adviser asserted that he had told a member of the board to put the meeting off until after the court's decision. A Paramount executive refuted the claim, stating that a delay "was never suggested by a single solitary person. Such behavior would have been irresponsible," he said. "The board had an obligation to consider QVC's revised proposal and it appropriately did so." The official company line came from a spokesperson who huffed that the ruling was "wrong on both the facts and the law."

It was the board's behavior at the November 15 meeting that Judge Jacobs had faulted, and now Paramount was left with no recourse but to wait and see whether the supreme court would review its case. Many Wall Streeters were putting their money on Diller and QVC, but at least one investment banker sounded less certain. "It's not a slam dunk," he said. Another seemed to agree when he said, "In the end a lot will depend on what is in Barry and Sumner's heads, and no one can know that."

Even if the chancery court's decision were to be reversed by the supreme court, most people in the financial community were counting on both companies to up their offers. Several analysts polled by the *New York Times* felt that QVC was in a better position to put up more money. The question was left hanging as all concerned waited to find out whether there would be a rematch.

The sense of relief was almost palpable at 15 Columbus Circle when the court agreed on November 29 to hear Paramount and Viacom's appeal. But Liz Barron, an analyst with S.G. Warburg, said she believed that the chancery court ruling would be upheld, and that the two competing companies would have to increase their bids. "The onus for the next move is on the shoulders of Viacom," she commented. "It is hard to say if it will match QVC or top it."

The court set the oral arguments for December 9 and informed the attorneys that each side would have one hour to plead its case. As the date approached, tempers flared on both coasts. *Newsweek* took note of what writer Charles Fleming called "the war of words . . . in what has become the most interesting and acrimonious takeover battle in years."

Covering the battle in a December 6 article entitled "Barry Diller Scores at the Buzzer," Fleming reported, "Redstone has derided Diller as a jewelry merchant who would bring nothing tangible to Paramount. Diller, in an interview from his Malibu, California, home had few kind words for Viacom. 'The issue isn't whether you get *Beavis & Butthead* [a Viacom show] and can make a movie out of it,' Diller said. 'The great "strategic alliance" idea balances itself out by a whisker. Does [Viacom] have anything that Paramount can't otherwise get? They say yes. I say that ain't true.'"

On the eve of the supreme court hearing, a whole new issue suddenly surfaced. News accounts reported that WMS Industries, a Chicago-based company that produced pinball machines and arcade video games under the brand names of Bally and Williams, had purchased approximately 500,000 shares of Viacom stock between the end of September and mid-October. What made these purchases so controversial was that Sumner Redstone was WMS's biggest shareholder.

"It seems on the surface that an affiliated company was supporting Viacom's share price at a time when the share price was critical in valuing the return in Viacom," commented Jessica Reif, a media analyst with Oppenheimer & Company.

Her concern was echoed by another media analyst, David Londoner of Wertheim Schroder & Company, who said, "Here is a company, WMS, that apparently has no history of buying stocks, which then goes and buys Viacom at an unusual time. At the very least, it looks unusual."

Had the value of Viacom's stock, so crucial to the resolution of the merger, been manipulated by Redstone? QVC charged that WMS, acting on behalf of Viacom, had bought the stock to increase its value and thus sweeten the deal for Paramount. Viacom and WMS executives contradicted the allegation. Redstone, they said, had only just heard of the charge himself.

"We expect to prevail on appeal," Viacom had boasted after the Court of Chancery ruled against it. Their expectations were dashed on December 9, when the Delaware Supreme Court found in favor of QVC only several hours after the case had been argued before it. The court upheld the chancery court's invalidation of Paramount's attempts to scare off other prospective bidders and concluded that Paramount had failed to fulfill its duty to its shareholders by seeking the best possible deal.

"This is a stinging rebuke to the Paramount management and board for not taking shareholder rights seriously," commented

Professor Larry Cunningham of Cardozo Law School. "In recent years, Delaware courts have wavered between protecting management and supporting shareholders. This decision is clearly intended to support shareholder rights."

A front-page story in the *New York Times* called the ruling "a personal defeat for Martin Davis, chairman of Paramount, who has long been an adversary of his former employee, Barry Diller, chairman of QVC."

The Delaware Supreme Court's opinion which was written by Chief Justice Norman Veasey, was an unqualified win for QVC. The Court ordered Paramount to accept other bids and to pursue the best possible price on behalf of its shareholders.

The opinion also spelled out the responsibilities of Paramount's board, and the areas in which the board failed to live up to its fiduciary duties: "Since the Paramount directors had already decided to sell control, they had an obligation to continue their search for the best value reasonably available to the stockholders. This continuing obligation included the responsibility, at the October 24 board meeting and thereafter, to evaluate critically both the QVC tender offers and the Paramount-Viacom transaction. . . . We conclude that the Paramount directors' process was not reasonable, and the result achieved for the stockholders was not reasonable under the circumstances."

QVC was cited for having "persistently demonstrated its intention to meet and exceed the Viacom offers, and frequently expressed its willingness to negotiate possible further increases."

The court then went on to state "It should have been clear to the Paramount Board that the Stock Option Agreement, coupled with the Termination Fee and the No-Shop Clause, were impeding the realization of the best value reasonably available to the Paramount stockholders. Nevertheless, the Paramount Board made no effort to eliminate or modify these counterproductive devices, and instead continued to cling to its vision of a strategic alliance with Viacom."

Paramount's directors were particularly harshly reprimanded because, said the court, when they met on November 15 to "consider QVC's increased tender offer, they remained prisoners of their own misconceptions and missed the opportunities to eliminate the restrictions they had imposed on themselves. Yet, it was not 'too late' to reconsider negotiating with QVC. The circumstances existing on November 15 made it clear that the defensive measures, taken as a whole were problematic. . . . Nevertheless, the Paramount directors remained paralyzed by their uninformed belief that the QVC offer was 'illusory.'"

Viacom was not spared from being chastised by the court's judgment, which described the company as "a sophisticated party with experienced legal and financial advisors, [that] knew of (and in fact demanded) the unreasonable features of the Stock Option Agreement. It cannot be now heard to argue that it obtained vested contract rights by negotiating and obtaining contractual provisions from a board acting in violation of its fiduciary duties. . . . We reject Viacom's arguments and hold that its fate must rise or fall, and in this instance fall, with the determination that the actions of the Paramount Board were invalid."

Finally, the court concluded, "The realization of the best reasonable value available to the stockholders became the Paramount directors' primary obligation under these facts in light of the change of control. . . . Rather than seizing those opportunities [of QVC's unsolicited bid], the Paramount directors chose to wall themselves off from material information . . . and to hide behind the defensive measures as a rationalization for refusing to negotiate with QVC or seeking other alternatives. Their view of the strategic alliance likewise became an empty rationalization as the opportunities for higher value for the stockholders continued to develop."

Diller had watched the televised hearings from his QVC office. "It's hard not to be gratified by the court's decision," he told a reporter for the *New York Times* that night. "For three months we have argued consistently that we deserved a fair hearing. We started the process putting more money on the table. We ended putting more money on the table."

Davis was not talking for the record. But a statement issued by Paramount said that the company would cooperate with the decision. "We will promptly establish procedures applicable to all bidders for an orderly and fair process."

An auction date would have to be set by Paramount. And there was still the messy matter of Sumner Redstone's alleged purchases of Viacom stock through WMS that would have artificially inflated the price of the stock.

QVC, however, was now a legitimate contender, and by December 11 it had received notice from Paramount that a board meeting had been scheduled for December 13 to establish the ground rules of the auction. A Paramount executive, said to be "close to the board," told the *New York Times* that the meeting was expected to be "long and difficult."

Wall Street was predicting that Viacom would raise its bid. But Diller beat Redstone to the punch when he increased his offer on December 20 to $92 for 50.1 percent of the shares, the other 49.9 percent to be paid in securities, for a total value of $11 billion. By the time the closing bell rang that day on Wall Street, QVC's stock had slumped, making the bid worth only $10.2 billion, about even with Viacom's last bid in October.

The Paramount board endorsed Diller's bid the next day. Diller finally had his merger agreement. Viacom had until January 7 to counter with a higher offer or withdraw. Both sides had until February 1 to submit their final bids.

On a trip to the Caribbean island of St. Bart's on a rented yacht, Diller crunched the numbers and decided that Paramount wasn't worth a penny more than $10 billion in cash and stock. When he returned on January 3, he told his partners, "[Paramount] is, with a real stretch and some real hard work, worth what we've offered, but I'm not going to offer any more."

Viacom waited until its January 7 deadline to announce an $8.4 billion merger with Blockbuster Entertainment that enabled Viacom to raise its cash portion of the Paramount tender to $105 a share. Despite the sweetened offer, Wall Street continued to favor Diller, and the Paramount board also maintained its preference for QVC. A friend of Redstone's reported that as eager as Redstone was to win his prize, he was not prepared to overpay to achieve his goal. If Redstone couldn't win, said the friend, he would try to bluff Diller into overbidding for Paramount, then quietly leave him to pick up the overpriced pieces.

Viacom increased its offer again on January 18 to $107 a share for 50.1 percent of Paramount shares and stock, plus warrants and contingent value rights (CVR) or a "collar" for the remainder, bringing the total value to $9.56 billion. The blended bid averaged out to $82 a share in cash and securities, less than Diller's blended bid of slightly over $87 a share, but with more cash up front and a guaranteed floor. The collar secured the value of Viacom's bid at $12 a share if Viacom stock failed to reach a certain level within three years of the merger. The device was a two-edged sword that could cost Viacom an additional $1 billion if they had to make good on it—a very real possibility with Viacom stock dropping. To make up the difference, Viacom might have to issue more shares, devaluing their offer for Paramount.

With the collar as added incentive, the Paramount board switched sides and endorsed Viacom's bid on January 21. Diller sat on his $10.2 billion offer but threw in more cash and reduced the stock portion; he still offered less cash value for the Paramount stock than Redstone. Ignoring the pleas of his key advisers, he refused to follow Redstone's strategy and adopt a collar for his deal.

On February 1, the closing day of the auction, the closing market price of QVC's cash and stock bid was worth $10.6 billion, while Viacom's was worth $10.2 billion. However, Viacom's collar, which would protect Paramount shareholders, plus its pending merger with Blockbuster, gave Viacom the edge. Behind the frantic bidding, Paramount quietly recorded a $40 million loss for the quarter ending January 1994.

The future of Paramount was now in the hands of its stockholders who had two weeks to decide to which side they would tender their shares. Diller distracted himself during that period by attending the New York premiere of the critically panned *I'll Do Anything,* directed by James Brooks. After the screening, Diller was spotted at the concession stand, where Steve Martin, Kevin Kline, and Phoebe Cates were filling up on soda and popcorn. "Is it free?" asked Diller. A reporter for *Entertainment Weekly* quipped, "Guess working at QVC is rubbing off."

Polly Platt took a different view of Diller's appearance at the premiere during what had to be one of the most anxious weeks of his life. "We had this $50 million dollar flop, and Barry was right up there," she said. "He was very much at Jim's side and at the party afterwards. Most people in Hollywood run from failure."

Diller began telling friends that his bid for Paramount had been transformed into "the deal from hell." The last shots had been fired, the final salvos volleyed. There was nothing left to do except wait for the body count. The war officially ended at midnight on February 15. Most experts—and suddenly, *everyone* was an expert—felt the vote could go either way. Beyond the obvious issue of money, the choice lay between what media stock analyst Lisbeth Barron of S.G. Warburg & Co. called Viacom's "breadth of assets" which gave the company's bid "a psychological solidity" and Diller's assertion, as reported in the *Wall Street Journal,* that "he could wring more long-term value from Paramount's assets than Viacom" because he had a "track record for creating entertainment properties."

The shareholders were ultimately persuaded by the lure of the bottom line, rather than by promises of rosy things to come. When all the votes had been counted, Viacom emerged the victor, having garnered 75 percent of Paramount's stock to create what would be America's second-largest media empire. Redstone's telephone lines were tied up with messages from friends and colleagues, including Hollywood lobbyist Jack Valenti, Time Warner's Gerald Levin, and Tom Pollock, head of Universal Pictures, who called to applaud his achievement. "Congratulations on your glorious victory. From your fair-weather friends at MTV," said the card that came with the bottle of Veuve Clicquot champagne that was delivered to Redstone's office.

"Might Made Right," cried the front-page headline of *The Wall Street Journal* on February 26. The story boiled down to this: "The big guy won. . . . For all the talk of clashing egos and grand corporate alliances, it was sheer size and financial clout that determined the outcome of the $10 billion takeover battle for Paramount Communications, Inc." One investment banker, quoted in the *Journal* article, said that QVC's bid for Paramount "was like the minnow swallowing the whale."

QVC's year-end stock market value of $2.04 billion was not much more than a third of Viacom's $5.6 billion year-end stock market value. No one could deny, however, that the minnow had put up a hell of a fight. Asked about the conquest that had cost $2 billion more than his original offer, Redstone described the protracted battle as "cruel, abusive and sometimes ridiculous," adding, "It's a marriage made in heaven, dragged through hell on the way to consummation." On the other hand, he said of Diller, "There's no lingering ill-feeling. I consider myself a lover, not a hater."

Diller tried to shrug off the defeat. "Life is mistakes," he said. "We got into an auction. We stopped bidding. We take the consequences." But Redstone, still smarting from the financial wounds inflicted by Diller's bid, had the last word: "It isn't as if there's another Paramount. We got the last Paramount."

Martin Davis, who had launched and supported the merger with Viacom, and who had been assured by Redstone in September that he would be CEO of Paramount/Viacom, soon learned that he had no future role in the new company. "You may look forward to hearing from me a great deal in the future," he tersely announced to his staff. The day after the auction, Viacom's stock fell sharply, reflecting the over-priced cost of the merger. (Ironically, QVC's stock rose.) Redstone had his work cut out for him, beginning with Paramount Pictures, whose two recent Christmas movies, *Wayne's World 2* and *Addams Family Values*, had both failed to live up to the studio's expectations.

The big question, both on Wall Street and in Hollywood, was what lay ahead for Barry Diller. In the immediate aftermath of a major professional setback, all he would commit to was that he intended to build his QVC kingdom into multimedia empire. "Down and Out in Beverly Hills? Get Real," scoffed *BusinessWeek*, analyzing the fallout. Peter Dekom, a Hollywood lawyer, predicted, "Clearly, Barry Diller is going to be at the top of a lot of lists" of people hoping to find partners to initiate entertainment industry takeovers.

Diller refused to fuel the conjecture, except to say, "We're not going to discuss it at any time until an opportunity presents itself that we think is worthwhile." He admitted that QVC had "lost time" because of his involvement in the takeover fight, but the company was still in good health, with a positive prognosis for future growth and expansion.

"One of the things I learned long ago about auctions," Diller said, "was that it's not about ego or talent. It's simply about raising your hand for the next bid. . . . We went for five months tilting at this windmill. There will be others. . . . They won. We lost. Next!"

17

Breakfast at Tiffany's

The Bid for Black Rock

"Even in defeat, Mr. Diller's star is shining bright," said *The Wall Street Journal* the day after Viacom was declared the winner in its bid for Paramount. As the weeks passed, and Diller labored to clean up the messes left uncared for while his energies had been absorbed in the takeover battle, the guessing game continued: What media giant would become the next object of Diller's desire? NBC, MCA, and Time Warner were all considered likely candidates. A Diller adviser, affecting Diller's oblique style of self-expression, would say only, "You have to be opportunistic about these things."

Until the next great opportunity came knocking at his door, Diller's immediate agenda focused on a possible merger with rival Home Shopping Network, the still pending $500 million investment by BellSouth, and the nature of John Malone's involvement in QVC. And then there was the matter of CBS. . . .

Diller and Laurence Tisch, the 71-year-old chairman of CBS, had been exploring a CBS-QVC merger even before the final results were in on Paramount. The main sticking point was the $6 billion price tag for an all-cash purchase that Tisch had hung on CBS. It seemed unlikely that Diller could raise anywhere near that amount.

But the idea of a Diller-CBS matchup stayed with Tisch, who had known Diller since 1974, when Diller was at Paramount and Tisch was chairman of Loews Corporation movie theaters. They had first discussed network television and programming in the spring of 1986. Tisch, then in the process of buying a 25 percent stake in CBS, wanted to educate himself about the entertainment industry and journeyed to Hollywood to pick the brains of top executives.

Six months later, Tisch was elected chief executive officer of CBS. He was an odd choice to head up a network. The son of Eastern European immigrants, Tisch and his brother Robert grew up in the Flatbush section of Brooklyn. He graduated from New York University, served in the Army during World War II, then dropped out of Harvard Law School after his first semester to work for his parents who had just opened a hotel in Lakewood, New Jersey. By the late 1960s, he and his brother had parlayed their experience in hotel management into a chain of luxury hotels and resorts in Atlantic City, Manhattan, and southern Florida.

Early on, Tisch developed a name for being a shrewd and tough-minded negotiator. His first foray into Wall Street occurred in 1958, when he bought stock in Loews Inc., a group of 102 movie theaters that had just been spun off from Metro-Goldwyn-Mayer. He quickly developed an avid appetite for finding undervalued companies that could be bought on the cheap. A year later, he and his brother controlled 28 percent of Loews and had become involved in the day-to-day management of the company's assets and operations; he was elected chairman of the company in 1960.

Seven years later, the Tisch-controlled Loews Corporation owned 108 movie theaters, 12 hotels and motels, and had earned $15.8 million in profit for the most recent fiscal year. As the 1960s drew to a close, Tisch decided to diversify his business acquisitions, beginning with the Lorillard Corporation, a manufacturer of cigarettes. From there, he moved on to insurance company stocks, savings and loans associations, the Federated Department Stores and, in 1979, the Bulova Watch Company.

A devoted husband and father, Tisch and his wife Billie raised their four sons to work hard and be mindful of money. Andrew and Jimmy followed their father into the family business; Tommy devoted himself to managing the Tisches' finances and philanthropic ventures; Daniel went to work on Wall Street, first at the investment banking firm of Salomon Brothers, then at the arbitrage firm he established in 1989.

At the start of the Reaganomic Wall Street go-go era of the 1980s, Loews' annual revenue was $3 billion, an increase of 30 times what it had been 10 years earlier. Midway through the decade, at the urging of his son Daniel, Tisch began buying stock in CBS, and it was then that he first talked television with Diller. Eight years later, while Diller was trying to keep his hand in the Paramount merger game, they were still pursuing the subject.

CBS had just achieved its best fiscal year in its history, with profits of $326 million. It had also just completed its third year in a row as the front-runner in prime-time ratings, thanks to such hits as *Murphy Brown* and *60 Minutes*. To complete its year of triumph, it had scored a hat trick in the preceding television season by winning not only the prime-time ratings race, but daytime and late night, as well. The network could also point with pride to its most recent—and very expensive—addition to its lineup in the person of David Letterman.

It had suffered a significant blow to the corporate ego, however, in December, 1993, when the upstart Fox Network had nabbed the rights to televise the National Football League games. NFL football had been a CBS fixture for 38 years, but the network was losing up to $150 million a year on the deal, and Tisch refused to match what he considered Fox's inflated price for the franchise.

There were other problems to be faced at Black Rock, as the network's New York headquarters at Sixth Avenue and 52nd Street was known. CBS's hit shows were losing ground in the ratings race. The *CBS Evening News,* once the domain of the venerable Walter Cronkite and now anchored by Dan Rather, regularly alternated between second and third place. Tisch was criticized for getting rid of the network's nonbroadcasting divisions, including the lucrative CBS Records and regional cable sports networks, and investing the money from the sales in Treasury bills rather than expanding into other areas of the industry. Recently, he had become the butt of Rush Limbaugh's scorn, when Limbaugh had talked about "the three major networks—four, if you count CBS."

He was also being faulted for resisting the lure of cable TV. The other three networks had already taken the plunge by buying shares of cable channels, but Tisch was wary of the changes in the telecommunications industry. In the summer of 1993, when the networks lost a battle to force cable channels to pay for the rebroadcasting of network programming, Tisch questioned the wisdom of purchasing a cable channel. Howard Stringer, Tisch's hand-picked choice for president of CBS Broadcasting, repeatedly spoke out about the strength of broadcasting and network television, in contrast to cable broadcasting.

"That was a disaster," Tisch said, referring to the fight for cable fees. "We are at a loss as to what the cable industry does want, short of our abject surrender."

Tisch was growing increasingly tired of an industry that "once again was showing its proclivity for a lack of spending discipline." He felt frustrated with what he saw as an illogical approach to the economics of running a network, as exemplified by Fox's retail price purchase of the NFL package.

What he badly needed in the early spring of 1994 was a graceful way to leave CBS. But first he had to find a worthy heir to replace him, someone who could restore the luster to the once-gleaming Tiffany network, so-called because of its former spare-no-expense policy of elegance and generosity.

It was Danny Tisch who set the ball in motion. "The genesis of the deal was during the course of the Paramount-QVC-Viacom fiasco," he told Christopher Winans, a former *Wall Street Journal* reporter and a biographer of Tisch. "During that period, I spoke to Marty Lipton [Diller's attorney and an old friend of Tisch's] who was representing QVC and said, 'If you think that's attractive, you should take a look at CBS. I can't believe Paramount is worth anywhere near these numbers. You ought to be able to do a transaction at CBS.'"

Most people in the industry expected Diller to bide his time before he made his next move. That didn't stop the Diller-watchers from gossiping about his future plans. One rumor appeared in George Rush's April 1 "People" column in the *New York Daily News:* "Media mogul S.I. Newhouse is said to be quietly exploring a takeover of Time Warner Inc. with the help of CAA shotgun Michael Ovitz," wrote Rush. "One potential partner might be Barry Diller, the QVC chief who's already contemplating his own assault on the company."

Was it true, or just an April Fool's joke on the media industry? Said Rush, "Diller, who hopes to put his QVC programming on the interactive network TW is developing, has roundly denied having grander designs."

The next month, Diller spoke to Don West and Mark Berniker of *Broadcasting and Cable.* Diller, who was hailed by his interviewers as among "the half-dozen individuals who have had the greatest influence on television in the last decade," sounded like

a man who had fully committed himself to QVC and the cable culture. "Right now most people look at home shopping and say,
'Crummy, down market, zircons, dolls,' etc., And the visual image
of home shopping is somewhat poor. The work that my company
can do over the next couple of years is to change that," he declared.

As usual, he was disconcertingly vague when asked to spec-
ulate about the future of the communications industry. "I think
the picture is murkier," he said. "We've made enough progress to
know some of the words now. Like information superhighway, in-
fobahn, roadkill, on ramps, off ramps—all tasked to a technology
that's not there yet. It's even more misleading when it's real than
when it was just a big rosy piece of hype."

Invoking the buzzwords of the technocrats he had decried to
Ken Auletta little more than a year before, Diller spoke of "coaxial
cable compression," "telephony," "telcos," and "smart agenting."
Asked to define the latter, he replied, "We mean a service that in
short order will know the areas of your interest, your pocketbook,
your disciplines, and will act as a filter to bring you goods and services you would not be able to get any other way. We believe that
what a computer does that is of use to a normal person is to act as
their homework helper, which is what a smart box, i.e., a computer, can do with today's technology."

QVC was already in the midst of developing a "smart agent"
network called Q-online, to be transmitted via a PC modem.
Diller's estimates of the service's potential audience made QVC's
present viewership look positively anemic. "There are probably
a solid four million people who use online services on a regular
basis and another couple of million who use them a little bit," he
gloated. "And then there are several million more who access via
the Internet."

Diller also seemed to have given considerable thought to the
role of the so-called "smart TV" as opposed to the PC. He anticipated computers becoming ever more user-friendly. "Eventually

the computer's going to come up and the television set's going to come down, and they'll meet in the middle," he said. In the scenario he favored, the typical home would have a computer "with a relatively small screen that you'll task as a workstation kind of environment. But the majority of people will be . . . watching and accessing and interacting with a large-screen television tasked to a smart box, tasked to a pipe with huge data capability, two-way."

Reminded that market penetration by the cable industry was holding at less than 65 percent, Diller predicted that the number would rise to over 90 percent once the cable companies resolved their hardware problems. He foresaw two wires coming into each home—"a telco twisted pair and a cable coax. The result will be we'll have real competition, video and telephone competition."

As for what *his* next step might be, and what he foresaw for the future of television, Diller took the Zen approach of being in the moment: "I can't comment on what's next. Because I think you should comment on what is, not what will be." And then, suddenly, he shed some light on his thoughts about where he saw his place in the industry.

"My interests are to be involved in as many aspects of media as are available and interesting. And I'm not talking about retailing. I do not . . . plan and I haven't heard anything that says to me that electronic retailing . . . is the further definition, widest definition of television that I'm going to engage myself in. It's the narrowest. . . . I'm not by any degree making a judgment about it because I think it can be great and a huge business. . . . But the definition of my interest goes way beyond electronic retailing."

His statement of intent was as clear as if he had hired a plane to skywrite it for everyone to read. And in case anyone missed the message, he spelled it out even more bluntly in QVC's 1993 annual report. "We will continue to look at the world of multimedia with prudent but eager interest," he said. If a worthwhile acquisition made itself known, "we will pursue it aggressively."

293

As for the Paramount episode, "We thought it was a onetime opportunity to acquire a remarkable group of assets that were undermanaged. When the price, in our opinion, proved too high, we passed."

Despite the costs of the takeover battle, the company was in good shape. Revenues had risen 14.2 percent to $1.22 billion in 1993. But the stock had dropped over 20 points since the tender offer had been defeated, down to 29¼ by mid-May.

On his wish list for the future of QVC: "Growing ever faster" by means of various new projects that would "put the QVC stamp on electronic retailing and all its natural offshoots throughout the world."

Diller reiterated his "smart agent" theme at the Promax and Broadcast Designers Association conference, held in New Orleans during the first week in June. "When we find an easy, national way to send information back and forth that is powered by a smart computer, we'll open up the world," he said. "We won't go from 70 channels to the 500 that scare you, but to one channel. One that accesses thousands of possibilities and opportunities."

QVC was a primitive template for what the future of communications promised. The home shopping network had "almost converged the television, the computer, and two-way communications." Rival technologies, media hype, and the industries themselves were to blame for stalling the development of the hardware that could elevate the convergence of the systems to their next level.

Each of the players "has a different view of his place in the communications hierarchy," he said. "Computer nerds think . . . Hollywood has to move to Silicon Valley because entertainers need computer expertise. Moviemakers think they'll be the real winners, since they know how to reach mass audiences. The telephone companies with their massive switching capacity and cash flow remain convinced that they'll come out on top. And cable executives are afraid they won't."

Sounding like the spokesperson for a motivational tapes infomercial, Diller urged industry executives to "plunge in. Get confused. Embrace the technology."

Consciously or not, he had neglected to mention the television networks. Yet they were guilty of the same hubris evidenced by the other members of the communications industries. And Laurence Tisch was in the forefront of those least likely to embrace the technology. Nevertheless, he was already deep into discussions with Diller about a CBS-QVC merger.

"I'm not selling," Tisch insisted on June 2. "One of the reasons I find this a very interesting business is because it's so dynamic." But he was still reeling from the recent defection to Fox of eight affiliates, including two major market stations in Detroit and Atlanta.

Whether he was playing coy or being legalistic, he was determined that the transaction between CBS and QVC not be perceived as an auction that was open to all comers. Nor did he want the deal to be subject to a long, drawn-out FCC investigation, which was why the proposal stressed that there would be no "change of control." The key was to position the deal in such a way that it could be defined as a "strategic alliance" and thereby preclude his having to consider the merits of other offers. Diller had taken Paramount and Viacom to court in part to demolish their claim to a strategic alliance; now he had to hope that no other suitors would surface to do the same to him.

Martin Lipton worked closely with Diller and Tisch to structure the merger. Most of the details were hammered out by June 10. The deal would be worth $7.1 billion, with CBS shareholders to receive a cash dividend of $175 a share. Tisch would own 53.6 percent of the new company, which would be called CBS. QVC shareholders would own 46.4 percent, and they would get a combination of common and nonvoting preferred stock. The Loews Corporation, 31 percent of which was owned by Tisch and his family, would come out with approximately 10 percent of the new company. Diller would have a 4.7 percent stake and a seat on CBS's board of directors; he would also be named CEO and president, while Tisch would remain as chairman for no more than two years.

Lipton's formula provoked great enthusiasm in the Tisch camp. "Marty came up with this new structure and sat down with my father and myself and Jimmy at Loews and went over the new proposal," said Danny Tisch, "and we could find nothing wrong with it."

Diller gave it his nod of approval as well. Toward the end of June, he went to a dinner party in Manhattan where he was pestered with queries about what he planned to do next. "I'm onto something," was all he would say. Also present at the party were Don Hewitt, executive producer of CBS's *60 Minutes,* and Hewitt's wife, reporter Marilyn Berger. "Barry, you really should come around the show more often," said Berger. Diller grinned slyly. "Oh, I'll be around," he said.

That same week, he was named to the Television Academy Hall of Fame, along with other TV notables, including Oprah Winfrey. For Diller, said a friend, the honor was tantamount to "being embalmed." He wasn't quite perceived as a has-been, but he was still stuck in Pennsylvania, spinning fantastic tales of what could be to anyone who would listen. He craved an arena that would return him to the vanguard of the entertainment industry and give him the means to make his dreams reality. CBS appeared to be the perfect solution.

The next step would be to discuss the deal with, and get the support, of Brian Roberts. But a leak to the media ruined the plan. On June 29, Jimmy Tisch was informed by the CBS newsroom that the Associated Press had run an item reporting rumors about a possible merger with QVC. Moments later, a call came in from the *New York Times,* seeking confirmation of the story.

There was no choice but to call a news conference for the next day, at which Diller and Tisch jointly discussed "a possible business combination." Tisch made sure to mention that "Barry will be the boss." The press release quoted Tisch as saying that the merged companies would be "devoted to the creation of first-rate original programming."

Although the two men talked about a strategic merger and synergy, when pressed to define what that synergy and strategies might be, Diller would only comment, "There are some here for sure; I don't know where they are yet. To say now would be an idiot's game." However, he added, there would be no home shopping shows on CBS. "The goal isn't to fudge them together."

Diller made an effort to show a friendly face to some of the people he hoped would soon be working for him. He telephoned Dan Rather, and later, accompanied by Howard Stringer, paid a visit to the CBS broadcast offices on 57th Street. That night, David Letterman made the merger the subject of his Top Ten list, which featured "Ways CBS will be different after merging with QVC." Number ten on the list was this line: "You know that stopwatch on *60 Minutes*—It's yours for $49.94!'" Relentless as always, Letterman quipped, "Goodbye Tiffany network, hello Kmart network."

While America was laughing at Diller and Tisch's expense, the press was excitedly touting the merger. The *New York Times* declared, "Diller's Comeback Stuns But Hardly Surprises." In a generally laudatory article, Diller was described by Joe Roth as "the most forthright, brilliant, strong-headed person I've ever met in my life. He's thoughtful, mercurial, and suffers fools with as short a fuse as anyone I've ever met." Jeffrey Katzenberg went even further. "Even in the hyperbole of Hollywood, where there's a new flavor every week, Barry is in a league in which he does not really have any peers."

A few lone voices wondered whether Diller's often testy and imperious management style would fly at CBS. Lest Diller's reputation for ruling like a despot go unnoted, *The Wall Street Journal* described an incident that had occurred at QVC, where workers were unaccustomed to the temper tantrums that Hollywood took for granted. At Diller's request, a QVC employee had brought to his office a tray of rings that Diller wanted to show to some guests. "That's not what I wanted, you idiot!" Diller shouted. "I'm not an idiot!" the hapless employee shot back.

Both companies' stock jumped 19 percent that day. Stock analyst Christopher Dixon of PaineWebber saw advantages on both sides of the deal. "They are saving each other," he said.

But some in the industry were surprised by Diller's choice of partner. Less than 18 months earlier, he had remarked that owning a network "would be fun. But even as I say it, I bore myself." Since then, he had predicted that television would be led into the next century "by the cable systems." Why then, asked the cynics, would he want to sell himself to a network?

Perhaps his failed bid for Paramount had taught him a lesson in humility. Now he was extolling broadcasting as "a huge growth business." There were definitely growth opportunities for QVC inherent in the merger. The annual increase of the company's revenues had declined by 50 percent since the first quarter of 1993. A large part of that drop was attributed to startup costs for new home shopping ventures in Mexico and the United Kingdom. "Can We Shop?" a show hosted by Joan Rivers for QVC, had lost the company $831,000.

The company's net revenues had risen only 8.4 percent during the first quarter of 1994, with only 1.1 million new subscribers joining the network. The 4.3 percent growth rate was lower than it had been the previous two years. Penetration of the American market had reached 80 percent of all homes wired for cable. Was it any wonder that Diller was eager to piggyback QVC onto CBS's ability to reach of over 90 million homes?

Another plus was that the demographics of CBS's audience—upscale, with money to spend—were perfect for QVC's new, higher-priced Q2 (with Diane Von Furstenberg as creative planning director) and on Q shopping services. (Though retailers who had viewed tapes of Q2's programs gave them mostly negative reviews.)

There was also the possibility of airing QVC programs on CBS, either during prime time in place of advertising, or at off-peak hours. Or the shopping network could tie in its merchandise with a specific programming event, the precedent for which had been set when QVC sold $250,000 of soccer-related items on ESPN after a World Cup soccer match.

An executive with Malone's TCI described one scheme that could have been the stuff of Diller's fantasies. "Think about running a 30-second ad after a top-rated show like *Northern Exposure.* The ad says, 'Anything you just saw on the show we can sell it to you.' Then selling on TV gets interesting."

As for CBS, the company "had to do something to break out of the doldrums," said Christopher Dixon. "With this move they enter the modern age—albeit laughing, kicking, struggling, and crying. They are now where they need to be to be able to compete in the rapidly developing broadcast world of the '90s."

A merger with QVC would bring to CBS the one very important element it was missing—leadership. Tisch was a superb manager and trader, and he had diligently studied the television industry. But he had come to it as an outsider, and he lacked the feel for and fascination with programming in all of its many facets that CBS needed to drive its engine into the next century. "It's that vision thing," said Harold Vogel of Merrill Lynch. "His idea of a vision is another year of winning the ratings war, and that's it. That's not the way you grow a network."

Diller, on the other hand, seemed to have been born with a passion for programming. He had been trading in the creative market, conceiving and exchanging ideas since he was 20 years old, and he came with a blue ribbon seal of proven experience. "CBS will now be looking for results, said a cable executive who was familiar with the specifics of the proposed merger. "It's a risk, but one Barry knows well."

Bishop Cheen, an analyst with Paul Kagan Associates, gave high marks to a Diller-led CBS. "Diller will create synergy by wearing three hats," he said. "Number one, the network hat, and there he's a Hall of Famer. Two, the programming hat: He will create good and cheap programming. And third, merchandiser—a hat that has never been worn at CBS with any great authority. He'll merge two favorite American pastimes: shopping and watching TV."

"He's probably the one executive that just about everybody in the industry would salute," declared Larry Gerbrandt, Cheen's colleague at Paul Kagan Associates.

With Diller installed in the executive suite, Tisch could clean out his desk knowing he had left the company in excellent hands. He could say goodbye to Black Rock without being faulted for his choice of successor.

Harold Vogel called the QVC merger, "Tisch's exit strategy." Acknowledging Tisch's dilemma because of the leadership void that existed at CBS, Vogel said that Tisch "was having a problem closing out. This is one way of solving that problem."

Tisch's colleagues in the broadcasting industry agreed. "I think it's a very shrewd exit for Larry," said NBC's president, Robert Wright. "If he had simply announced that the company was going to issue a $175 a share dividend—equal to sixty percent of the market value of CBS—people would have said, 'The company is going nowhere. There is no vision. There is no future.' By combining his taking out a huge dividend and gluing on QVC, he gives it a sense of a future and takes away the sting. The market is happier with Barry Diller glued on."

The dividend would be huge, indeed. Assuming the deal went through, Loews would walk away with $550 million profit in pure cash and still keep a stake in CBS that was roughly estimated to be $700 million. One expert in the mergers area, quoted in *The Wall Street Journal,* called the deal a "creative way for Mr. Tisch to harvest the majority of the market value of his stock in cash at a time when CBS is under siege."

Tisch held yet another trump card in Diller. QVC's chairman was probably the single person in the industry most capable of revitalizing CBS's legitimacy in the eyes of its all-important affiliates. The timing could not have been better or more crucial. For all the networks, the upcoming fall television season was shaping up to be one of the most contentious that industry veterans could recall. Local stations in at least 12 markets were planning to shift their affiliations, which could cause no end of confusion for viewers trying to find shows that were suddenly appearing at a new place on the dial. Time Warner and Paramount were planning to launch their own networks by January. Some analysts were predicting that the ABC prime-time lineup was strong enough to displace CBS, the leader for the past three years.

During his years at Fox, Diller had ruffled more than a few affiliate feathers because of what had been viewed by many stations owners as his cavalier approach to their needs. Nevertheless, his reputation as a CEO who could deliver the ratings and his particular genius for programming could not help but benefit CBS's attempts to find new affiliates, at the very least to replace the eight it had lost.

"Are you going to walk away as an affiliate when Barry Diller is about to come on board?" John Reidy, an analyst with Smith Barney, asked rhetorically. "I think his arrival stops the hemorrhaging on that score."

Sunbeam Television Corporation, which owned WHDH in Boston, had planned to switch its allegiance from CBS to Fox. But the company started having second thoughts after the merger was announced. Its Miami station, WSVN, had moved from NBC to Fox during Diller's tenure there and had developed into the market leader in terms of profits.

Sunbeam's executive vice president, Robert Leider, was circumspect about whether WHDH would be moved. "We're still studying the situation," he said, then went on to admit that the presence of Diller "adds another element to it." He was more outspoken in his appraisal of Diller, calling him "one of the most brilliant people in broadcasting today," who "understands the importance of affiliates."

Tisch, speaking in May at CBS's affiliate meeting, had declared that the network had "just begun to fight." The affiliates sounded more convinced now that Diller would be coming on board to lead them into battle. One CBS executive described what he called an "ongoing lack of comfort" on the part of the affiliates with Tisch's nonbroadcasting background. "Everyone is anxious to hear from Mr. Diller about what he sees for the affiliate-network relationship," said Bill Sullivan, the chairman of the CBS affiliate board and president of KPAX in Missoula, Montana.

CBS's head of affiliate relations, Anthony Malara, said that Diller was "not at all swayed" by the encroachment on broadcasting's territory that cable services had been making of late. But the competing networks professed concern about a union between the two species.

"The fact that a significant block of ownership is in the hands of cable operators is dangerous and should not be permitted," said an ABC official. Robert Wright of NBC took a more judicious tone when he commented, "It certainly scares a lot of people here."

For the most part, however, reactions within the industry were positive, and it was generally agreed that the merger was a blessing for all concerned. "Here you put together two companies that seemingly were in trouble," said one television executive. "QVC is basically a single great executive with an asset that has no future. CBS is a great asset with a great future but an executive that has no vision. So it was a perfect marriage."

A similar assessment came from Mario Gabelli, an investor in media properties who was also a Paramount shareholder. Gabelli said, "I think it's a good deal for everybody. Tisch gets away from CBS, and Diller gets the opportunity to enlarge an asset."

When Tisch and Diller were jointly interviewed for an article that appeared in the July 1 *Wall Street Journal,* Tisch skirted the issue of what Diller might do to expand the scope of CBS's influence. "Barry is going to be the boss here. He's going to run the company," was all he would say. As for himself, "I've enjoyed it immensely," he said, referring to his eight years with CBS. "It's time to move on. I might have stayed longer if a person like Barry Diller hadn't come along. I wanted to make sure the future is ensured. This is the perfect timing for me."

He also engaged in some fence-mending with his long-time opponent, John Malone, against whom he had often testified in Washington regarding the demands of the cable industry. Mindful that Malone, through his 13 percent interest in QVC, would have a 4.8 percent share of CBS, Tisch told the *Journal,* "I think John Malone is brilliant. Very smart, but tough."

One of Diller's former employees was more specific when he addressed the question of Diller s plans for the network. "He'll use CBS as he uses QVC. Barry has a big dream. He'll use this as a step, not as the end of the game. He'll buy a studio. He'll buy a publisher." Although Diller maintained that he would not go on a firing spree, others predicted that he would slash overhead and initiate a round of cost-cutting that would inevitably lead to jobs being eliminated.

In a conversation with Ken Auletta of *The New Yorker,* Diller emphasized program production as the area in which he hoped to expand CBS's activities. "I tend to speed up everything," he said.

"My tendency is to go faster rather than slower." And although CBS had considered, then rejected a plan to start a cable news service the previous fall, Diller was also looking forward to competing with CNN by developing an around-the-clock news operation. "I think that the news divisions are underutilized. All of them. They have really remarkable resources."

Both Diller and Tisch were anxious to see the merger go forward, but the stakes were far higher for Diller. Tisch could always find another buyer for CBS. Diller would have no choice but to return to QVC to consult his shopping list, which kept getting shorter, for the next media opportunity in which he could invest his future.

"We got the last Paramount," Redstone had jeered, but a network was the next best thing—perhaps even better. Diller was "more excited now than he was when he was trying to buy Paramount," said David Geffen. "I've never heard him like this. He said to me recently, 'This is my destiny.'"

If such were the case, his fate could hang on the court's determination as to whether CBS was for sale. Tisch continued to reiterate his position about the merger, reciting as if it were his mantra, "This company will not be shopped. This deal will not be shopped. We are not selling. We are simply merging two companies, and it's a genuine merger."

Many Wall Street analysts, however, disagreed. "CBS is clearly in play," said Bruce Thorp, an analyst with PNC Bank. "This deal implies that it's open to all comers." Raymond Katz, an analyst with Lehman Brothers, concurred with Thorp. "The company is definitely in play," he maintained. "CBS has essentially said it is very amenable to going out and doing a business combination, changing its ownership and capital structure."

Others talked about the unduly low price tag, suggesting that the company was worth $400 a share, not the $336 per share value at which the QVC offer priced out. *Time* magazine reported on July 11 that Diller's adversary, Marvin Davis, "could find a CBS deal seductive," but Tisch vowed that "he would never sell his stock to Davis."

Other reports mentioned Disney as a possible CBS suitor. Because of the antitrust issues raised by a studio's purchase of a network, Disney would have to get government approval, a long and potentially fruitless process. Nevertheless, Diller took the rumors seriously enough that he called his old friend Michael Eisner to ask if he was interested. Eisner led him to believe that Disney would stay out of QVC's way. But when queried by Ken Auletta about whether he thought Eisner might try to steal his prize, Diller equivocated. "I don't know. I hope not. It's tough for any studio to do."

But not so tough that he wasn't worried. "I'll make it as difficult as I can," he threatened. Then he turned philosophical. "If we get another bid, we get another bid."

Richard Corliss, in a *Time* magazine piece dated July 11, examined whether CBS was for sale from a slightly different perspective. He cast doubt on Tisch's avowals regarding the made-to-order fit of the deal when he wrote, "Diller may even have to convince himself that Tisch—a proud man, stung by accusations that he is a timid blunderer in the high-speed world of entertainment commerce—is not using the Diller name to entice a corporate behemoth with a fatter wallet."

Indeed, the word was that Tisch had already tried to back out of certain aspects of the agreement. But Tisch sounded sincerely committed to QVC, playing the optimist to Diller's realist. "This transaction is so right for both companies I don't anticipate another bidder coming in," he said.

The boards of the two companies were set to meet separately on July 13 to vote on the merger proposal. Unless Davis, Eisner, or some other industry heavyweight crashed the party, it seemed likely that Diller would finally fulfill his ambition. A notoriously impatient man, he had been forced at least to pretend equanimity in the face of so many roadblocks during his crusade to secure himself a seat at the top of the media industry. The CBS deal, which Martin Lipton had tailor-made to fit the needs of both companies and their chief executives, appeared too tightly constructed to encounter any setbacks.

But if timing was all, then Diller and Tisch were still not home free. Too much could happen in what had to feel like the interminable two-week period between the announcement of the deal and its consummation.

One TV industry executive expressed what had to be Diller's concern about the time lag when he pointed out, "It's not like the board is coming in tomorrow ratifying to do it. It's not coming in for another ten days! You've got the July Fourth weekend—what do you think is going to happen over that time? A lot of meetings. You can name ten possible suitors for CBS: All the studios that could afford to pick up a $5 or $6 billion tab, telephone companies, how many is that right there?"

As the countdown to the meetings commenced, Diller surprised Tisch with a new set of demands for a stock option package. Tisch, well-known for his corporate parsimony, was irritated by what felt to him like a last-minute attempt on Diller's part to put even more money in his pocket. "The chemistry got bad," said a member of Tisch's staff who was involved with the deal. "Barry negotiates like a bully. 'If I don't get this and that, the deal's off.' That doesn't sit well with Larry."

Christopher Winans, who interviewed Tisch and his family for *The King of Cash*, an unauthorized biography of Tisch, described the situation as follows:

"Diller was insisting on getting stock options for certain nonexecutive employees, not the kind of issue one allows to get in the way of the opportunity of a lifetime. But Diller was abrasively demanding. The sense was that he wanted to assume the throne like an anointed king. He failed to see the value of keeping his ego in check during talks with Larry, who had always viewed an overinflated ego as an obstacle in business."

Diller tried to play down the dispute, characterizing it as a "QVC matter"; he was, he said, "not aware" that it had become a problem in the merger discussions. "This isn't going to stop the deal," said someone else close to the situation. "This is a little glitch and it will all get resolved."

Whereas Winans understood the issue to be about stock options for QVC employees, others said that Diller's quibbling was solely on his own behalf, in an attempt to push his personal wealth into the big-digit column to compete with David Geffen. Still others defended Diller by pointing out that when putting together a deal, he usually tended to his own financial interests after all the other details had been resolved.

One insider, expressing a different view from that offered by the Tisch camp, said that accepting the deal as it was initially conceived "would make Barry a fool. . . . The deal was driven by him. . . . Sure, they [Mr. Tisch and his allies] would like to get Barry as cheaply as possible."

Diller's concerns about the stock options were rendered moot on July 12. On the eve of the board meetings, he returned from a meeting in Los Angeles with CBS personnel, flying in to Teterboro Airport in New Jersey on his Gulfstream jet. He was met there by Ralph and Brian Roberts who handed Diller a letter in which they announced Comcast's intent to launch a takeover of QVC. Comcast was offering a total package of $44 a share for the QVC shares it didn't already own, $6 per share above CBS's bid for a total value of $2.2 billion.

Their discussion was "cordial," Brian Roberts said later; he and Diller even drove into Manhattan together. But Diller's carefully laid plans for CBS had been suddenly and definitively torpedoed by the Robertses' decision to top the CBS bid.

The Wall Street Journal called Comcast's move a "stunning strike," but Diller professed not to be shocked by the company's eleventh-hour intervention. Brian Roberts had been his greatest ally at QVC—in fact, the person most responsible for bringing Diller to Pennsylvania. More recently, however, Roberts had made no secret of his growing disaffection with Diller's high-flying schemes to crossbreed QVC with a network.

Neither he nor his father had been boosters of the CBS deal. They were both true believers in cable, and the merger, said Roberts, "represents a fundamental departure from our strategic view of the company's future." Unlike Diller, who was searching for a larger arena in which to ply his talents and interests, the Robertses were still enthusiastic about home shopping.

Moreover, they wanted to preserve their control of programming which would have been threatened by the CBS deal because their 15 percent stake in QVC would have been shaved to 5 percent in the new company. "The sale of QVC to CBS, which was clearly going to be, would have made us a disenfranchised minority investor," said Brian Roberts.

Wall Street gave the Comcast bid mixed reviews. Jessica Reif of Oppenheimer preferred the combined assets of QVC and CBS to QVC by itself. "Is this the best use of his [Roberts's] cash?" she asked.

John Tinker of Furman Selz, Inc., putting a different spin on the offer, called it "a very shrewd move by Comcast," and positioned the Robertses in a win-win position. "The bottom line," he said, "is that electronic retailing is a very valuable business with great growth prospects. Comcast either gets control of a major player—QVC—or if QVC comes into play, they get bought out at a higher price. That's better than having no control at a merged CBS-QVC."

A money manager who owned stock shares in all three companies shared Reif's viewpoint. He accused Comcast of "muddying

the waters" and rated the bid only "marginally better from an economic standpoint." Besides, he said, "longer term I would rather
have a $38 stock with the asset base of QVC and CBS and the lead-
ership of Diller." Although Comcast's offer was higher by $6, he also
favored the CBS deal because it was a tax-free exchange of stock.

Tisch heard about the deal at a CBS board dinner and immediately opted out of engaging in a costly takeover battle. "It wasn't
in our interest to stay in the picture," he said. "We aren't in the
counter-bid business." Within 24 hours, he was revealing an ambitious agreement with Westinghouse Broadcasting Company that
would turn over affiliation of three stations to CBS and would ultimately pave the way for a merger between the two companies.

Diller, who stood to make approximately $75 million in pre-
tax profit on his initial $25 million investment, put on his best
game face and called QVC's offer "a legitimate offer which should
be respected." QVC would "look at the other options we have," at
the board meeting that had been called to vote on the CBS merger.

As for Diller's own options, Brian Roberts said, "We would be
delighted if he stays," but few people expected Diller to remain at
QVC. His relationship with the Robertses had soured beyond the
point that he could continue to forge a future together with them.

It was time to move on again.

Two days after the Roberts had killed his dreams for CBS, Diller
joined the power elite of the entertainment, communications, and
information industries at Herbert Allen's annual media conference
cum weekend romp in Sun Valley, Idaho. Among the more than one
hundred guests were Rupert Murdoch, Sumner Redstone, Bill Gates,
Michael Eisner, Edgar Bronfman Jr., then head of Seagram, Michael
Ovitz, David Geffen, and John Malone. In between rounds of golf,
fishing, hiking, and white-water rafting, they had all come to talk
deals, settle pending legal cases, and exchange information.

What should have been a victory celebration had turned into
an upscale job mart for Diller. "There are a lot of people here that

Barry can talk to," said one participant. But at least one of those present was holding a grudge against Diller.

Still smarting from the battle they had waged the previous fall and winter, Sumner Redstone said, "I once considered Diller a real friend. That's history. I would be a hypocrite if I said that I didn't have some strong feelings about what he did. He did what I wouldn't have done."

When Diller and Redstone ran into each other in Sun Valley, Diller said "I hope you don't feel I victimized you . . . I didn't intend to hurt you." Redstone said, "That's a strange statement—you did."

Diller had more important matters to concern himself with than Redstone's animosity. He was still trying to thwart the sale of QVC to Comcast. His campaign suffered a major disappointment when BellSouth decided to let lapse its option to invest $500 million in QVC. Without their backing, he lacked the resources to top Comcast's offer. His name also kept coming up as most likely to buy CBS, now considered for sale. "Don't count out Diller, who is forming a group to resume his quest for the CBS plum," said an investment banker who predicted that Diller would ally himself either with BellSouth or TCI.

It seemed, however, that his destiny lay elsewhere than at QVC or CBS. In hindsight, David Geffen saw it thusly: "QVC could never be enough for Barry. It was the first step in Barry's going to work. It was the beginning, not the end."

Six months later, Comcast bought QVC, and Diller departed West Chester, Pennsylvania, richer by $100 million. CBS was for sale—even Laurence Tisch was now prepared to use the "S" word—but its price had risen to $5 billion. Despite the profit he had realized from the Comcast takeover, Diller still didn't have enough to make his own deal. He would have to go searching once again for that elusive partner who was willing to bankroll a hefty percentage of a deal, yet allow Diller to call the shots.

18

Silver King

Barry Diller had already built one network from the ground up. Now it appeared, on August 25, 1995, that he would attempt to recreate that feat with his purchase of a 20 percent stake in Silver King Communications. The St. Petersburg, Florida-based company owned 12 little-known independent television stations in small markets, as well as 27 stations on the UHF band. In buying into Silver King and becoming the chairman, Diller was reuniting with his former QVC partner, John Malone, whose Liberty Media's Home Shopping Network was distributed by Silver King.

Diller invested $5 million of his own funds and, in an arrangement worked out with Malone, also got 70 percent of TCI's voting shares, thus giving Diller control over Silver King. At last, at the age of 53, Diller finally was his own boss—albeit of a kingdom that consisted mostly of outlets for Home Shopping Network.

Financially, the deal was a very good one for him: he would receive two separate bonuses, one to be paid on August 24, 1996, the second on August 24, 1997, each worth approximately $2.5 million—exactly the cost of his investment. He would also receive up to $1 million to cover any taxes he might owe from purchasing his shares. Diller agreed to waive a salary, although he would be reimbursed for any company-related expenses that he incurred.

Dennis Bovin, a vice president at Bear Stearns, expressed Wall Street's faith in Diller, when he said, "The media industry is at a point of maximum uncertainty. People don't know what's going to define the future so they focus on individuals with track records who they think know more than they do."

Nevertheless, there were many on the Street who doubted whether Silver King was the right vehicle. Although the stock rose almost 53 percent immediately after the announcement of his investment, by the following week it had dropped 14 percent. "It's just so much baloney that he can start a network out of those lousy assets he's got," said Dennis McAlpine, an analyst with Josephthal Lyon and Ross, in an article by Ron Grover that appeared in the September 11, 1995 *BusinessWeek*. Diller countered the criticism, saying, "The station group has great distribution coverage, and it really is a bit of a blank sheet. It's what you write on it."

Diller's plan for Silver King was to create a national network of "distinct and separate voices," although the company did not yet produce most of its programming. He intended to devote the next year or so to creating shows of local interest, including sports and news, possibly in conjunction with the hometown or regional newspapers. He also hoped to renegotiate the company's contracts with Home Shopping Network so that more air time would be available for actual programming.

He explained his rationale for the network he hoped to build in an interview with Bruce Handy in the February 25, 1996, issue of *Time* magazine. "I firmly believe," he said, "you build a network not nationally, but locally. The idea is to build local TV stations with programming that serves the local market. Once you've done that, a national TV program service is possible.

"Am I interested in a national voice? Probably—sure I am. But that's not what I'm trying to do. My job is to say, 'Is there a local voice? Can I be of service? Can I get you?' Local broadcasters all look exactly the same. Local newscasts are terrible. Except for weather and sports, they're uninformative. They should just have one master shot of police and ambulances and yellow police tape because that's all they run."

Soon after, Diller acquired Savoy Pictures Entertainment, a money-losing movie and television studio, for $210 million in stock. Diller was undecided as to whether Savoy would continue to produce movies. Its recent offerings, such as *Last of the Dogmen* and *Exit to Eden,* were flops by any definition. But the company had $140 million in cash and securities that Diller planned to use to upgrade his stations.

Savoy also brought to the Silver King network four television stations—in Honolulu, New Orleans, Green Bay, and Mobile, Alabama—that were signed to become affiliated with Fox in 1996, which would give them the advantage of Fox's lucrative football and baseball packages.

The structure of Diller's network took further shape when it was simultaneously announced that, in a stock swap with Liberty Media Corporation, he would gain control of Home Shopping Network. Liberty, which owned the largest share in HSN, would exchange 41 percent of its stake and voting control for an interest in Silver King. Diller would be named chairman of Home Shopping Network.

A plan to merge the two companies was announced on August 26, 1996, in a deal that was valued at $1.27 billion, with Silver King buying Home Shopping Network. "This opens up our options for acquisitions, for use of available cash flow, and for securing an additional line of credit," said a spokesperson for Silver King.

Diller's strategy for the new company was to create new programming and further his acquisitions. Will he succeed in transforming a hodgepodge of weak TV stations into a viable network on a par with CBS, NBC, ABC, and Fox? The answer is an unqualified yes, provided he continues to receive the help and support of people like John Malone.

What is the future for Diller and Silver King? Programming is already under way to be launched in 1997. "We are on track," Diller says. "Do we know what sort of programming we are planning? Yes. Are we ready to talk about it? No."

From anyone else, such talk might be considered the fevered inventions of a manic imagination. But Diller, who for much of his more than 30-year career had been the hired gun of wild-eyed entrepreneurs, is regarded by most on Wall Street and in Hollywood as a media genius of unparalleled vision. He is, after all, the man who successfully created a new TV network for the first time in 40 years. He was the mentor and role model for some of the most progressive and powerful leaders in the entertainment world today.

At Fox-TV one executive says, "His ghost still walks the halls here. There are certain management practices that still exist from the Diller era." Another former Fox executive, Sandy Grushow, now president of Tele-TV, describes Diller as being head and shoulders above other entertainment executives in intelligence, ability, and vision.

Producer James Brooks said, "I was there when Fox was a minute-and-a-half from going under. But Barry brought it off. It wasn't an act, it wasn't manipulation. It was sheer force of will."

In October 1996, in *Vanity Fair's* second annual report on the "Top 50 Leaders of the Information Age," Diller was listed in thirteenth place, up three places from last year, behind media stars that included Bill Gates; Rupert Murdoch; Michael Eisner; Gerald Levin, Chairman and CEO of Time Warner Inc.; Herbert Allen; John

Malone; Sumner Redstone; David Geffen, and Michael Milken. In the accompanying thumbnail sketch, he was described as "smart and . . . cool and the other guys want to hang out with him."

The pattern has been the same throughout. Diller comes into a unsettled situation and applies his unique combination of unsurpassed imagination, aggressive management style, and workaholic energy to save the floundering ship. In each instance, he does what has to be done, and what no one else seems capable of doing.

In pursuit of his own company, since leaving QVC, Diller has rejected the opportunity to run two major Hollywood studios; both Edgar Bronfman, Jr., of MCA and Michael Eisner at Disney invited him to join them. Instead, he has opted to pull together a group of marginal TV stations to create the seventh TV network. His motivation fascinates and eludes his many observers.

As Diller himself phrased it, "Do I wonder why I have this need to keep proving myself? No. Yes. From this enthusiasm to total failure is a crooked-straight line. A lot of it has to do with willfulness, whether you're capable of imposing your will on the process. To the extent that you insist, you at least have a prayer."

One of his close associates who has also worked for Laurence Tisch and Rupert Murdoch offered this comparison of the three men:

> There are striking differences between him and other major industry executives. He is a unique person. I have worked in recent years with two other quite strong and different executives: Larry Tisch and Rupert Murdoch, as well as Diller.
>
> Each of them has a passion about getting business judgments right—making smart business judgments and making independent judgments. Murdoch is completely focused, listens, makes decisions and then executes them. Diller will talk through a decision and converse about it at much greater length and then a decision will emerge. That is, a decision will be reached which is the product of that conversation.

Murdoch is not an autocrat in the sense that he doesn't listen. He will listen. . . . Diller is a consensus maker. He is not politically trying to get to a consensus because the word "consensus," in the normal parlance, means trying to get everybody's point of view the same. Diller's way of acting is to try and get everyone's point of view right. I think there's a difference. One is trying to come to a *right* judgment and consensus builders are trying to come to a *common* judgment.

Right is a judgment about a particular matter. I think in the end, people who have worked with Diller would say it's Diller's judgment. Diller would say a right judgment is a right judgment, and a wrong judgment is a wrong judgment. There is, he believes, an objective standard of what is right and wrong. And it is not necessarily the consensus view; not necessarily the common view.

Diller is intriguingly not a particularly large risk taker. Diller is perceived as a risk taker. Taking risks is what he does for a living, but it is different with Tisch and Murdoch. Maybe it's because with Tisch and with Murdoch, it is their money. When you make a movie, you do take a risk, but if it ain't your $35 million it's a risk of is your judgment right or is your judgment wrong. Murdoch will not make fine calculations of risk. Rather he will seize opportunities and say, "I don't know how big the risk or the opportunity is, but I know the opportunity's big and I don't know exactly how to exploit it, but I know I've got to get there."

This same executive believes that Diller's decision-making process is much longer and contemplative than that of other executives. This, says his former colleague, accounts for why Diller didn't do more with QVC other than to use it to try and buy Paramount and CBS. He thinks that Diller's decision-making style kept him from moving QVC to a next higher level and exploiting the opportunities that were present.

"He is exasperating and fascinating," his colleague said. "Fascinating because his mind is so marvelous and so intriguing. Working with him, you learn how to think, as well as learn the business.

Exasperating because he can be as tenacious as a goddamn pit bull and say, 'No, I want to keep talking until we get it right.'"

His longtime close friend, Diane Von Furstenberg, attempted to shed some light on his character with this analysis: "It's not about greed with him. It's ambition. It's vision. That makes him different and makes him a nice person."

Many of those who have worked with Diller and endured—some would say survived—his abrasive management style might argue with Von Furstenberg's equating his ambition with niceness. He himself describes his creative style as "bashing idea against idea to get stuff out of yourself and other people."

Early in his career, while at ABC, he experienced firsthand the concept of confrontation management and the need to defend one's viewpoint, both of which he now routinely demands of his colleagues. As he tells it,

"One fateful day, my boss at ABC threw me a script and said, 'Read this and tell the producer what you think.' I was terrified. That producer was the emperor of television and he had something like eleven shows on the air. I studied the script. I hated it. When the producer cornered me, I croaked out my opinion—an inarticulate, incompetent response. The guy let me have it up one side and down the other. That's when I discovered the secret to success: Plunge into the uncomfortable; push or be lucky enough to have someone push you, beyond your fears and your sense of limitations."

Diller guards his personal life very closely. His relationship with his family and his feelings about his dead brother are tightly held secrets. He maintains intimate relationships with a small, tight-knit group of friends, to whom he is extremely loyal. He speaks his mind, and he has paid a price for his forthrightness.

Alan Sternfeld, who had worked with him at Fox, said of Hollywood and Diller's place in it, "This is a town not known for its candor. It's a small town and the reverberations tend to be rather loud. It's a town of enduring relationships or lack of same. I saw Barry briefly in September of '94 at the TV Academy Hall of Fame Induction Ceremony.

"There were a half a dozen other people being inducted, Oprah Winfrey, Howard Cosell, I don't remember the whole list. And all of the other inductees were there with a small group of family and friends and had somebody to wish them well upon them receiving their statue. Barry seemed to be very much alone. I don't recall that he was, in fact, there alone. But in terms of who stood up for him—there were no warm, glowing tributes in the presentation to him. It was a very matter-of-fact recitation of his accomplishments. He stood alone from the rest of that little group."

Diller is a risk taker in his personal life as well as in his professional life, almost to the point that he sometimes seems to have a death wish. He has a penchant for speed; one story told about him goes back to his days at William Morris, when he was asked to act as driver for Abe Lastfogel. At one intersection, Diller slammed on the brakes with such force that Lastfogel slid out of his seat and onto the floor. Diller had to get out of the car and help his boss get resettled before they continued on to Lastfogel's destination.

Diller loves fast cars—he owns a Jaguar, a Mercedes, a Porsche, and a BMW—and high-powered motorcycles. His close friends call him a thrill seeker who drives and skis like a madman, ignoring the marked trails, the warning signs, and common sense. In Manhattan, his idea of excitement is to drive his BMW the length of the island at high speeds.

"Driving here is wonderful," he insists, "especially if you want to go fast. There's nothing greater than starting at 125th and Second Avenue and going down to 30th Street. You can hit the lights and you have six lanes to maneuver in."

A classic example of the complexity of the private Diller occurred in 1993 during his battle to seize control of Paramount Communications. Despite the high stakes involved, Diller disappeared from the corporate field of battle at a crucial period in the negotiations. The New York media community was buzzing with speculation as to where Diller was and what he was doing.

Only his closest friends were aware that Diller was not holed up somewhere in New York plotting the next step in his takeover strategy. He was, in fact, in a quiet hospital room in Los Angeles, at the side of a beloved friend who was dying of AIDS.

A Diller confidante said, "Barry was having brutal conversations with the doctor. He didn't think his friend was being given proper treatment. The doctor had to take Barry to lunch, to explain things, to get him settled down. Barry had been involved in AIDS-related causes, but now he was losing someone he loved. He was very frustrated. For the first time in his life, he had come across something he had absolutely no control over.'

There are some who believe that this break in his battle for Paramount lost Diller the momentum he needed to win the takeover bid—that Diller had let his feelings for his friend lose him one of the most coveted prizes of his life. Others think he dropped out of the Paramount fight because the price had risen too high.

Indeed, in the case of Paramount, he seems to have won by losing. In August 1996, Viacom reported that earnings in the second quarter had fallen more than 22 percent, due in part to lower revenue from the television and movie programming divisions. Of its four principal business units the networks and broadcasting division was the only one to show gains in operating cash flow.

"Difficult comparisons with 1995 should not obscure the significant progress Viacom has made in the second quarter toward achieving our ambitious long-term objectives," said Sumner Redstone, Viacom's chairman.

The numbers speak for themselves, however, confirming the belief that Diller was wise to quit the Paramount battlefield when he did. Insiders have a seldom-discussed reason for taking seriously Barry Diller's attempt to build a network from a group of

UHF television stations most people can't even find with their channel changer, and it has nothing to do with what he's done in the past. Rather, it's what he didn't do.

Diller is one of the few executives in the entertainment business who can raise billions of dollars with just his name and vision as collateral. His singular status among Wall Street investors is the result of two decisions he made: to throw in the towel during the bidding war for Paramount, and to decide not to top Westinghouse's bid for CBS. In both cases, entertainment executives say, Diller sent the kind of signal investors like—that he will forgo a dream when the price gets too high.

For a lesser man, the loss of Paramount might have been a devastating blow, but Diller seems blessed in his ability to cope with adversity. "Failure is hard," he says, "But the real payoff is if you can figure out how to get over the fear of it, how to live with it and, ultimately, how to use it to push ahead. In my experience, one of the secrets of success is to embrace failure. I'm talking about real failure. Failure so close you can taste it, so strong that your clothes reek of it—the kind of failure that makes people pretend they don't know you. That sort of failure is the best thing that can happen to you if you want to run your company creatively."

Yet, referring to the luminaries gathered at Herbert Allen's retreat, he said, "I think that there's probably nothing in the shared experience other than a need to succeed and probably an even greater need not to fail."

Diller has earned his right to speak with such authority on the subject. Nevertheless, Wall Street continues to have faith in the man whom it regards as counterintuitively imaginative. Analysts and investors are intrigued by what he is doing, as well as by what he has not done. As *Los Angeles Times* reporter James Bates observed,

"With Diller in this new venture [of Silver King], the issue is not money, because Barry has been the winner even when he has been the loser in recent years and is millions of dollars richer from these various deals. No, what is at stake now is ego—particularly how Barry perceives he is seen by the likes of David Geffen, Sandy Gallin, and Diane Von Furstenberg. As Geffen puts it, 'Diller would rather die than fail.'"

Former protégé, Jeffrey Katzenberg—cofounder with Steven Spielberg and David Geffen of DreamWorks SKG—says, "It's not always clear to the rest of us where he's going, but for his entire career, Barry Diller has been a pioneer and a visionary—able to see over the horizon. He's building another network that will be neither conventional nor predictable. When Barry steps up to the plate, he hits a grand slam."

Diller understands perfectly how to play the game and when the rules can be broken. He will do what has to be done to integrate creative software and distribution channels with the necessary hardware.

"The networks are on a path of vertical integration without any question," he says. "They have to do that. The world is heading toward certain kinds of concentration. The financial interest rules [government ban on networks owning and syndicating programs that has been recently lifted], appropriately, are no longer relevant. The networks have to have vibrant production facilities. Now, if they're doing it correctly, they also ought to sell programs to anybody who will buy them. It's good for the health of the business. I think the other networks will do it increasingly."

Diller believes that the traditional modes of earning profits in the communications and entertainment industries are potentially obsolete. There are several barriers to positioning companies for survival and growth in the new and far less regulated worlds of information and entertainment.

One is the mindset of those in the industry. During the peak years of the movie industry, for example, the executives in charge frequently resisted producing a salable product. Each new technological innovation—sound, color, television, videocassettes—made Hollywood's entertainment product more attractive to the consumer and, therefore, more salable.

Yet most Hollywood moviemakers vigorously fought each of these technological innovations. Similarly, many people in the business today don't have Diller's grasp of and enthusiastic response to technology, both of which are essential to the goal of getting the product to the consumer and making a profit from it.

What Diller saw in the mating of QVC and CBS, which most people in the industry did not, was what is now becoming a buzzword among communications, media, and content-provider experts—"convergence." That was the phenomenon that Diller saw when he discovered, almost by accident, the concept of the shopping channel.

The sale of 29,000 of Von Furstenberg's dresses in a matter of a few hours was due to a synergy that traditional software and hardware makers hadn't achieved. The entire process of program transmission and profit collection was one smooth, uninterrupted flow, instead of being segmented into several separate parts that were handled by unrelated companies.

"I was really fascinated," said Diller, "before the word "convergence" became so overhyped and overused, at a place where—in a primitive way—the telephone, the television and the computer fused together."

The creative software combined with the network distribution hardware is the solution Diller sees to the primary challenge of the future that the industry faces. The fusion of television, telephone, and computer is the solution he envisions to the second challenge, namely, how to make a profit from the information superhighway. The concept is still more potential than reality, but Diller is thoroughly convinced that the ultimate winners will be those companies which "own the wire"—the phone line, cable TV line, fiber-optic multiuse line—going into the home or office where the consumer must be reached.

Under our present system, the communication and entertainment product and the wire are paid for indirectly either through advertising or flat fees for cable television service or both. As Diller points out, in a way this is the best of times for the television industry with more advertising dollars than ever flowing into the companies that create and deliver electronic media.

However, advertisers are rethinking how to get their message to the consumer in the most cost-effective way. Television is generally the most effective form of advertising; the total number of cable-connected homes is rising; and Americans spend more time watching direct satellite, cable, and network TV than almost anything else they do in their leisure time. For many, this is also true of the workplace, in part because corporate downsizing and other factors make home and workplace one and the same. Advertisers are retreating from the print media, which haven't been able to capture a significant percentage of the new generation. Print readership is sinking; the illiteracy rate is rising.

But Diller believes that for over-the-air, broadcast TV networks this is also the worst of times. "The fact is that the three-network share is down enormously. All of the networks, it seems to me, are mining the same field. They are more than adept at programming the correct demographics and I think that, over a period of time, that's going to erode things even further."

Diller's comment on the downward trend of network audiences was underscored by the Nielsen Media Research report issued April 19, 1995, just nine days after Diller made his observation. The report showed that, despite the popularity of blockbuster shows such as *ER, NYPD Blue, 60 Minutes, Seinfeld, Friends,* and *Frasier,* the three broadcast networks' combined share of the American audience had dropped again. This decrease had gone from 61 percent to 57 percent, and the majority of the lost audience had migrated to cable television.

Part of the reason for this continuing trend is similar to what happened to motion pictures when, for a long time, Hollywood concentrated on films that appealed to teenage boys. Today, the networks are focusing on appealing to the 18 to 49 age market because this segment of the population has disposable income and traditionally spends the most money. In 1996, however, the baby boomers started turning 50 at the rate of one every seven seconds. With those demographics, network television will drive away both the young and the old.

The availability of cable television has led to the fractionalization of the audience. What once was a communication and entertainment product delivery system dominated by the three networks, now is a system that has 36 or more channels depending on the cable provider. What happened to network radio after World War II is now happening to network television; the industry is becoming more generalized in its programming while each channel is becoming more specialized except for the four, free, over-the-air broadcast network channels. Diller sees the need for the broadcast over-the-air networks to return to what the three of them were some years ago—distinct personalities or networks each with its own identifiable character and brand of programming.

"The truth is that the best network services are those that are distinct and have personalities onto themselves. In history, CBS, the Tiffany network, had a particular style and point of view about what it did. You knew what NBC was. NBC was the network that started color television, did all sorts of live events, was very much involved in show business. And, ABC was the hip shooter who would try anything. Those distinct, carved-out personalities were part of branding which is now going more toward the center line demographic.

"I think that as you go into the future, you have to be about something and the something you have to be about is something that is honest to yourself. You really can't ask research, you can't ask the witch doctors in television."

One of Diller's most passionately held views about broadcasting and movie production is that a company has to have a position, a discrete identity. It has to stand for something to communicate and bond with its viewers if it is going to gain their loyalty and survive in a time of multiple television services.

For Diller, this also relates to his views on how to earn profits. For over-the-air broadcasters, profits traditionally have come through selling advertising; and for cable television broadcasters it was through collecting a flat monthly fee. Both of those methods are remote from the actual display and pitch for the products advertised. It is here that Diller sees the beauty of selling a product directly at the moment of on-air display, with the distribution system or television network getting a share of the sale.

This point-of-display/point-of-purchase approach has great appeal to both the advertiser and the network. For the advertiser, sales cost would no longer be some ephemeral formula or rating book figure. It would be directly related to the effectiveness of the advertising medium. For the television operator, it can mean more profit because the lackluster items would be winnowed out as unprofitable to advertise, and the hot items would be pushed ever harder. In addition, the television operator could control fulfillment of the orders. Diller sees the method as a means to get more income, more quickly, by using a proven, although relatively rudimentary system of the sort now used by QVC, combined with a seductive entertainment package.

This concept was the reason Diller had such strong, positive feelings about the CBS-QVC deal. Later, he would say regretfully, "Clearly, I wanted the CBS transaction to proceed. QVC and CBS were a great combination. I think the danger for broadcasters is one day the cable operator is going to figure out—through an interconnect—how to sell in the local market with enormous effectiveness."

Barry Diller's vision of the future was triggered by his becoming acquainted with computers through the use of his Apple PowerBook. He put this hands-on experience together with what he had learned at ABC, Paramount, Fox, and QVC to focus on the multimedia future of entertainment and communications. He foresaw that together, QVC and CBS could provide the matchup of the hardware and software of tomorrow, and open up an abundant new flow of earnings.

The alliance didn't happen, however, because while he was focused on the technology, he forgot about the human factors at work even at the highest corporate levels.

Diller's view on how he has achieved his record is, "What all my experiences have had in common is a battle, a holy war, between process and expertise. Expertise is a pack mentality that concludes something can't be done or that it must be done this way. Process, on the other hand, is ignoring the doomsayers and optimists alike."

What motivating force drives Diller to continue fighting the pack mentality as fiercely and stubbornly as he does? Alan Sternfeld considered the question of what drove Diller so hard to keep looking for the next great deal.

"He's a brilliant dealmaker," Sternfeld said. "I could only presume one of the net consequences of all of the effort is his personal reward. But he sees the big picture and defines, for himself, a very large goal where others would probably be overwhelmed by the daunting nature of the proposition to create a fourth network.

"I understood the difficulty for him not having a monument to his name. What would be his legacy? The idea that he founded the fourth network—people forget that. He's friends with some very affluent people, particularly David Geffen, and while we don't have to pass the hat for Barry, there's a big difference between being an employee and being a principal. And I think it's pretty clear that he reached a point in his 50s when he wanted to become not only a principal, but he wanted to set a new challenge for himself on the dawn of a new technological age.

"The design was at hand for him at QVC—just sounded terrific. Whether it was always a plan for him to use it as a base to approach CBS or some other network I can't say but, well, I think he's looking to build an empire for himself."

Barry Diller has said that his favorite movie is Orson Welles's classic *Citizen Kane,* the story of a newspaper publisher, modeled after William Randolph Hearst, and his rise to power. On his deathbed, Kane whispers one word—"Rosebud"—the trade name of a much loved sled that was taken from him as a child and had come to symbolize all he had lost in life.

It is unlikely that Barry Diller will ever reveal to light his "Rosebud"—the source that feeds his inner strengths and weaknesses, that forces him to keep fighting beyond the point at which others would have given up. His father, Michael, was a builder of homes in southern California. Perhaps it's no coincidence that Diller is also a builder. He works with ideas and numbers rather than hammers and nails, but what he does best and enjoys most is not all that dissimilar from what his father did. He creates a structure where none existed previously, carefully builds on the framework, constantly measures and calculates to ensure that the structure will hold. Did Michael ever build his dream house? Will his son someday build his?

A rival Hollywood mogul spoke admiringly of Diller as "not a person to count out. Look at what he's done in his life. This guy wants to be the president of the world. He wants to be the king of media. He wants to be richer and more powerful than David Geffen. This is one tough, brilliant son-of-a-bitch."

Notes

Introduction

1 Description of filming of *The Last Tycoon* is based on Elia Kazan's recollections, in Elia Kazan, *A Life* (New York: Anchor Books, 1989), pp. 765–781.

3 "The most influential man in Hollywood": Biographical details about Thalberg, are found in Ethan Mordden, *The Hollywood Studios* (New York: Fireside, 1989), pp. 101–117.

4 John Higgins, "QVC's Diller Sees a Diamond in the Rough," *Multichannel News* (January 19, 1993), p. 1.

4 "Dominated by the interests of cable": Ibid.

5 "His next move": Elizabeth Jensen, Mark Robichaux, and Greg Steinmetz, "Is CBS in Play Now? If Merger Is 'Strategic' What Is the Strategy?" *Wall Street Journal* (July 1, 1994), p. 1.

5 Laura Landro, "Diller's Need for Control Stalls Search for an Empire," *Wall Street Journal* (July 14, 1994).

6 Ronald Grover, "How Much Room Is There for Barry?" *BusinessWeek* (September 11, 1995).

6 *The Economist* (September 2, 1995), p. 57.

6 "However his plans for the future": Kevin Sessums, "Interview," *Playboy* (July, 1989), p. 51.

7 "There are no end of stories" Richard Corliss, *Time* (July 11, 1994), p. 48.

7 "But he defends himself": Sessums, op. cit.

7 F. Scott Fitzgerald, *The Last Tycoon* (New York: Charles Scribner's Sons, 1941), pp. 134-135.

Chapter 1   An Issue of Privacy

11 "Barry Diller is often": Sessums, op. cit.

11 "I have never": Ibid.

11 "Unlike most of his peers": Christopher Byron, "Mogul in a Mess," *New York* (November 1, 1993), p. 30.

12 "Diller's profound sense": Sessums, op. cit.

15 "By Diller's own description": Ibid.

16 "Everything I ever learned": Ibid.

17 Information about Donald Diller was taken from police and court records, Los Angeles County.

Chapter 2   The Mailroom and Beyond

23 "In 1961, Barry": Sessums, op. cit.

24 "You know how people": Ibid.

26 "He was smart": Leonard H. Goldenson, *Beating the Odds* (New York: Charles Scribner's Sons, 1991), p. 327.

27 General information on history of ABC, ibid.

29 "Disney turned in desperation": Ibid., p. 124.

30 "Tisch put Goldenson together": Ibid., p. 259.

32 "Diller was excited about": Ibid., p. 333.

Chapter 3   Reinventing the Wheel

37 Goldenson, op. cit., p. 333.

38 Ibid., p. 347.

40 "Eisner had grown up": Ron Grover, *The Disney Touch* (Homewood, IL: Business One Irwin, 1991), pp. 26-28.

41 "Two years later, having moved': Joe Flower, *Prince of the Magic Kingdom* (New York: John Wiley & Sons, 1991), p. 39.

42 "Before long, Eisner": Ibid., p. 44.

44 "That's a very tough subject": Goldenson, op. cit., pp. 345-346.

45 "Like many classic Hollywood": Ibid., pp. 363-365.

47 "Long before *Roots* captured": Byron, op. cit. p. 30.

48 "Pierce remembers their conversation": Goldenson, op. cit., p. 356.

49 "When Diller reported": Ibid.

Chapter 4 At the Movies

60 John Brooks, *The Go-Go Years* (New York: Weybright and Talley, 1973), p. 170.

60 "Bluhdorn also talked": Ibid., p. 172.

61 "His investment in Paramount": Priscilla S. Meyer, "Gulf & Western after Bluhdorn," *Forbes* (March 14, 1983), p. 42.

62 "Diller liked working for": Alex Ben Block, *Outfoxed* (New York: St. Martin's Press, 1990), p. 56.

62 A. D. Murphy, "Diller New Par Head," *Daily Variety* (September 23, 1974), p. 1.

64 "A spate of spectacular": Sessums, op. cit.

66 "Film critic Vincent Canby": William Goldman, *Adventures in the Screen Trade* (New York: Warner Books, 1983).

67 "He took similar risk with": Vincent Canby, *New York Times* (October 30, 1976).

68 "His unconventional methods": Flower, op. cit., p. 66.

68 "Donald had been arrested": Ibid.

69 Author's interview with Tereza Mendoza.

Chapter 5 The "Killer Dillers"

74 "One of his greatest successes": Goldenson, op. cit., p. 348.

75 "The two men were in many": Sessums, op. cit.

75 "Eisner, on the other hand": Flower, op. cit., p. 69.

76 "The one thing you cannot": Ibid., p. 68.

76 "Despite their privileged": Ibid., p. 78.

77 Dawn Steel, *They Can Kill You But They Can't Eat You* (New York: Pocket Books, 1993), p. 126.

78 "*Reds,* on the other hand": Sessums, op. cit.

79 "In fact, Diller pushed his": Pierce O'Donnell and Dennis McDougal, *Fatal Subtraction* (New York: Doubleday, 1992), p. 268.

79 "Another key member of": Flower, op. cit., pp. 73-74.

83 Steel, op. cit., p. 126.

86 Grover, op. cit., p. 32.

86 "It was at Paramount": Sessums, op. cit.

Chapter 6   Aboard the Twentieth-Century Express

92 "Many of them feared": O'Donnell, op. cit., pp. 71-78.

92 "Three years later": Ibid.

93 "After all his years": Block, op. cit., p. 56.

93 "Charles Bluhdorn had been": Meyer, op. cit., pp. 41-42.

94 "For one thing, it meant": Block, op. cit., p. 57.

94 "He and Davis had gotten": Bryan Burrough, "The Siege of Paramount," *Vanity Fair* February, 1994, p. 129.

95 "He had headed up": Flower, op. cit., pp. 121-122.

95 "Diller and Davis, on the other hand": Burrough, op. cit., p. 129.

95 "Paramount Pictures was having": Flower, op. cit., p. 122.

96 "One colleague at the time": Rod Lurie, "More Power," *LA Magazine* (December 1993), p. 106.

96 "Diller's contract was due": Burrough, op. cit., p. 129.

97 "The attention seemed only": Block, op. cit., p. 58.

97 "Twentieth Century-Fox got": Block, op. cit., pp. xxi-xxv.

103 "David Geffen was by far": Fredric Dannen, *Hit Men* (New York: Times Books, 1990), pp. 129-133.

104 "No wonder then that Diller": Flower, op. cit., pp. 125-126.

105 "It was Fred Silverman": Goldenson, op. cit., p. 362.

105 "The five-year contract": Block, op. cit., pp. 60-62.

106 "I felt horrible": Sessums, op. cit.

Chapter 7   Setting the House in Order

109 "Diller got his first hint": Block, op. cit., p. 68.

109 "Diller was in for more": Ibid.

110 Aubrey Solomon, *Twentieth Century-Fox* (Metuchen, NJ: Scarecrow Press, 1988), footnote for p. 204.

113 "Diller could have quit": Block, op. cit., p. 79.

Chapter 8   Creating the Fourth Network

121 Substantive information in this chapter regarding Barry Diller and his relationship with Rupert Murdoch at Fox is taken from Block, op. cit.

131 "In December 1985": Block, op. cit., p. 113.

132 "Michael Eisner and Jeffrey Katzenberg": Grover, op. cit., p. 161.

133 Author's interview with Michael Moye.

Chapter 9   Truth or Consequences

141 "He even went so far": Sessums, op. cit.

142 Author's interview with Moye.

144 Author's interview with Matt Groening, 7/18/95.

145 Author's interview with Polly Platt, 5/31/95.

146 "The very same qualities": Block, op. cit., p. 175.

147 Author's interview with Alan Sternfeld, 7/6/95.

Chapter 10   The Plots Thicken

153 Author's interview with Sternfeld.

157 Substantive information in this chapter regarding the Fox network is taken from Block, op. cit.

160 Author's interview with Moye.

166 Author's interview with Doug Wick, 5/11/95.

Chapter 11   "Don't Have a Cow, Man"

169 Author's interview with Groening, op. cit.

Chapter 12   In Development Hell

181 "It took a solid": Block, op. cit.

182 Author's interview with Platt.

189 Author's interview with Groening.

190 Author's interview with Sternfeld.

194 "But it wasn't necessarily": Block, op. cit.

196 "Twentieth Century-Fox Films paid": Lisa Gubernick, "Barry's Been Distracted," *Forbes* (January 18, 1990).

196 Author's interview with Wick.

198 "Others, however, took a far": Gubernick, op. cit.

198 "Roth was Diller's fifth": Ibid.

Chapter 13   Saying Goodbye

203 "On February 24, 1992": "After the credits, the debits," *The Economist* (February 29, 1992).

205 "Geffen's approach to the": Dannen, op. cit.

205 "He rejected offers from": Ibid., p. 320.

208 Author's interview with Platt.

Chapter 14   The Odyssey

213 "He had an unbelievable": Ken Auletta, "Annals of Communication," *The New Yorker* (February 22, 1993).

214 "Rob Glaser, Microsoft's": Ibid.

216 "In August, Diller": Burrough, op. cit.

219 "Meeting at Malone's": Auletta, op. cit.

220 "Despite his reservations": Ibid.

221 "Washington communications": Lis de Moraes, "Diller Calls It Quits at Fox," *Hollywood Reporter* (February 25, 1992).

221 "Diller's vision of programming": J. Max Robins, "Hollywood Bets That Barry Won't Tarry," *Daily Variety* (March 2, 1992).

221 "The prospect of having": Ibid.

222 "Other rumors": "Barryball," *Daily Variety* (September 14, 1992).

222 "Taking over Time Warner": Liz Smith, "Barry Diller Rumor Denied," *Los Angeles Times* (September 4, 1992).

222 "Orion Pictures": "Diller's Next Deal," *California Business* (Summer 1992).

222 "Ronald Perelman": Alan Citron and John Lippman, "Barry Diller: Up to What with Whom?" *Los Angeles Times* (March 18, 1992).

222 "Other productions": Emily Yoffe, "Diller's Hollywood Shuffle," *Newsweek* (March 9, 1992).

223 Brian Lowery, "'Where's Barry' H wood Bored Rooms Wonder," *Daily Variety* (July 8, 1992).

223 "David Geffen promised": Richard Corliss with reporting by Salley B. Donnelly and Martha Smilgis, "The Miracle Mogul Walks Out," *Time* (March 9, 1992).

223 "The 'whatever' finally": Auletta, op. cit.

225 "That was the clincher": Lurie, op. cit.

225 John Higgins, "QVC's Diller Sees a Diamond in the Rough," *Multichannel News* (January 18, 1993).

226 "Malone and Brian Roberts": John Higgins, "Diller Shopping Trip Ends with QVC," *Multichannel News* (December 14, 1992).

226 "Since at the time of the deal": Mark Landler and Ronald Grover, "How Far Can Barry Go? Very Far, It Seems," *BusinessWeek* (July 26, 1993).

227 "On December 10, Diller shocked": Higgins, op. cit., December 14, 1992.

Chapter 15   "What's the Idea?"

234 "For nearly a year": John Lippman, "Shopping Network's Potential Attracted Diller," *Los Angeles Times* (December 11, 1992).

235 J. Max Robins, "Diller's New Diamond: No Cubic Zirconium," *Daily Variety* (December 14, 1992).

236 "The advertising industry": Risa Bauman, "A New Dawn for Home Shopping," *Direct* (January, 1993).

238 Higgins, op. cit., January 18, 1993.

239 Steve McClellan, "Diller: Broadcasters Will 'Go out of Business' unless Compulsory License Is Eliminated," *Broadcasting* (January 27, 1992).

242 "Diller wants to persuade QVC": Auletta, op. cit.

242 Ed Martin, "Take That, Barry: on *Larry King* and *Donahue,* Ordinary People Confront Media Moguls," *Inside Media* (April 28, 1993).

243 "Ed Martin, reporting on": Ibid.

243 Michael Schrage, "Disconnected: After Seeing Barry Diller's Plan for the QVC Home Shopping Network, It's Hard to Believe This Is the Same Man Who Created the Fox Network," *Adweek* (March 15, 1993).

Chapter 16   Of Paramount Importance

247 "Barry Diller had an unlikely": Burrough, op. cit.

253 "Nobody was more cognizant": Ibid.

254 "Davis and Malone met": Ken Auletta, "The Last Studio in Play," *The New Yorker* (October 4, 1993), p. 80.

254 "The proposed merger": 1994 Del. LEXIS 57. Supreme Court of Delaware, 637 A.2d; 1994 Del. LEXIS 57; Fed. Sec. L. Rep. (CCH) P98, 063.

255 "Davis and Redstone accompanied": Byron, op. cit.

255 "I never thought it would happen": Auletta, op. cit., October 4, 1993.

255 "Seeking to forestall": Burrough, op. cit.

256 Kurt Andersen, "Ego Is of Paramount Importance," *Time* (October 4, 1993), p. 71.

257 "Davis sounded matter-of-fact": *Broadcasting & Cable* (October 24, 1993), p. 7.

257 "Diller took pains": "Indecent Proposals," *The Economist* (September 25, 1993).

257 "A Viacom executive": Bill Hewitt, "Day of the Hunter: Brash, Brilliant, Abrasive, Barry Diller Mounts a Bold Power Play for a Company He Can Call His Own," *People* (October 11, 1993).

257 "Diller's friends and colleagues": Lurie, op. cit.

257 "One friend, who preferred": Hewitt, op. cit.

258 "Joan Rivers, wary perhaps": Ibid.

259 "On October 5, Diller": Lurie, op. cit.

259 "Von Furstenberg preferred": Ibid.

266 "Rumors were flying": Michael Meyer, *Newsweek* (November 1, 1993).

267 "October 28, Diller sent": Geraldine Fabrikant, "Paramount-QVC Talks Said to Be Unproductive," *New York Times* (November 2, 1993).

268 Fabrikant, op. cit., November 5, 1993.

268 "She also speculated that": 1994 Del. LEXIS 57, op. cit.

269 "Industry analysts voiced questions": Ibid.

271 "The same day, a QVC": Fabrikant, op. cit., November 18, 1993.

271 "The consensus on Wall Street": Fabrikant, op. cit., November 19, 1993.

271 "As he awaited the": Burrough, op. cit.

272 "'Wow!' said Diller": Fabrikant, op. cit., November 25, 1993.

272 "At this moment of his": Burrough, op. cit.

272 "The Court of Chancery": Fabrikant, op. cit., November 29, 1993.

273 "In his 61-page": Fabrikant, op. cit., November 25, 1993.

274 "A Paramount executive refuted" Michael Janofsky, "Ruling on QVC Bid Faces an Expert Review," *New York Times* (November 26, 1993).

274 "The official company line": Charles Fleming, "Barry Diller Scores at the Buzzer," *Newsweek* (December 6, 1993).

275 "The sense of relief was": "Court Will Hear Appeal in Paramount Case," *New York Times* (November 30, 1993)

276 "It seems on the surface": Fabrikant, op. cit., December 8, 1993.

278 "This is a stinging": Fabrikant, op. cit., December 10, 1993.

278 "Diller had watched": Ibid.

279 "QVC, however, was now": Fabrikant, op. cit., December 11, 1993.

281 Jessica Shaw, "Cheap Thrills," *Entertainment Weekly* (February 18, 1994).

281 Author's interview with Platt.

281 Randall Smith, "Wall Street's Final Analysis: Might Made Right," *Wall Street Journal* (February 26, 1994).

282 "Redstone's telephone lines": "Sumner at the Summit," *BusinessWeek* (February 28, 1994).

282 "QVC's year-end stock": Ibid.

282 "The shareholders were": Ibid.

283 "Diller refused to fuel": Ibid.

Chapter 17   Breakfast at Tiffany's

287 "A Diller adviser": Ibid.

290 "There were other problems": Richard Corliss, "The Barry and Larry Show," *Time* (July 11, 1994).

290 "He was also being faulted": "CBS Reported in Merger Talks with QVC; Diller Would Head Network," *New York Times* (June 30, 1994).

290 "That was a disaster": Christopher Winans, *The King of Cash* (New York: John Wiley & Sons, 1995), pp. 255–256.

290 "Tisch was growing": Ibid., p. 264.

292 "As usual, he was disconcertingly": Don West and Mark Berniker, "Barry Diller: TV's Smart Agent," *Broadcasting & Cable* (May 23, 1994).

294 "Diller reiterated his": John Eggerton, "'Smart Agent' Is Smart Thinking, Says Diller; QVC Head Has Seen Communication's Future, and It's Powered by a Computer," *Broadcasting & Cable* (June 13, 1994).

295 "I'm not selling": *New York Times* (June 30, 1994).

295 "Martin Lipton worked": Winans, op. cit., pp. 265–266.

296 "Diller gave it his nod": Corliss, op. cit.

296 "That same week": Ken Auletta, "Back in Play," *The New Yorker* (July 18, 1994).

297 "There was no choice": Winans, op. cit., p. 267.

297 "Although the two men": Elizabeth Jensen, Mark Robichaux, and Greg Steinmetz. "Is CBS in Play Now? If Merger is 'Strategic,' What Is the Strategy?" *Wall Street Journal* (July 1, 1994).

298 "Both companies' stock": Auletta, op. cit., July 18, 1994.

299 "There was also the possibility": "Next: CBS and QVC," *The Economist* (July 9, 1994).

299 "An executive with Malone's": Jensen et al., op. cit., July 1, 1994.

299 "As for CBS, the company": *New York Times* (June 30, 1994).

299 "A merger with QVC would": Corliss, op. cit.

299 "Diller, on the other hand": Johnnie L. Roberts, Randall Smith, and Mark Robichaux, "CBS, QVC Are Said Close to Agreement on a Merger," *Wall Street Journal* (June 30, 1994).

300 "Bishop Cheen, an analyst": Corliss, op. cit.

300 "Tisch's colleagues in the": Auletta, op. cit., July 18, 1994.

300 "The dividend would be huge": Johnnie L. Roberts et al., op. cit., June 30, 1994.

301 "Are you going to walk": Elizabeth Jensen, "CBS Battle to Keep Affiliates May Gain Potent Weapon in Form of QVC's Diller," *Wall Street Journal* (July 5, 1994).

302 "Tisch, speaking in May": Johnnie L. Roberts et al., op. cit., June 30, 1994.

302 "The affiliates sounded more": Elizabeth Jensen, op. cit., July 5, 1994.

302 "The fact that a": Auletta, op. cit July 18, 1994.

302 "For the most part": Corliss, op. cit., July 11, 1994.

303 "A similar assessment": Auletta, op. cit., July 18, 1994.

303 "One of Diller's former": Ibid.

304 "Many Wall Street analysts": Jensen et al., op. cit., July 1, 1994.

305 "But not so tough that": Auletta, op. cit., July 18, 1994.

305 "Then he turned": Jensen et al., op. cit., July 1, 1994.

305 "Indeed, the word was": Ibid.

306 "One TV industry executive": Corliss, op. cit.

306 "As the countdown to": Winans, op. cit., p. 268.

307 "Diller tried to play down": Johnnie L. Roberts, "QVC's Diller Is Said to Seek Sweetener Via Stock Options in CBS Merger Deal," *Wall Street Journal* (July 12, 1994).

307 "One insider, expressing": Ibid.

307 "Diller's concerns about the stock": Winans, op. cit., p. 269.

308 "Neither he nor his father": Laura Landro, Johnnie L. Roberts, and Mark Robichaus, "Comcast Offer for QVC Kills CBS Merger," *Wall Street Journal* (July 13, 1994).

308 "Moreover, they wanted to": "Comcast Plays Spoiler," *BusinessWeek* (July 25, 1994).

308 "John Tinker of Furman Selz": Landro et al., op. cit., July 13, 1994.

309 "Two days after the Roberts": Mark Landler and Ronald Grover, "Herb Allen's Media-Fest: Suddenly, a Star Is Unborn," *BusinessWeek* (July 25, 1994).

310 "When Diller and Redstone": Elise O'Shaughnessy, "This Is Now," *Vanity Fair* (October 1994).

310 "Diller had more important matters": Gene G. Marcial, "Diller, Disney and CBS?" *BusinessWeek* (August 8, 1994).

310 "It seemed, however, that his destiny": Auletta, op. cit., July 18, 1994.

Chapter 18   Silver King

313 "Financially, the deal was": Jeffrey Daniels, "Diller Gets Silver King for Practically Nothing," *Baseline* (August 30, 1995).

315 "The structure of Diller's": Sallie Hofmeister, "Diller Expected to Take Over Cable Firm," *Los Angeles Times* (November 25, 1995).

317 "As Diller himself phrased it": Bruce Handy, "Diller Doing It His Way," *Time* (February 26, 1996).

319 "Many of those who have": Ibid.

319 Author's interview with Sternfeld.

320 "Diller is a risk taker": Kim Albert, "The Menace Diller Show," *Entertainment Weekly* (July 22, 1994).

321 "Indeed, in the case of Paramount": Associated Press, "Viacom Posts Profit Decline of 22% in Second Quarter," *New York Times* (August 1, 1996).

322 "Yet, referring to the luminaries": O'Shaughnessy, op. cit.

Index

ABC Television, *see* American
   Broadcasting Company (ABC)
A.C. Nielsen Company, 135
Acquisitions:
   Capital Cities/ABC, 125
   Savoy Pictures Entertainment, 315
   Silver King Communications, 313–314
A Current Affair 194
Advertisers:
   Fox Network, 123–124, 156–158
   television industry and, 324–325
Airplane!, 86
Allen, Herbert, 250, 258, 309
Allied Artists Picture Corporation, 92
Alternative programming, at Fox
   Broadcasting Company, 134, 153–166,
   173. *See also specific programs*
American Broadcasting Company (ABC):
   broadcast movie rights, 28–29
   Capital Cities acquisition, 125
   children's programming, 42
   color television and, 30
   development of, 22–23
   merger deal with ITT, 27, 33, 37
   miniseries, 3, 43–45
   Movie of the Week, 3, 39–41
   senior programming executive at, 47
   soap operas, 42
   as vice-president of, 3
America's Most Wanted, 195, 221
Ancier, Garth, 125–126, 133–134,
   53–154, 156, 159–161, 165, 170,
   188. 192

Andersen, Kurt, 256
Anderson, Frances, 16
Animated series, *see Simpsons, The*
An Officer and a Gentleman, 86
Archduke of Programming, 157
Arrow, 259
Aubrey, James, 65–66
Auletta, Ken, 241–243, 262, 292, 303
Avildsen, John, 77

Babes, 173
Bad News Bears, 67–68
Barron, Liz, 275, 281
Barton, Peter, 252
Baskin, Stuart, 269
Bates, James, 322–323
Baxter, 173
Beatty, Warren, 75, 78–79
Bell Atlantic, 262–263, 265
BellSouth, 265–266, 268, 287
Berger, Marilyn, 296
Berniker, Mark, 291
Beverly Hills Cop, 86
Big. 166, 196, 208
Big-budget films, 64–65
Block, Alex Ben, 116, 150, 183, 188, 195
Blockbuster Entertainment, 280
Bluhdorn, Charles:
   death of, 91–92
   Paramount acquisition, 60–61
   professional characteristics, 93–94
   relationship with, 62, 68, 85, 95
   working for, 3, 38, 47–49, 57, 65

Bluhdorn, Yvette, 93
Bolger, Ray, 22
Bovin, Dennis, 314
Box Office Attractions Film Rental
    Company, 97
Boyd, Michael, 226
Brandt, Gary, 188
Broadcast movie rights, 28-29
Broadcast News, 145, 166, 183, 208
Bronfman, Edgar, Jr., 317
Brooks, James, 132-133, 145, 161, 166,
    169-170, 174-175, 208, 281
Brooks, John, 60
Brown, David, 110
Burrough, Bryan, 257, 264
Byron, Christopher, 258

Cable television, 223-224, 324-325. *See
    also* QVC
Cannell, Stephen, 133, 148, 161
CBS-QVC merger, 5-6, 288-291, 295-310,
    328-329
Censorship, Fox Broadcasting Company,
    142, 176
Cheen, Bishop, 300
Cheers, 86
Chiat Day, 149
Childhood history, 13-14, 16
Chris-Craft, 57, 99
CinemaScope, 98
Citizen Kane, 329
Clinton, Bill, 237
Cocoon, 110-111
Cohn, Harry, 56
Cohn, Jack, 56
Color television, impact of, 29-30
Columbia Pictures, 55-56
Comcast:
    CBS-QVC merger, 216, 224-226,
        308-310
    QVC takeover, 310
Cops, 221
Corliss, Richard, 305
Cunningham, Larry, 270, 277

Davis, Martin:
    acquisitions, 247-249
    leadership at Paramount, 4-5, 59-60,
        92, 104, 111, 249-250
    QVC and, 250-255
    Viacom/Paramount merger, 250-283
Davis, Marvin:
    CBS-QVC merger, 264, 304-305
    relationship with, 105, 136, 264

Twentieth Century Fox acquisition, 57,
    96-97, 100-101
Davis, Ossie, 45
Decision-making strategies, 146, 189
Dee, Ruby, 45
Dekom, Peter, 126, 149, 283
Dickson, W.K.L., 54
Die Hard/Die Hard 2, 196, 198-199, 208
Digital-compression technology, 235, 240
Diller, Bernard, 12
Diller, Donald, 17, 68-70, 74
Diller, Michael, 12-15, 73, 329
Diller, Reva Addison, 13, 15
Diller, Richard, 13-14, 16, 73
"Diller drive," 16, 85
Disney, Roy, 29
Disney, Walt, 29
Disney Company, 111-112, 132, 305
Dixon, Christopher, 298
Dolgen, Jonathan, 111, 113
Down and Out in Beverly Hills, 173
DuMont, Allen B., 27

Educational background, 17, 23-24
Eisenberg, Jerry, 40
Eisner, Michael:
    at ABC, 40-42
    Bludhorn, Charles and, 94-95
    CBS-Disney merger and, 305
    comparison with, 75-76, 117, 317-318
    Disney Company and, 111-112
    as protege, 74-75
    relationship with, 85, 96, 317
    successes of, 86
Elephant Man, The, 79
Empire Strikes Back, The, 99
Employees, relationship with, 83-85

Fabrikant, Geraldine, 268
Family:
    history of, 12-17
    relationship with, 17, 68-70
Family Ties, 86
Farrier, Brenda, 184
FCC investigations, 184-185, 295
Feuer, Cy, 59
Field, John, 236
Fin-Syn rule, 222
Flashdance, 82-83
Fleming, Charles, 275
Flower, Joe, 76
Forrest Gump, 81
Fox, Inc., 4, 206-207

Fox, William, 54–56, 97
Fox Broadcasting Company:
  hiring process, 124–126
  management team, 126
  news broadcasts, 182–183
  NFL football, 290
  prime-time series, scheduling, 154–156
  programming philosophy, 156
  programming strategy, 184–185
  reasons for leaving, 203–209
  turnaround of, 195–196
Fox Film Corporation, 97
Fox Films, 196, 198
Fox Movietone, 55
Fox-TV, development of, 188–199, 208.
  See also Fox Broadcasting Company
Freeman, Mike, 239
Friendly, Fred W., 31

Gabelli, Mario, 303
Gallin, Sandy, 103, 206
Gardiner, Michale, 221
Gates, Bill, 214
Geffen, David, 24–25, 75, 102, 109,
  204–206, 223, 249, 257, 304, 323,
  329
Geneen, Harold, 30, 33
General Electric, 219–220
Gerber, David, 222
Gerbrandt, Larry, 300
Glaser, Rob, 214
Godfather, (I and II), The, 63, 66
Gold, Stan, 104
Goldberg, Gary David, 194
Goldberg, Joanne, 148
Goldberg, Len, 3, 26–27, 31–32, 38–39,
  41, 124, 134, 196, 198
Goldenson, Leonard, 22, 28–29, 33,
  37–38, 42
Goldfish, Samuel, 55
Goldman, William, 76
Goldwyn, Sam, 55, 62
Goldwyn Pictures, 55
Gordon, Larry, 102, 111, 130
Gordy, Berry, 49
Grease, 86
Greenhill, Robert, 250, 254
Griffith, Andy, 23
Griffith, D. W., 54
Groening, Matt, 144, 146, 169–177, 189,
  208
Grover, Ron, 77, 86, 314
Grushow, Sandy, 316
Gulf & Western, 4, 92, 94

Haber, Art, 70
Haley, Alex, 45–46
Hall, Arsenio, 187
Hard Copy, 221
Harris, J. Ira, 100
Harris, Kathryn, 261
Haverty, Larry, 258
Hays, William, 14
Heaven Can Wait, 86
Heaven's Gate, 58
Hendricks, John, 242
Higgins, John, 238
"High concept" creations, 77
Hirschfield, Alan, 96, 99, 101, 109
Home Shopping Network:
  QVC and, 6, 252–253, 287
  Silver King Communications and,
    313–315
Home video market, 101, 113
Horn, Alan, 130–131
Horsley, David, 54
Huggins, Roy, 38–39
Hughes, Howard, 57

Independent Moving Picture Company,
  54
Inner life, 11
Interactivity, importance of, 260

Jacobs, Jack, 272, 274–275
Jaffe, Stanley, 102
Jessel, George, 22
Jobs, Steven, 214, 223–224
Johnson, David, 125
Judelson, David, 93

Kalcheim, Harry, 23
Katleman, Harris, 112, 122
Katzenberg, Jerry, 79–81, 85, 95–96,
  297
Kellner, Jamie, 124–125, 159
Kennedy, Edward, 181
Kennedy, Joseph P., 21, 57
Kerkorian, Kirk, 65–66
Kern, Jerry, 251
"Killer Diller," 6, 73–87, 189, 204, 206
King Kong, 67
Kinney National, 57
Klein, Calvin, 75, 103
Kluge, John, 115–116, 222
Krim, Arthur, 38

La Bonte, C. Joseph, 99
Ladd, Alan, Jr., 98–99

Laemmle, Carl, 54
Lansing, Sherry, 101
Lasky, Jesse L., 54
Lastfogel, Abe, 21–22, 25–26, 320
Last Tycoon, The, 1, 7
Late Show Starring Joan Rivers, The,
    134–137, 139–150, 186
Lauder, Harry, 21
Lazar, Swifty, 204
Leavitt, Ron, 133–134, 142, 162, 164–165,
    173
Leider, Robert, 302
Levy, Norman, 111
Liberty Media Corporation, 226, 313, 315
Lippman, John, 220, 233
Lipton, Martin, 271–272, 295–296
Loew, Marcus, 54–55
Loews Corporation, 288–289, 300–301
Londoner, David, 276
Looking for Mr. Goodbar, 86
Lucas, George, 78
Lurie, Rod, 103

McAlpine, Dennis, 314
McKay, Bruce, 130, 148
Madison Square Garden, 94, 258
Magic Kingdom, 29
Make Room for Daddy, 23
Malara, Anthony, 302
Malle, Louis, 145
Malone, John:
    Paramount/Viacom merger, 215–219,
        223, 225–227, 233–235, 250–254,
        261–263
    Silver King Communications and, 313
Malone, Leslie Ann, 217
Management philosophy, 86
Management style:
    description of, 81
    development of, 32
    hands-on approach, 183
    impact of, 111, 209
    influences on, 26
Mancuso, Frank, 95, 104
Maney, Kevin, 207–208
Married . . . With Children, 4, 142, 149,
    160–163, 165–166, 172, 194, 221
Marsh, Paul, 207
Martin, Ed, 243
Martin, Ernest, 59
Mayer, Louis B., 55–56, 62
Media Lab, 214
Mendoza, Teresa, 68–69, 73
Mengers, Sue, 75–76

Mergers:
    ABC-ITT, 27, 33, 37
    CBS-Disney, 305
    CBS-QVC, 288–291, 295–310, 328–329
    Paramount/Viacom, 253, 254–284,
        321–322
    TCI-Bell Atlantic, 262–265, 268
Metro-Goldwyn-Mayer (M-G-M), 55–56,
    65–66
Metro Pictures, 55
Meyer, James, 235
Mickey Mouse Club, The, 29
Miniseries, 3, 43–45
Monash, Buddy, 111–112
Moore, Tom, 32
Morris, William, 21–22
Movie industry, *see specific movie studios*
    blockbuster films, 64
    historical perspective, 54–56, 63
    impact on, 67
    mindset, 323–324
Movie of the Week, 3, 39–41, 43
Movie studios:
    acquisitions, 57–58
    development of, 55–56, 97
    decline of, 57
    survival of, 58
Moye, Michael, 133–134, 142, 154,
    160–166, 173
Mr. President, 173
Murdoch, Rupert:
    acquisitions by, 181–182
    career development, 122
    comparison with, 317–318
    at Fox Broadcasting Company, 124, 181,
        199
    history of, 121
    settlement from, 209
    at Twentieth Century-Fox, 114–117
Mutchnick, Brenda, 158

NBC, development of, 29
Negotiation skills, 37–38
News Corporation, 199, 204, 207
Niche programming, 166
Nichols, Mike, 75, 166, 197
Nielsen Media Research, 325
Nielsen ratings, 157–158, 166
Norris, Floyd, 274
North Wilton Report, The, 187, 194

Ordinary People, 79, 86
Oresman, Donald, 251, 267, 269
Orion Pictures, 222

Ostrager, Barry, 270
Outfoxed, 188, 195
Ovitz, Michael, 268

Paley, William, 28-29
Paramount Communications, 247, 256, 264
Paramount Pictures:
    acquisition by Gulf & Western, 57, 60-61
    as chairman, 3-4, 46, 49-70
    financial problems, 59-60
    successes at, 86-87
    Viacom merger, 253, 254-284, 321-322
Phillips, Julia, 12
Pierce, Fred, 44, 48
Platt, Polly, 145-146, 169, 182-183, 208,
    281
Porter, Edwin S., 54
Presley, Elvis, 23-24
Private life, importance of, 11-17,
    319-321
Proteges, 74
Pudney, Gary, 41

QB VII, 44
Q-online, 292
QVC:
    acquisition/merger of Home Shopping
        Network, 236, 252-253
    bid for Paramount, 266-284
    CBS merger, 288-291, 295-310, 324,
        327-328
    Comcast deal, 6, 216, 225-226
    as corporate partner, 5
    impact on, 234-238, 259-260
    initial interest in, 214-215, 225,
        231-233
    partnership with, 4, 224-244
    programming strategy, 239-240
    Q-online, 292
    success factors, 243-244, 294
    vision for, 241-242

Raiders of the Lost Ark, 78-79, 86
Rakolta, Terry, 162, 164-165
RCA, 29
Reds, 78-79
Redstone, Sumner, 5, 251, 253-255, 257,
    260-261, 276, 279-280, 282-283,
    304, 310
Reidy, John, 301
Reif, Jessica, 207, 235, 308
Relationships:
    with Marvin Davis, 105, 136, 264
    with Michael Eisner, 85, 96, 317

with employees, 83-85
with family, 17, 68-170
with friends. 75, 206, 214-215, 225,
    232-233, 259, 299, 318
with Rupert Murdoch, 4, 158, 177, 204
Reputation, 6-7, 85
Rich, Marc, 57, 100-101, 110, 113, 115
Rich Man, Poor Man, 44
Risk-taking, generally, 320. *See also*
    Acquisitions/Mergers
Rivers, Joan, 126-137, 141-144, 146-150,
    258, 298
Roberts, Brian. 6, 215-216, 223-227,
    233-235, 252-253, 264, 296, 307-309
Roberts, Ralph, 215-216, 223-224, 227,
    233-235, 307
Robins, J. Max. 220
Rohatyn, Felix. 253, 256
Roots, 45-46
Rose, Frank, 24. 26
Rosen, Steven, 260-261
Rosenberg, Edgar, 126-137, 141-144,
    146-148, 150, 224
Ross, Steve, 222, 256
Roth, Joe, 198, 297
Rubell, Steve, 102-103
Rule, Elton, 48
Rush, George, 291

Sammeth, Bill, 128
Samuel Goldwyn Productions, 92
Sand, Barry, 187
Sarnoff, David. 28-29
Sassa, Scott, 125, 158, 184, 193, 242
Saturday Night Fever, 77, 86
Savoy Pictures Entertainment, 6, 315
Segel, Joseph, 224-226
Shrage, Michael, 243-244
Siegel, Herbert, 57, 60, 99-100
Silver King Communications, 6-8,
    313-329
Silverman, David, 175
Silverman, Fred, 105
Simon, Norton, 30
Simon and Schuster, 94
Simpson, Don, 80-81
Simpsons, The, 4, 169-177, 243-244
Siris, Peter, 236
$64,000 Question and Twenty-One, The,
    23
Smith, Ray, 263-264
Snyder, Richard A., 94
Sound of Music, The, 98
Spelling, Aaron, 40

Spielberg, Steven, 40, 78
Standards and Practices, Fox Network, 175–176
Stanfill, Dennis, 98–101
Starger, Marty, 39, 43
Star Trek-The Motion Picture, 79–80, 86
Star Wars, 98–99
Steel, Dawn, 6, 77, 81–83
Steinberg, Saul, 99
Sternfeld, Alan, 147, 153–160, 166, 189–192, 319, 328
Stoddard, Brandon, 46
Strategic alliances, 295. *See also specific mergers*
Stringer, Harry, 290, 297
Sunbeam Television Corporation, 301–302
Syndication, 44, 122–123
Synergy, 260–261

Tartikoff, Brandon, 126, 154–156
TCI (Television Cable, Inc.), 215, 217–219, 237, 242, 251
TCI-Bell Atlantic merger, 262–265, 268
Television industry:
    advertisers in, 324–325, 327
    color television, impact of, 29–30
    development of, 22–28
    growth of, 56–58, 63
    viewing trends, 325–326
Temperament, 83–85, 127, 184
Tentpole movies, 79
Terms of Endearment, 86
Thalberg, Irving, 2–3, 6–7, 56, 79
Thomas, Danny, 17, 23
Thomas, Marlo, 17, 26–27, 75
Thorp, Bruce, 304
Tiffany network, *see* CBS
Tinker, Grant, 156
Tinker, John, 308
Tisch, Danny, 296
Tisch, Laurence:
    CBS-QVC merger, 5, 30, 288–291, 295–297, 299–306, 310
    comparison with, 317–318
Tracey Ullman Show, The, 144, 149, 161, 166, 170, 172, 193–194
Turner, Ted, 261
Twentieth Century-Fox:
    acquisition of, 100
    CEO at, 105–117
    historical perspective, 56–57, 97–98
    problems at, 101–103
21 Jump Street, 148–149, 161, 194

United Artists, 57
Universal Studios, 39, 54, 58–59
Urban Cowboy, 86

Van Doren, Charles, 23
Van Meter, Jonathan, 127
Veasey, E. Norman, 273
Velvet Mafia, 103
Viacom, 5, 124, 253–254, 256, 321–322. *See also* Paramount/Viacom merger
Vogel, Harold, 299–300
Von Furstenberg, Diane, 75, 206, 214–215, 225, 232–233, 259, 299, 318

Wachtell, Herbert, 269–272
Walt Disney Productions, 58–59, 104. *See also* Disney Company; Eisner, Michael
Warner, Jack, 28
Warner Bros., 55, 57, 103
War of the Roses, 172, 208
Wasserman, Lew, 37, 39, 58–59
Watson, Ray, 103
Weekend at Bernies, 172
Weisbord, Sammy, 25, 31
Weltman, Phil, 25, 31
Weltner, George, 59
Wendle, Kevin, 125–126, 159–160, 192–193
West, Don, 291
Westingouse Braodcasting Company, 309, 322
Wick, Doug, 166, 196–197
William Morris Agency, employment at, 3, 21–22
Williams, Edward Bennett, 100
Winans, Christopher, 291, 306–307
Winger, Debra, 75
Wizan, Joe, 102
WMS Industries, 276
Wolper, David, 45–46
Working Girl, 166, 196
Wright, Robert, 300, 302
Wyser-Pratte, Guy, 266

Yablan, Frank, 75
Yoffe, Emily, 223
Young Guns 2, 199

Zanuck, Darryl F., 98, 110
Zanuck, Richard, 98
Zukor, Adolph, 54